THE HUMAN
IN A DEHUMANIZING
WORLD

D1603453

THE HUMAN
IN A DEHUMANIZING
WORLD

Reexamining Theological Anthropology and Its Implications

Jessica Coblentz
and Daniel P. Horan, OFM
Editors

**THE ANNUAL PUBLICATION
OF THE COLLEGE THEOLOGY SOCIETY
2021
VOLUME 67**

ORBIS BOOKS
Maryknoll, New York 10545

ORBIS BOOKS
Maryknoll, New York 10545

Fathers and Brothers
MARYKNOLL™

Founded in 1970, Orbis Books endeavors to publish works that enlighten the mind, nourish the spirit, and challenge the conscience. The publishing arm of the Maryknoll Fathers and Brothers, Orbis seeks to explore the global dimensions of the Christian faith and mission, to invite dialogue with diverse cultures and religious traditions, and to serve the cause of reconciliation and peace. The books published reflect the views of their authors and do not represent the official position of the Maryknoll Society. To learn more about Orbis Books, please visit our website at www.orbisbooks.com.

Library of Congress Cataloging-in-Publication Data

Names: Coblentz, Jessica, editor. | Horan, Daniel P., editor.
Title: The human in a dehumanizing world : reexamining theological anthropology and its implications / Jessica Coblentz and Daniel P. Horan, OFM, editors.
Description: Maryknoll, New York : Orbis Books, [2022] | Series: The Annual publication of the College Theology Society ; 2021, volume 67 | Includes bibliographical references. | Summary: "CTS annual volume focusing on dehumanization and theological anthropology, in such areas as sexual harassment, racial justice, and decolonization"—Provided by publisher.
Identifiers: LCCN 2021057576 (print) | LCCN 2021057577 (ebook) | ISBN 9781626984578 (trade paperback) | ISBN 9781608339204 (epub)
Subjects: LCSH: Theological anthropology—Christianity. | Christianity and culture. | Theology, Doctrinal.
Classification: LCC BT702 .H86 2022 (print) | LCC BT702 (ebook) | DDC 233/.5—dc23/eng/20220107
LC record available at https://lccn.loc.gov/2021057576
LC ebook record available at https://lccn.loc.gov/2021057577

Contents

Introduction

Jessica Coblentz
and Daniel P. Horan, OFM

Christianity is an inherently human enterprise. The central tenet of our faith tradition is the belief that the God who created the world freely entered into that same world as one of us, a human being. Theological anthropology, that subdiscipline of theology that focuses on what our tradition has to say about human personhood, touches on all aspects of Christian theology—ethics, history, sacraments, liturgy, scriptural interpretation, etc.—and therefore stands at the heart of theological reflection.

And yet, like all areas of theological inquiry, theological anthropology is never static, concrete, or immutable. In the Anselmian tradition of understanding theology as *fides quaerens intellectum*, we continually strive to understand better the faith tradition we profess. We continue to learn more about who we are and who we are called to be through engaging in historical *ressourcement* of the tradition and correlating the best of scientific, social, and historical discovery to our theological reflection. In an age marred by so many dehumanizing forces—including colonialism; white supremacy; exploitative capitalism; and sexual assault, harassment, and abuse—a perennial question surfaces anew: How ought Christians understand what it means to be human? This volume brings together essays and plenary addresses delivered at the 2021 College Theology Society annual convention that sought to address this fundamental query in some form, particularly in light of the forces and realities of dehumanization in our contemporary world.

The unique circumstances in which the 2021 convention took place further highlighted the need for critical engagement with the tradition in order to respond to the dehumanizing "signs of our times" (*Gaudium et Spes* 4). Among these signs was a renewed public awareness of the inherently white supremacist and structurally racist culture that exists in the United States. This convention took place less than a year after the police murder of George Floyd, which sparked a fire this time that led to a widespread embrace of the Black Lives Matter movement that publicly decries racial dehumanization. None of us could have imagined the January 6th insurrection that took place at the United States Capitol, which marked the end of the Trump presidency—itself a catalyst of dehumanizing policies and practices. Nor could we have anticipated the rampant individualism and disregard for the lives of others on display as the COVID-19 pandemic swept the globe, resulting in the deaths of millions of humans—the ultimate form of *de*humanization—and the suffering of billions more. Though miraculous scientific innovation made vaccines available to many by the start of the 2021 convention, the CTS wisely opted to meet virtually for this gathering for the second year in a row.

In addition to addressing many of these events and themes, the essays in this volume take up the challenge of reflecting theologically on what it means to be human in a time and context that can be so frequently dehumanizing. The authors in this volume model what it means to do theological anthropology in diverse and creative ways, drawing on the best resources within Christianity while also critically engaging culture, society, and our own faith tradition.

Overview of the Book

We have organized the essays collected here into three parts. Part I, which focuses on reexamining the academic subdiscipline of theological anthropology in view of contemporary dehumanizing realities, presents essays from the convention that invite us to renew our understanding of the human person from within the Christian tradition. David de la Fuente brings together the work of Paul Ricoeur and of Willie James Jennings to reimagine the human "after whiteness." Through an analysis of the place of anger in the Black Lives Matter protests, on the one hand, and in the January 6th insurrection, on the other, plenary speaker Cristina L. H. Traina elucidates an inductive and relational theological anthropology grounded in emotion. Plenary speaker Karen Kilby explores recent theological debates about the relationship between sin and suffering; she identifies patterns in contemporary thought concerning their relation and argues for the important place of social or structural sin in theological reflection on suffering. Cynthia L. Cameron sketches and analyzes the nascent theological anthropology of youth in *Christus Vivit*, Pope Francis's fourth apostolic exhortation and the culminating document of the 2018 meeting of the Synod of Bishops. Contending with critics of Karl Rahner's theological anthropology, Jack Louis Pappas engages the carnal phenomenology of Maurice Merleau-Ponty to present a Rahnerian humanism that is postmodern and Christocentric. Part I concludes with Martin Madar's exploration of how a strengthened dialogue between theological anthropology and ecclesiology can inform the Catholic Church's self-understanding.

Part II contains those essays that interrogate the ways in which the Christian tradition and its practitioners have contributed to dehumanization, particularly as it concerns the deleterious consequences of Christian action in the church, academy, and society. Tracy Sayuki Tiemeier interrogates how Western academic comparative theology reinforces White Christian supremacy and exhorts a decolonization of the field through engagement with the work of An Yountae. The Christian fascism that has stoked the rise of the new right and led to the violence of the January 6th insurrection is the focus of Derek Brown's essay, where he argues that Christian fascism demands resistance strategies unfamiliar to the existing American "resistance" movement. Next, Donna Freitas's *Consent: A Memoir of Unwanted Attention* is the subject of a four-part discussion that challenges theologians to confront the realities of sexual harassment in theological education. Drawing on trauma studies and recent scholarship on the cultures of sexual exploitation that shape women's lives, Julia Feder contextualizes Freitas's experiences of stalking and sexual harassment by a professor-priest during doctoral studies. Julie Hanlon Rubio situates Freitas's story within the networks of gender, sex, and power that shape clergy sexual abuse of all kinds and which all Catholics—including those in theological education—must confront. Jason King calls for an ethics of being a mentor in view of the systemic dangers of academic mentorship that Freitas's story exposes. Donna Freitas concludes the discussion of her memoir with a call to theologians to focus on the survivors of abuse in the academy who are among them—survivors like Freitas herself, who presents a new set of questions for theologians as they contend with abusers and their institutions. Part II closes with an essay from Ish Ruiz that argues for an embrace of the ministerial contributions of LGBTQ+ educators in Catholic schools—a needful alternative to the recent firings of several of these educators in the US Church.

The final part of this volume turns to essays that engage those resources within the theological tradition and Christian praxis that contribute to resisting dehumanization in our contemporary world. Plenary speaker Andrew L. Prevot begins the section with a Black theological reading of Angela of Foligno's *Memorial*, which he offers as a spiritual resource for "those whom this world annihilates." Todd Whitmore demonstrates how a return to the theological understanding of kinship that first grounded the work of Oaklawn Psychiatric Center in northern Indiana at its Mennonite beginnings can address shortcomings of the clinical "therapeutic" approach to treatment that prevails in Oaklawn's addiction treatment programs. From central Minnesota on lands of the Dakota people, Colleen Mary Carpenter identifies storytelling as an important practice for affirming the history and humanity of the Native communities of Minnesota and for opening the possibility of creating a just community for all who do and will live there. Marjorie Corbman examines how Judith Malina—a Jewish actress, theater director, and friend of Dorothy Day—understood theater as a ritual of resistance to dehumanizing structures. Building on Pope Francis's discussion of consumerism in *Laudato Si'*, Sara Bernard-Hoverstad situates consumption within the wider context of consumer practices in today's economy and argues for a pragmatic strategy to empower agents to engage in market reform. Ending Part III and the volume as a whole is Andrew Staron's look at what the writings of Annie Dillard impart about the nature of creation—in all its brutality—and our proper response to it. Staron's meditation on Dillard's literary artistry extends to readers a call to not only attend to our aching world but also to bless and hallow it.

Acknowledgments

A publication such as this requires the efforts and generosity of so many individuals. We thank Mary Doak, the president of the College Theology Society at the time of the 2021 convention, who not only encouraged us but also stepped in as the *de facto* executive director of the convention amid leadership changes in the Society. Without the exceptional contributions of executive coordinator of digital media Dana Dillon and of board member Katherine Schmidt, the 2021 convention simply would not have happened. Dana and Katherine planned and oversaw all the digital logistics for the virtual convention with skill, composure, and good humor. Because of them and all those who participated in the online convention, it was an inspiring success despite the challenging circumstances of the global pandemic. Special thanks go to our plenary speakers at the convention: Andrew Prevot, Cristina Traina, and Karen Kilby. All were generous as the convention logistics shifted, and they offered inspiring and incisive remarks that we are thrilled to share in this volume. We also thank the many other authors in this volume, all of whom have been a pleasure to work with and whose writings have captivated us throughout the editorial process. The many other scholars who submitted their work for possible inclusion in this volume presented us with a very difficult selection process. We thank them for their offerings and thank all those who lent us a hand in the selection process by serving as reviewers. Lastly, thanks to Reid Locklin, the Society's editor of research and publications, and to Jill Brennan O'Brien at Orbis Books, for their editorial assistance and care in bringing this volume to fruition.

PART I

REEXAMINING THEOLOGICAL

ANTHROPOLOGY IN VIEW

OF DEHUMANIZATION

Recognizing the Human *After Whiteness*

Hermeneutics, Anthropology, and Scripture in Paul Ricoeur and Willie James Jennings

David de la Fuente

I am haunted by the question that Willie James Jennings poses at the beginning of *The Christian Imagination*: Why did white Christians from the same town not know him, not recognize Jennings and his family as fellow Christians?[1] This prompts me to ask: Why do I also fail to recognize others as fellow human beings to whom I owe love and justice?[2] It has become clear that any theological imagining of the human must address race—more particularly, whiteness, which Willie James Jennings identifies as the "signature reality of the modern condition" as well as the disease afflicting the Christian imagination.[3] This makes theology itself an area of struggle for naming and confronting the evil of racism.[4]

To take up that struggle, I propose turning to Paul Ricoeur and Willie James Jennings as resources for reimagining the human. My thesis is that reimagining the human after whiteness can be fruitfully accomplished by mediating between the hermeneutical and anthropological resources found in their works. Ricoeur's thought offers a philosophical "prefiguration" for a race-critical hermeneutics of suspicion, and Jennings's thought provides the full "refiguration" of the self by clarifying the disfiguring effects of whiteness.[5] To demonstrate this, I proceed by first examining the intersecting themes of anthropology and hermeneutics in each thinker. I then gather insights in their treatment of anthropology and narrative in order to conclude with the special case of Scripture as that narrative that can disclose a possible world for shared human life "after whiteness."

Ricoeur: Anthropology and Hermeneutics of a Wounded Capable Self

Like his French contemporaries, Paul Ricoeur is part of the tradition that asks, "Who comes after the subject?"[6] Ricoeur uniquely reimagines this human subject by way of a carefully mediated hermeneutic philosophical anthropology of the "capable self." While attesting to our fundamental capacities to act, Ricoeur sees the self as a "wounded *cogito*" due to the legacy of the "masters of suspicion": Freud, Marx, and Nietzsche. Yet Ricoeur insists that this capable self can be realized if it passes through the hermeneutics of suspicion which eventually enable a "second naïveté."[7]

Ricoeur's first major insight about the wounded capable self is that it is not transparent to itself. Though his career begins in a Husserlian mode that affirms "direct" phenomenological access to the will in its positive valences (that which I can do or can will), Ricoeur later observes two related problems that chasten knowledge of the self. One dimension of this is that any accounting for the will's fallibility and the experience of evil proceeds by way of symbols that require interpretation (namely myths). The second dimension stems from a philosophical reading of Freud and of psychoanalysis. Freudian psychoanalysis brings about the "crisis of the philosophy of the subject" because "it makes consciousness not a given but a problem and a task. The genuine *cogito* must be gained through the false *cogitos* which mask it."[8] The critique of false consciousness through psychoanalysis demonstrates that the self is not transparent to itself; it depends on the scrutinizing process of interpretation.[9] Yet it is also the case that in Freudian psychoanalysis, the goal "is that the one who is analyzed, by making his own the meaning that was foreign to him, enlarge his field of consciousness, live better, and finally be a little freer and, if possible, a little happier."[10]

The second major insight in Ricoeur's account of the self is that it must be thought of reflexively and as intrinsically ethical in relation with the other, or as "oneself *as* another." This is in part due to the paradoxical relationship between selfhood as *idem* identity (sameness amid change) and *ipse* identity (sameness across change, self-constancy). As revealed through grammatical analysis and through the semantics of action, selfhood as *ipse* identity is reflexive: By attesting that I, a self, can act, it is implied that I am imputable—that another can hold me to my word, that they can count on my character. This means that selfhood implies the other so much so that one "cannot be thought of without the other, that instead one passes into the other."[11] The consequence of this is that any account of selfhood must also pass over to ethics, which Ricoeur understands as "aiming at the good life with and for others in just institutions."[12] This includes the proximate other with whom that good life is shared in friendship and the distant other who shares the good life through a historical community's institutions, which protect and guarantee justice—the good life for all.

This brings us to the threshold of a third insight in Ricoeur regarding "narrative identity" and selfhood. Put simply, the self is constituted and "refigured" by narrative, and the capacity of narrative to perform this refiguration involves the same process of the hermeneutics of suspicion. Ricoeur calls this "distanciation," which works in two ways. With regard to the text, the fixation of discourse into a text generates a distance between the author of that text and its meaning. For the reader, distanciation is from one's real world so that one can enter into "the world of the text." Given the first type of distanciation, a creative interplay can take place that "refigures" the reader who encounters that text. Thus, Ricoeur observes, "To understand is not to project oneself into the text but to expose oneself to it; it is to receive a self enlarged by the appropriation of the proposed worlds that interpretation unfolds. . . . In reading, I unrealize myself."[13]

There is finally an important interrelationship with selfhood, text, and alterity that Ricoeur explicates through the themes of memory and mutual recognition. For Ricoeur, memory is the "womb" of history and therefore "the guardian of the entire problem of the representative relation of the present to the past." Memory has a unique role in safeguarding the narrative function of history by opening up to justice, such that the duty of memory is "to do justice, through memories, to an other than the self." This is not a generic "other," but points to every other to whom one is obligated across history. Historical consciousness and identity place the self in debt to historical others, especially the "victims" of history who are "other than ourselves."[14]

Ricoeur's philosophical self is not atomized, nor is it a masterful subject. It is a self chastened by personal experiences, wounded by its awareness of finitude, and soberly instructed by the other to whom one is accountable.[15] Such an account facilitates attention to the witness and memories of othered persons, as well as their recognition as "my fellow human being."[16] What remains is to refigure Ricoeur's philosophical anthropology in light of race.

Jennings: Anthropology
and Hermeneutics *After Whiteness*

To fully refigure the self as "oneself as another," an account of race and, specifically, of the pervasive reality of whiteness is needed. Just as Ricoeur has licensed a hermeneutics of suspicion as a vital step in actualizing the capable self, Willie James Jennings has also argued for the essential role of race studies and critique of whiteness as that reality that inhibits authentic encounter with the other as "my fellow human being." Naming this condition makes it possible to clear away the dehumanizing characteristics of human life in the West and also makes it possible to theologically retrieve an authentic doctrine of creation that views human and creaturely diversity as gift.[17]

It is important to note that an interrogation of race does not just expose historical injustice. Rather, in a manner analogous with Ricoeur's movement from suspicion to action, Jennings observes that race criticism can also "make possible a freer space within which theology might explore its collaboration with formations of identity in modernity." It does so in three ways: First, interrogating race and whiteness opens up more comprehensive ways of grasping the modern condition of theology. Second, it also allows for sustained analysis of whiteness and theology. Finally, it clarifies the "intellectual ecologies within which we do theology."[18] In each case, what will emerge is a recognition of the formative power of whiteness.[19]

What, then, is whiteness? Jennings explains that it is not about "a person or a people. . . . [I]t was and is a way of being in the world and a way of perceiving the world at the same time. Whiteness was and is a way of imagining oneself as the central facilitating reality of the world, the reality that makes sense of the world."[20] It is the means of a "deformed building project" centered on imposing a vision of maturity.[21] This account of whiteness hearkens back to the question of the subject in philosophy. As Jennings observes, "Whiteness is difficult to define because it emerged from the site of that centered European subject and reflects the constituting realities of that centered subject position: a subject that is not vulnerably objectified but carries the power to classify, categorize, and order hierarchically."[22] He adds, "Whiteness emerged from the colonial period forward not simply as a way to identify explorers, colonialists, and proto-Europeans, nor simply as a descriptor for those designated white, but also as a way of seeing, that is, a structuring structure."[23]

This account resonates with the harrowing findings of historical interrogations of race in virtually every field of study: it was—and is still—operative in theory and practice in medical and scientific knowledge, in accounts of history and culture, in laws and the designs of cities, and even in professional sports.[24] As a way of seeing and forming others, whiteness has especially painful effects on the Christian theological imagination and on theological education. In this realm, Jennings draws on experiences and memories as an administrator and as a faculty member that demonstrate how whiteness operates in theological education in unstated norms of beauty and accomplishment, in the desire to compartmentalize the life of a scholar, in the inability to imagine racial, ethnic, cultural others and their gifts. Language is one major site of deformation: He recounts a debate among divinity school faculty about teaching "the scholarly languages" that did not celebrate the beauty of language but cast them as a means of "colonialist horror." Jennings also recalls how a poor evaluation of an international student's English writing skills unfairly failed to acknowledge that student's rich experiences and particular gifts in several other languages.[25]

For Jennings, the roots of the colonialist horror are deep. Jennings argues, as many others do, that imagination of the other stands or falls on the Christian's ability to preserve the link between Jesus and Judaism.[26] At stake is what Jennings calls the "original trajectory" of joining of Jew and Gentile—an unprecedented joining that is a pure gift. Any attempt at retrieving this trajectory would require a hermeneutic reversal in which the Gentile (the Christian) takes the position of a "second reader" theologically because Christians are those "outside Israel."[27] Such a disposition renounces the mastery of the Western subject, for theology should instead be about realizing "God's dream," not one's own design.[28]

Jennings has powerfully demonstrated how the emergence of race is so intimately tied with Christian logics that any hope of reimagining the human, or better, of recognizing the human other as "my fellow human being" depends on one's willingness to imagine life *after whiteness*. This involves not simply shedding the aesthetic dimensions of whiteness but also divesting the Western Christian self of its privileged place as interpreter. Christians are instead to be "second readers." It is this position that opens up the biblically communicated dream of ending hostility, something that is not only within general human capacities (in a Ricoeurian sense and by grace) but is also theologically speaking God's intention. To tutor this possibility, narrative—especially Scripture—can play a powerful role.

Ricoeur and Jennings on Narrative, Scripture, and the Self

Narrative, especially that of Scripture, looms large in each thinker's work. In Ricoeur's own admission, his thinking oscillates between "a Biblical pole and a rational and critical pole."[29] For both thinkers, Scripture as narrative is a source for reconfiguring the self as either a "summoned subject" or as one confronted by the demands communicated in Scripture.[30] From Ricoeur, one can derive a general understanding of Scripture as a source of narrative identity. That understanding is fully "refigured" by Jennings's interpretation of Scripture.

Despite maintaining a sort of professional distance from formal theology, Ricoeur treats religious themes extensively and considers the narrative power of Scripture as a special case for understanding the capable self. Thought "biblically," this self is what Ricoeur calls a "summoned subject," convoked and addressed by forms of discourse in Scripture such as prophecy, law, or poetry. What is more, reading Scripture is also about "the world of the text." Scripture enjoys a "semantic autonomy" that requires the same process of distanciation that applies to any other text. This means that interpretation involves attention not only to the place of historical criticism but also to the response of the reader. As readers, Christians affirm Scripture as normative while opening themselves to the "worlds" of the scriptural texts.[31] These texts are therefore sites that inform and orient memory, praxis for justice, and understanding of others.

Commenting on the literary and political force of the Bible in Protestantism, Jennings notes, "[The Bible] was the pedagogue that guided me in the joy of reading, writing, and discovery. . . . The Protestant story is the story of literacy in unanticipated hands, but with mixed consequences and mangled results."[32] At its best, the Bible indeed opens up life. At its worst, Scripture is subjected to use and abuse for imperialistic and racializing purposes during the colonial enterprise.[33] But the confrontation that Scripture brings can open up the imagination to an "original trajectory" of joining across difference and the need to reconfigure Christian reading of Scripture after whiteness. For Jennings, this is the vision of being "readers together, readers who in the very act of reading constitute an invitation to a shared life."[34]

That shared life is expressed in powerful ways in the Acts of the Apostles. Jennings's commentary on Acts emphasizes in continuity with historical criticism and empire criticism that Acts is a story, a "created" history, but one that beckons the reader into a different "historical consciousness" that follows the "created history" of Acts into a "revolution of the intimate." Put in somewhat Ricoeurian terms, the narrative function of Acts is to disclose a possible world in opposition to empire. The reader is summoned and called by the Spirit of God, who, according to the text, is "crumbling imperial design from within."[35] A resonance also emerges between Ricoeur's vision of "oneself as another" and Jennings's more theological thematic of joining, cultural intimacy. This is best conveyed in the Acts of the Apostles with its vision of cultural and linguistic hospitality and embracing of otherness and difference. As Jennings puts it, Acts narrates the story of the Spirit of God moving the disciples to overcome the aesthetic regime of empire, directing them "to those whom they would in fact strongly prefer never to share space, or a meal, and definitely not life together." It is a history that we learn and enter into, but only if Christians enter as second readers.

There is another concept that can open up the power of narrative. Besides the encounter with texts such as Scripture, there is also the interpretation of Scripture through preaching. But alongside this also stands a practice indicated by Ricoeur and enacted evocatively by Jennings. For Ricoeur, this entails a call to mutual recognition, both interpersonally and politically. Importantly, he calls for an "exchange of memories" as a means of enabling such recognition. This entails "taking responsibility, in imagination and in sympathy, for the story of the other, through the life narratives which concern the other." Through the exchange of memories, "it is a matter . . . of helping one another to set free that part of life and of renewal which is found captive in rigid, embalmed, and dead traditions."[36]

Such an exchange is already operative in the United States among those who are willing to listen to and amplify the voices naming the disfiguring effects of whiteness and the intersecting experiences of oppression. This concept also seems to capture Jennings's interventions in theological reflection and education: By offering his own memories, Jennings invites the kind of exchange that can continue to render visible what whiteness would obscure about theological education and the malformations that continue to plague the Christian imagination. This has a clarifying effect that destabilizes the "masterful" Western self and opens up a more authentic recognition of the human other in their particularity and diversity.

Conclusion: On Recognizing the Human

In this essay I have deliberately chosen to bring into dialogue a white Western male thinker alongside a Black thinker because of resonances in their accounts of the human and the task of recognizing the human. Despite differences in discipline and methodology, I find here evocative resources for reimagining the human precisely because they (and surely many others) prioritize imagining the human with an eye toward preserving difference. I also am consciously working to address practical concerns in church, academy, and the wider public: In each sphere one can encounter resistance to discussion of race. The ongoing coronavirus pandemic further demonstrates a refusal to consider human others. Though Ricoeur never formally addressed race, one could recast Ricoeur's hermeneutic philosophical anthropology as a means of receiving and amplifying the work of Jennings and many other scholars. For Ricoeur, the other has to be visible, and there is a demand to recognize every human other as those to whom love and justice are due. Also important and helpful is the dynamic of Ricoeur's thought: despite insistence on the boundaries between philosophy and theology, Ricoeur's insights often take one to the threshold of the theological so that the whole frame of the capable self, thought alongside others and informed by the power of narrative, can find refiguration in the theological.

This is where Jennings's insights carry the promise that many see in Ricoeur's work by explicitly addressing the false consciousnesses that inhibit recognition of the human. Where whiteness threatens to homogenize, silence, and subjugate, there is a trajectory that can guard against it. It is possible to recognize the other as one's "fellow human being." Speaking theologically, for Jennings, this recognition is nothing less than intimacy and joining of people through their difference. As he powerfully notes, this is God's dream—a dream that, if recognized, can turn the Christian imagination away from whiteness.

Notes

[1] Willie James Jennings, *The Christian Imagination: Theology and the Origins of Race* (New Haven, CT: Yale University Press, 2010), 3–4.

[2] This phrase is derived from Paul Ricoeur's plea for an authentic "encounter with the other, my fellow human being." Ricoeur, "Epilogue: Personal Capacities and Mutual Recognition," in *Philosophical Anthropology*, Writings and Lectures, vol. 3, ed. Johann Michel and Jérôme Porée, trans. David Pellauer (Malden, MA: Polity, 2016), 290–95.

[3] Willie James Jennings, "Theology and Race," in *The Routledge Companion to Modern Christian Thought*, ed. Chad Meister and James Beilby (New York: Routledge, 2013), 783–94.

[4] Ibid., 783.

[5] Here I am drawing on Ricoeur's own concept of threefold mimesis as prefiguration (pre-understanding), configuration (the world of the text itself in its imaginative variations), and refiguration (the self that emerges from the encounter with the text). See Paul Ricoeur, *Time and Narrative*, vol. 1, trans. Kathleen McLaughlin and David Pellauer (Chicago: University of Chicago Press, 1984), 54–70.

[6] Jean-Luc Nancy, Introduction to *Who Comes After the Subject?* ed. Eduardo Cadava, Peter Connor, and Jean-Luc Nancy (New York: Routledge, 1991), 4.

[7] Paul Ricoeur, *The Symbolism of Evil*, trans. Emerson Buchanan (Boston: Beacon, 1969), 351. For the discussion of the "masters of suspicion," see

Ricoeur, *Freud and Philosophy: An Essay on Interpretation*, trans. Denis Savage (New Haven, CT: Yale University Press, 1970), 33.

⁸Paul Ricoeur, "A Philosophical Interpretation of Freud," in *The Conflict of Interpretations: Essays in Hermeneutics*, ed. Don Ihde (Evanston, IL: Northwestern University Press, 2007), 161.

⁹Paul Ricoeur, "Appendix: From Existentialism to the Philosophy of Language," in *The Rule of Metaphor: The Creation of Meaning in Language*, trans. Robert Czerny, Kathleen McLaughlin, and John Costello, SJ (New York: Routledge, 2003), 372–81.

¹⁰Ricoeur, *Freud and Philosophy*, 35.

¹¹Paul Ricoeur, *Oneself as Another*, trans. Kathleen Blamey (Chicago: University of Chicago Press, 1992), 3.

¹²Ibid., 180.

¹³Paul Ricoeur, "Hermeneutics and the Critique of Ideology," in *From Text to Action: Essays in Hermeneutics, Volume II*, trans. Kathleen Blamey and John B. Thompson (Evanston, IL: Northwestern University Press, 2007), 300–301. Also see the relevant essays in the same volume, "The Task of Hermeneutics," "The Hermeneutical Function of Distanciation," and "What Is a Text?"

¹⁴Paul Ricoeur, *Memory, History, Forgetting*, trans. Kathleen Blamey and David Pellauer (Chicago: University of Chicago Press, 2004), 87–89. I defer a fuller treatment of memory and recognition to the section on narrative.

¹⁵Ricoeur's life is marked by several traumatic moments: he was orphaned early on and raised by his paternal grandparents. He never had meaningful contact with his mother's side of the family. He was pressed into service during World War II and spent five years as a prisoner of war in Germany. Amid the delivery and preparation of his Gifford Lectures (published as *Oneself As Another*), Ricoeur's son Olivier died by suicide. Ricoeur was also predeceased by his wife. Though Ricoeur only occasionally acknowledged such experiences, many of his closest collaborators point out the obvious effect. See Charles Reagan, *Paul Ricoeur: His Life and His Work* (Chicago: University of Chicago Press, 1996).

¹⁶Ricoeur, "Personal Capacities and Mutual Recognition," 295.

¹⁷Willie James Jennings, "Reframing the World: Toward an Actual Christian Doctrine of Creation," *International Journal of Systematic Theology* 21, no. 4 (October 2019): 338–407.

¹⁸Jennings, "Theology and Race," 783.

¹⁹Jennings, *The Christian Imagination*, 290.

²⁰Willie James Jennings, "Teaching and Living toward a Revolutionary Intimacy," in *You Say You Want a Revolution? 1968–2018 in Theological Perspective*, ed. Susie Paulik Babka, Elena Procario-Foley, and Sandra Yocum (Maryknoll, NY: Orbis Books, 2019), 13.

²¹Willie James Jennings, "Can White People Be Saved? Reflections on the Relationship of Missions and Whiteness," in *Can White People Be Saved? Triangulating Race, Theology, and Mission*, ed. Love L. Sechrest, Johnny Ramirez-Johnson, and Amos Yong (Downers Grove, IL: InterVarsity, 2018), 28.

²²Jennings, "Theology and Race," 787.

²³Willie James Jennings, "Racism," in *The Oxford Encyclopedia of the*

Bible and Ethics, ed. Robert L. Brawley (New York: Oxford University, 2015), https://www.oxfordreference.com.

[24]For examinations of race in medicine, see John Hoberman, *Black and Blue: The Origins and Consequences of Medical Racism* (Berkeley: University of California Press, 2012); Deirdre Cooper Owens, *Medical Bondage: Race, Gender, and the Origins of American Gynecology* (Athens: University of Georgia Press, 2017). For a representative treatment of race in philosophy, see Andrew Valls, ed., *Race and Racism in Modern Philosophy* (Ithaca, NY: Cornell University Press, 2005). Days before this College Theology Society meeting commenced, the National Football League announced that it would cease the use of "race-norming" of cognitional capacities, which it had used as a defense against brain injury claims by Black players. See Associated Press, "NFL to Halt 'Race-Norming,' Review Black Claims in $1 Billion Concussion Settlement," *ESPN* (June 2, 2021), www.espn.com.

[25]Willie James Jennings, *After Whiteness: An Education in Belonging* (Grand Rapids, MI: Eerdmans, 2020), 52–54.

[26]Jennings, *The Christian Imagination*, 259–70. J. Kameron Carter also contends with whiteness by "sutur[ing] the gap between Christianity and its Jewish roots." Carter, *Race: A Theological* Account (New York: Oxford University Press, 2008), 4. Susannah Heschel demonstrates the historical consequences of the deliberate severance of Jesus from Judaism; see Heschel, *The Aryan Jesus: Christian Theologians and the Bible in Nazi Germany* (Princeton, NJ: Princeton University Press, 2008).

[27]Jennings, *The Christian Imagination*, 262–63; see also Jennings, "Theology and Race," 787; and Jennings, "Reframing the World," 393.

[28]Jennings, *After Whiteness*, 152.

[29]Paul Ricoeur, *Critique and Conviction: Conversations with François Azouvi and Marc de Launay*, trans. Kathleen Blamey (Malden, MA: Polity, 1998), 6. There is a fascinating overlap between Ricoeur and Jennings in their engagement with Barth, but unfortunately space does not permit a fuller exploration of the Barthian influence on their works.

[30]Ricoeur, "The Summoned Subject in the School of the Narratives of the Prophetic Vocation," in *Figuring the Sacred: Religion, Narrative, and Interpretation*, ed. Mark I. Wallace (Minneapolis: Fortress, 1995), 262–78. Willie James Jennings, *Acts: A Theological Commentary on the Bible* (Louisville, KY: Westminster John Knox, 2017), xv.

[31]Paul Ricoeur, "The Sacred Text and Community," in *Figuring the Sacred: Religion, Narrative, and Interpretation*, ed. Mark I. Wallace (Minneapolis: Fortress, 1995), 70.

[32]Willie James Jennings, "Protestantism," in *The Cambridge Companion to Religion and Literature*, ed. Susan M. Felch (New York: Cambridge University Press, 2016), 249.

[33]Ibid., 252.

[34]Ibid., 259.

[35]Jennings, *Acts*, 1–10.

[36]Paul Ricoeur, "Reflections on a New Ethos for Europe," in *The Hermeneutics of Action*, ed. Richard Kearney (Thousand Oaks, CA: Sage, 1996), 3–14, at 11–12.

"The Power of Anger in the Work of Love," Revisited

Theological Anthropology, Ethics, and Emotion

Cristina L. H. Traina

On May 25, 2020, police officers from Minneapolis's third precinct tried to arrest George Floyd on suspicion of passing counterfeit money at a corner store. Floyd died after Officer Derek Chauvin knelt on his neck for over nine minutes, despite his protest that he could not breathe. After a bystander video was released, large, mostly peaceful, racially diverse protest marches began in Minneapolis and across the country. But on May 28, part of the Minneapolis crowd attacked and burned the third precinct station, which many saw as a site and a symbol of institutionalized violence against people of color. Police had fled.

To be sure, we should not reduce the mostly peaceful Minneapolis protests to this violent action. Yet we can glean much for theology from the arson and the anger that led to it. Traditional moral theology provides tools for assessing and possibly justifying riotous violence ethically. We can extend doctrines of self-defense and just war or evaluate the arson as a justified action of last resort against a functionally, maybe selectively, tyrannical power. Sarah MacDonald and Nicole Symmonds have argued in addition that riotous violence can be an appropriate response to injustice and a virtuous intervention in the pursuit of social flourishing.[1] I assume that riotous violence is sometimes justifiable and instead inductively explore its etiology as an instance of politically expressed anger-seeking-justice for clues for theological anthropology.[2]

Below, I reflect on anger, particularly Black anger; on its expression; and on virtue. I invite contemplation of our interdependent creatureliness in conversation with the white theological heritage as well. Finally, I test these reflections against another event, the Capitol riot of January 6, 2021. In the end, I argue that our theological anthropology must begin with rather than arrive at our social and political nature. I touch on only some of the recent, rich literature on anger; broader reading would sharpen my descriptions, but my main focus is anger's implications for theological anthropology.

I begin with three framing thoughts. First, I do not intend to appropriate Black accounts of Black anger. Instead, I mean to hear Black anger and to reflect some of its consequences for moral theology and theological anthropology, noting resonances in Beverly Wildung Harrison's important article "The Power of Anger in the Work of Love" and many other works.[3]

Second, I refer to long-standing theological and ethical templates in white theological traditions not to "ratify" already authentic Black accounts of anger but to ask whether some of these templates might be adopted as analogies, correlates, or touchpoints for theological dialogue.[4]

Third, I am conscious of theological anthropology's double-edged sword. On the one hand, for example, the Catholic social justice tradition's emphasis on human dignity yields human rights criteria that can underwrite legal standards of justice. On the other, Black theologians have repeatedly demonstrated how Enlightenment-era anthropologies have served the interests of whites, especially white men, by denying people of color, especially women of color, fully human status.[5] Self-assured, reductionistic anthropologies usually christen some humans by excluding others. Even in its forceful claims for human dignity, theological anthropology must preserve self-critical humility and an openness to mystery and to the unknown.

Anger

Drawing on a tradition anchored by Aristotle at one end and contemporary theologians at the other, I define anger as my embodied emotional response to my perception that I (or someone else) has suffered an unjust harm or loss at the hands of other human beings. As Beverly Wildung Harrison said in "The Power of Anger in the Work of Love," "Anger is a signal that change is called for, that *transformation in relation* is required."[6] Anger can also be my response to my fearful perception that an unjust harm or loss is about to be inflicted.[7] It is a response to unjust human action, whether individual or systemic, but not to suffering from other sources. It is a passion or an emotion, not a virtue or a vice, even though it may become habitual; and it arises from an appraisal of factual evidence combined with a moral judgment about injustice. Even though this judgment inspires a desire to end the harm, it need not involve vengeance or a desire to cause the offender suffering.[8]

As Wildung Harrison, Audre Lorde, and many others have argued, anger is also a source of energy to fuel our battles against the injustices that awaken it. When we are exhausted or depressed, it bolsters our self-esteem and keeps us in the fight.[9] This energy comes not fundamentally from our aversion toward evil but from our generous desire for the good. Wildung Harrison calls it "a *vivid form of caring*": it arises from our love for others and for their thriving, our hope, and our ability to imagine a flourishing just beyond our current reach.[10] The hopeful, imaginative dimension of anger is what makes it an explicitly political and not just interpersonal emotion.

If anger is the appropriate human response to injustice, should we express it, and how?

Expressed Anger

In the early hours of March 29, 2021, Chicago police officer Eric Stillman shot and killed thirteen-year-old Adam Toledo in an alley. Adam's hands were up, although he may have ditched a gun seconds before he raised them. Just before video of the incident was released, Chicago mayor Lori Lightfoot warned that it told "a complicated and nuanced story" and urged everyone to "proceed with deep empathy and calm and, importantly, peace."[11]

We have heard this plea many times, usually from white actors. Whenever it is made, it conjures the unspoken ideal of "deliberative democracy," which has two ingredients. The first is that the people as a whole are responsible for establishing and maintaining justice, even when they delegate much of that task to elected representatives and to the judiciary. This distinction is important because, in a democracy, anger at systemic injustice obligates ordinary people to act or to confirm that someone else is acting; this is not medieval moral theology's background assumption.

The second, more problematic ingredient is the assumption that when an injustice occurs, everyone comes together on equal footing, analyzes the complex facts with cool objectivity, and reaches a rational consensus. This ideal of political interaction forbids high levels of expressed anger, in particular rage, because they disrupt both orderly discussion and the participants' ability to reason dispassionately.[12] On this view, the deliberative community should not entertain violence or even highly emotional appeals; only good manners and good arguments deserve a hearing and possibly the reward of reform.

This is why, as scholars like María Lugones have observed, the emotional registers of female anger and people of color's anger have had so little political uptake in a majority white democracy whose elected officials are usually white and male.[13] Those whose power questions righteous anger serve as gatekeepers, forbidding its expression.[14] This discipline of selective deafness has produced a victim practice of training, curating, and refining expressions of anger, slicing off their immediacy and urgency so that they fit within the boundaries of acceptable rational discourse. We could read Mayor Lightfoot's words about complexity and calm as disciplining the discourse, but we could also read them as disciplined by the discourse: a Black, lesbian mayor adhering to the standards of deliberative democracy to maintain credibility in the city of white Mayors Richard J. and Richard M. Daley. A quintessential example is August Wilson's depiction of Ma Rainey, who contains her rage just barely within the boundaries of white propriety to wring as much respect and justice as possible out of a white recording studio for her Black band.[15]

The mandate for mannerly argument harms victims of injustice in many ways. Here are two. First, it leaves an emotional remainder: the unexpressed anger at the injustice itself, which the demand for translation doubles. As Brittney Cooper argues in *Eloquent Rage*, victims frequently sublimate their anger into a "good political analysis," not realizing that this analysis is "a masterful cloak for the emotional work [they] haven't done" on both the immediate issue and the cumulative unjust injuries they have suffered in the past.[16] Second, as both Audre Lorde and Beverly Wildung Harrison wrote, one often turns this remainder of anger destructively inward and against one's companions because the risks of raging at its cause are too high.[17] Wilson's play illustrates this phenomenon as well.

The strategy of sublimation also leaves a moral remainder. If being the citizen of a democracy obligates one to seek justice for current victims, and one has presented a rational case for justice endlessly and protested peacefully without a meaningful, adequate result, must one not try something else, for their sake? As poet and essayist Hanif Abdurraqib said in response to Lightfoot's pleas for calm,

> What a foolish thing to say, when police murdered a 13-year-old with his hands up. Granted, in the States our social contracts are flimsy and don't mean anything anyway, but—you know, they've been broken many times over and don't really hold any water ... when they are broken so explicitly and egregiously and many people lied to uphold their breaking, including that mayor, I don't really want to hear a call for calm. That doesn't make sense to me.[18]

When uttered by powers that have repeatedly chosen not to listen and respond to the rational arguments that they themselves have required, "keep calm" is an empty demand. Expressed rage is sometimes the only remaining response, even when one cannot be sure it will succeed. As columnist Wesley Morris wrote last summer, "Black Americans have come in peace, they've come armed. They've just been trying to mind their business. Disappointment awaits, regardless. Anytime the racial temperature goes up and hell pays a visit to earth, the disappointment takes a holiday. And you fight."[19] Or as Brittney Cooper argues, "Rage is a legitimate political emotion"; "Sometimes the only thing that is in order is to act out of order. To turn up, show out, and disrupt."[20] Disruptive rage is not mainly a matter of self-expression, as if it were about an angry, harmed person unloading their "personal feelings." Rather, as South African theologian Jakub Urbaniak also argues, it is a mode of political communication about systemic injustice. It is another means to gain a hearing and receive an appropriate response, employed when deliberative methods have failed.[21]

If the political rage of speeches, blogs, marches, sit-ins, and/
or boycotts still produces no action to end the injustice, material
violence may be victims' only alternative. The Rev. Dr. Martin
Luther King Jr. famously said, "A riot is the language of the
unheard."[22] As Jermaine McDonald has written, King disliked
violence; he simply observed that ongoing, clearly analyzed,
uncorrected, systemic injustice eventually produces riots among
people who have exhausted all other strategic options for justice.[23]
A riot in response to injustice is evidence of the rioters' love of
justice and flourishing; their witness to violent injustice; and their
transformative strategy to end it.

This etiology of expressed anger shows why, when another's
rage is a witness to unanswered injustice, we must both confirm
that judgment in our own rage and express it politically, possibly
considering violent action against a violent oppressor.[24] Such rage
has consequences for our ideas of virtue.

Virtue

For Thomas Aquinas, a virtue is "a good quality of the mind, by
which we live righteously, of which no one can make bad use."[25]
Anger, on the other hand, is a passion or an emotion aroused
by our perceptions of others' unjust actions; it is praiseworthy
passion when it is proportionate to the slight.[26] MacDonald and
Symmonds join Macalester Bell in arguing that righteous anger
is virtuous: "anger is intrinsically a 'form of excellence' in character" when it "expresses opposition to evil."[27] In general, just
anger must adhere to the other virtues: prudently thorough in
fact-finding and honestly accurate in analysis; just and loving in
concern about the persons harmed; prudent in the direction and
expression of anger only toward those who damage the vulnerable, but not toward others; and proportionate to the degree of
injury suffered or threatened—including violent expression when
the need is urgent and other channels have been exhausted. Anger
at injustice also arises from the virtues of solidarity and courage. Brittany Cooper ties anger to the virtue of hope, because it
imaginatively paints a vision of the just world we want to create,
and to joy (the reward of virtue), which arises from our internal
vocational clarity about our fight to build that world and even
from that fight itself.[28]

Yet anger can also be vicious: culpably misinformed, sloppy in its thinking, aimed at scapegoats, and in both degree and expression either excessive or (as has often been true of white responses to racism) deficient in proportion to the harm inflicted or threatened.[29] Violent anger that is random or harms people who are not violent actors is also unvirtuous. Vicious anger transgresses truthfulness, charity, and prudence.

Beyond this distinction between virtuous and vicious anger, theologians and philosophers continue to struggle with three questions. First, even when righteous, sustained, expressed rage passes the initial tests of virtue, is it good for the people who practice it? Does it promote their flourishing? Second, is it good for the future of their society? Does their collective behavior promote communal flourishing? Finally, if we have reservations about these questions, can we truly say that sustained expressed rage is virtuous?

I agree with Lisa Tessman that sustained rage normally impedes the justly angry person's own flourishing in important respects.[30] Righteous rage that is repeatedly answered with disappointment rather than victory is exhausting. Morris describes the no-win cycle: "You fight because you're tired. Yet you're tired because you've been fighting. For so long. In waves, in loops, in vacuums, in vain."[31] As Lorde, Cooper, and others demonstrate, extended bouts of anger at ongoing injustice can transform us into anti-social, paranoid, hostile beings who cannot sustain relationships or collaborate politically.[32] The larger the number of people contorted by rage, the greater the cost to the future community. For this reason, some scholars draw the line of legitimate rage here: the behavior of a virtuously angry person seeking change should never violate the values they want a just community eventually to uphold.[33]

Others, like Symmonds and MacDonald as well as Tessman, argue that behavior that compromises personal flourishing is virtuous if it improves social flourishing: sustained anger, even riotous anger, is virtuous if it moves society closer to justice, even when the cost to the angry person herself is high.[34] In this view, the standard by which we should measure the virtue of justice in a democratic society is active, intentional work to deliver to all what is due to them.[35] This work is likely to be fueled by anger born of love, to be messy, and to be risky and even harmful to the practitioner. Workers for justice will nearly always become misshapen in the course of their own efforts largely because their world both resists change—extending their anger—and punishes them for their efforts at change. This is the burden of their virtue.

Importantly, victims of oppression who lead the effort for justice are triply burdened: materially by the injustice itself; psychologically, morally, and spiritually by the demand to be rational and by the angry, risky, warping effort to undo the injustice; and finally by the demand that they themselves correctly analyze the source of the injustice before protesting against it or attacking it.[36] Seen from this angle, the epistemological privilege of the oppressed that is intended to elevate victims becomes an additional burden: victims are charged with writing the recipe for their own liberation. Thus, privileged people's failure to address systematic injustice is triply unjust: they escape the injustice, the effort of analyzing its cause, and the labor and distress of correcting it.

Theological Anthropology

These reflections have implications for theological anthropology. As I hinted at the beginning, bias in anthropology's normative applications raises strategic questions about the whole project of describing humanity. From one angle, the problem is not society's definition of the human but its historical refusal to honor all people with that label. As Wesley Morris wrote, riffing on the Simply Red song, "If You Don't Know Me by Now,"

> If you don't know that a black man, calling for his mother, his dead mother, is so desperate for somebody to hear him that he's screaming for ghosts—or fears he's in the process of becoming one; if you don't know that we, too, can run for leisure and sleep for rest; if you don't know that this skin is neither your emergency nor an excuse to invent one, that the emergency has tended to be you—*by now*?—you will never, never, never . . . .[37]

A "correct" anthropology is worth nothing unless society honors it universally.

From the other angle, the issue is oppressive reductionism in the dominant definition of the human. Our discussion of anger dislodged an Enlightenment assumption—of which Catholic moral theology and Western Christianity generally are guilty—that emotionally cool reason is the epitome of human development.[38] The accompanying assumption is that even when felt anger is appropriate and even morally required, rage or strongly expressed emotion of any kind is characteristic of "undeveloped" people and societies and so is a tantrum, a sign of immaturity, proof that one has forfeited the right to be in the conversation.

These assumptions yield a series of contradictions and double standards that whites still use against people of color and men still use against women. As Amia Srinivasan writes, those most concerned to rule expressed anger out of public dialogue are those whose power expressed anger most threatens.[39] Finally, Brittany Cooper notes, the flip side of "the American project of suppressing Black rage" through a rationalist anthropology is "legitimizing and elevating white rage"[40]—that is, fear-driven anger that generates the lethal violence that it forbids to others.[41] Outwardly directed fear and expressed anger characterize "rational" white American public behavior, particularly against people of color, much more than they do Black American public behavior, particularly against white people. White people police Black expressions of justice-seeking anger, often excusing white, violent, unjust anger as "well-meaning," "mistaken," or "patriotic."

Under such circumstances, is there a way to engage theological anthropology in a liberatory mode? We must, beginning with inductive points. As Laura Alexander recently argued, embodied emotion and imagination are as essential to our humanity as reason.[42] Nearly everyone I have cited would say that emotions reveal truths at which logic might not arrive so quickly; the scholastics thought they were also necessary to move us to action. Imagination allows us to envision futures for which prudence has not devised the means. But rather than being subordinate to reason, emotion and imagination modulate reason as much as reason modulates them. They also connect reason to the body both through emotion's integral spirituality, physicality, and rationality and through the energy of "passionate," embodied action in the world.[43] This description is not radical; power and privilege acting in accord with it would be.

Second, reflecting on expressed anger as a form of communication signals that, whatever theory we may hold, our operative anthropology is far too individualistic. Righteous anger is a sign that human interdependence is the foundation, not the consequence, of the anthropological project. Like speech of any kind, expressed anger is connective; as Beverly Wildung Harrison said, it is about "hearing and speaking" in "reciprocity," about receiving what is said, about following it up with argument or action or collaboration for the sake of our common flourishing.[44] Communities form us holistically: our bodies, reason, emotions, spirituality, and ethics. We are originally and essentially beings who shape each other for better and worse, not inert atoms that occasionally collide. Wildung Harrison insisted that "we have the power through acts of love or lovelessness literally to create one another."[45] Our finitude (not to mention sinfulness) puts us essentially, deeply in need of everything others have to offer.

We can find resonance with these insights not just in theologies of the margins but in the canon of white theology. In the spirit of providing fodder for imagination, I suggest two strategies. To be clear, I do not cite them to ratify Black arguments for righteous anger or Black anthropologies. Instead, in the spirit of active listening to already justified arguments, I present them as potential bridges for crossing from one bank to the other or entries in a dictionary of idioms that proposes analogues to untranslatable sayings.

The first is a social, corporate vision of the image of God rooted in social trinitarian theologies. If we are not individually created in the image of God, we are not focused mainly on questions like these: Which of the creator's qualities do we analogously, individually incarnate and need to cultivate, and what personal rights do we thus possess? Rather, we image God by straining toward God's threefold image corporately, with graced energies and interdependencies flowing among us. We can grow into this identity only collaboratively. One instance is Joy Ann McDougall's revival of Jürgen Moltmann's eschatologically aimed concept of open friendship, with its mutuality, reciprocity, "communicative freedom," unity-in-difference, and advocacy for justice.[46] For Moltmann, "social relationships [patterned on the Trinity] are constitutive of true personhood."[47] This anthropology allows us to define sin theologically as ruptured relations among human beings that shatter God's reflection and action in humanity, breaching humanity's connection to God's life-giving action in the world.[48]

Sin is not merely disobedience or even failure to love. It disrupts *God's* project and identity.

The second lightly sketched offering comes from Thomas Aquinas: counsel. Counsel is part of prudence, or "right reason applied to action";[49] it identifies all the possible paths to the goal one is seeking.[50] Counsel is surprisingly underdeveloped and inconsistent in the *Summa*.[51] But in one long passage, Thomas tips his hand: it involves conversation.

> Counsel properly implies a conference held between several. . . . [I]n contingent particular cases, in order that anything be known for certain, it is necessary to take several conditions or circumstances into consideration, which it is not easy for *one* to consider, but are considered by *several* with greater certainty, since what *one* takes note of, escapes the notice of another. . . . Now the knowledge of the truth in such matters does not rank so high as to be desirable of itself . . . but it is desired as being useful towards action, because actions bear on things singular and contingent.[52]

Thomas clearly implies that the more inclusive the conversation, the more comprehensive the list of possible actions it can deliver to judgment and choice. Conferring involves listening to discover who is speaking, thoroughly hearing their words, and absorbing their practical implications. As Philip Lorish and Charles Mathewes write in a different context, true difference among the conversation partners is what makes seeking "insight from one another" so necessary in a world that poses "difficult, murky, and obscure" challenges.[53] Because Thomas provides no power analysis, it is important to add that the epistemological privilege of the marginalized obligates the powerful to listen first and hardest in this consultation; to reject both uncritical deliberative democratic and petition-and-response models of interaction; to commit to action for justice; and to maintain the conversation consistently, not just in emergencies.

Finally, theological anthropology must be tentative and humble. This is true for strategic reasons: as we have seen, power often deploys a definitive description of the human to exclude, or, failing that, it simply neglects to apply it at all. Given human sinfulness, we cannot behave as if we will ever be rid of this danger. For example, Vincent Lloyd argues that humanity—though certainly rational, emotional, and imaginative—is "ultimately unrepresentable": it is "a concept essentially defined by what it is not, marking what is in the world but never fully captured by it."[54] Not just because the dynamics of human culture reveal new elements of our humanity daily, not just because our perception is finite, not just because humans with power use definitions of the human against others, we must acknowledge that humanity exceeds every description we can make of it.

Reflecting on Gregory of Nyssa, Kathryn Tanner concurs for theological reasons. If we are made in the image of a malleable, incomprehensible God, we too are malleable and incomprehensible: "an apophatic anthropology is the consequence of an apophatic theology."[55] "By attaching ourselves to the incomprehensible," she argues, "we become incomprehensible ourselves."[56] Because we have "no definite nature to be true to," we shape ourselves, body and soul, by "the uses to which [we] put [ourselves]" depending on what we "care about," love, seek, or desire.[57] In such a view, any theological anthropology that is not apophatic is idolatrous. Tanner's theological anthropology also helps us to theologize the concept of burdened virtue that we met earlier. The end that shapes us, the use to which we put ourselves, *is* the self that we become: justice born of love. The scars that this work entails are carved in letters of righteousness. No one ever said that virtue had no cost.

The Capitol

On November 3, 2020, Joseph Biden won the presidency over incumbent President Donald Trump with only 51.3 percent of the popular vote in an election marked by multiple accommodations to the COVID-19 pandemic.[58] On January 6, the day that former Vice President Pence was to certify the results, Trump rallied with allies who believed that the reported electoral vote count was illegitimate. Afterward, a large group of mostly white supporters broke through inadequate police defenses, entered the Capitol, chanted threats to Congressional leaders and the Vice President, attacked police, and vandalized the building. Journalists and rioters filmed Capitol police "talking down" the rioters, leading them out of the building, and releasing them. Some members of Congress later compared the breach to "a normal tourist visit,"

labeled the invaders merely a "mob of misfits," and claimed that
Justice Department efforts to find and charge the rioters were
wrongly "harassing peaceful patriots across the country."[59]

The insurrection differed from the fire-bombing of Minneapolis's third precinct in several obvious ways. It was an attack on
the occupied seat of national government, not an empty police
station; it involved white rather than Black rioters (consider how
the Capitol police might have prepared and reacted had the rioters
been "irrationally angry" Blacks rather than rational, "patriotic"
whites); it involved threats of death against Congressional leaders
and the Vice President rather than destruction of symbolically
resonant property; it was fueled by culpable lies, culpably believed, rather than by long, documented historical experience of
race-linked police violence.

Our trip through anger and burdened virtue shows us further
differences. Minneapolis protesters were escalating their ongoing
effort to undo injustice by uttering their umpteenth—or umphun-
dredth—unheard cry against inadequate reforms of common,
documented police violence in Minneapolis. Insurrectionists were
making the last of only a few protests against a single, recent, apparent injustice; the issue was new, the existing evidence did not
support their claims, few nonviolent means had been tried, and
those that had were still in process. The Minneapolis protesters
who rioted attacked a symbol of that violence, the empty building
where the four officers involved in George Floyd's murder were
stationed. That is, their anger sought mostly transformation, not
retribution. In contrast, the Capitol rioters attacked the national
government, which does not oversee or adjudicate state election
processes. Their violence was retributive ("Hang Mike Pence!")
rather than communicative. Their aim was overthrow. It was vicious anger: not communicative but coercive.

In addition, the Minneapolis protesters—including the rioters—mostly aimed to undo racially unjust, injurious practices
and policies. The Capitol protesters seem to have been inspired
instead by the fear that the man who had protected their unjustly
superior status would no longer do so. That is, they were fighting
not for justice for all but for their own interests alone; they were
fighting not for the redress of injustice but for its preservation.
This was anger of presumption, not anger at exclusion.

And yet "a riot is the language of the unheard." If we image

God only in our mutual listening and collaboration for justice, some of us must listen to this riot as well. First, despite presumptive white privilege (especially in encounters with police), many whites who cheered the Capitol attack have, like other Americans, suffered losses: PTSD from military service in wars that had no apparent value in protecting the nation; the shrinkage of profitable farming, union manufacturing jobs, and full-time work; the mishandling of COVID-19.[60] Victims of the "wicked problem" of a globalized economy, they are angry about genuine injustices that they have suffered. [61] Their anger too signals true wrongs and deserves serious hearing, not self-serving manipulation by the powerful.

Second, the insurrectionists themselves appear to come from better-off regions in which they are in the political minority and believe that their neighbors do not hear their concerns.[62] To be sure, they transgressed the criteria of legitimate political anger: they attacked Congress for the wrong reasons and by the wrong means; they failed to measure their distress against the scale of justice and to analyze its true causes; and their coercive, violent tactics, culpable ignorance, and retributive intent are massive, vicious moral failings. None of these behaviors counts as righteous anger. Still, if their neighbors had invited them into dialogue, would some of them have stayed home? What responsibility did the majorities in their home precincts have to engage them in conversation across difference?

Conclusion

Riots of all kinds teach us that it is impossible to be good by ourselves. We can be good and seek good only together. We cannot even be human by ourselves. Any theological anthropology that begins with "the human person *in se*" and then proceeds to "the human in relation" is false. We must start where we usually end.

Riots of all kinds also remind us that virtuous anger fuels transformative work for social flourishing. But in keeping with a social, relational anthropology, riots are not only injustice alarms; they primarily signal catastrophically low social levels of listening, inadequate anger about injustice, and overly feeble efforts toward common flourishing. They are signs that people of privilege generally are failing to image God by collectively engaging their eyes and ears, their reason, their emotions, and their imagination and that too few people with privilege are individually deploying the social power that they hold. Importantly, many victims of injustice cannot riot or even press their cases: all the more reason that people with power must cultivate perception, reception, anger, and action routinely, acting consciously on our interdependence.

But this is not news. As Bryan Massingale argued twenty-five years ago, "black rage"—I would say, *all* rage—"must be transformed into a passion, that is, an anger which is *directed* and *focused* upon moral ends, *intelligent* in its execution, and *sustained* over the long haul pursuit of justice."[63] As Beverly Wildung Harrison declared, all those decades ago, "in a feminist moral theology, good questions are answered by something *we must do.*"[64] As a society, we must—still—collectively relieve the burden of transformation that we have loaded onto victims of injustice. We must—still—listen more and harder yet without requiring endless amounts of data before committing to a course of action. We must—still—awaken and sustain our anger. We must—still—deploy that anger in work for flourishing.

Notes

Thanks to all who suggested sources and commented on drafts: Antavius Franklin, William Hutchison, Stan Chu Ilo, Bryan Massingale, Richard Miller, Elsie Miranda, Karen Peterson-Iyer, Andrew Prevot, Stephanie A. Puen, and Jakub Urbaniak. To the extent that I failed to incorporate your suggestions, this essay is the poorer.

[1]Sarah MacDonald and Nicole Symmonds, "Rioting as Flourishing? Reconsidering Virtue Ethics in Times of Civil Unrest," *Journal of the Society of Christian Ethics* 38, no. 1 (2018): 25–42.

[2]In their analysis of non-US cases, Erica Chenoweth and Maria J. Stephan have argued that civil resistance to injustice is more effective than violence. See *Why Civil Resistance Works: The Strategic Logic of Nonviolent Conflict* (New York: Columbia University Press, 2011). Thanks to Richard Miller for this reference.

[3]Beverly Wildung Harrison, "The Power of Anger in the Work of Love: Christian Ethics for Women and Other Strangers," *Union Seminary Quarterly Review* 36 Supplementary (1981): 41–57.

[4]On the problematic white tendency to insist that Black rage be validated by white criteria, see Bryan N. Massingale, "Anger and Human Transcendence: A Response to 'A Rahnerian Reading of Black Rage,'" *Philosophy and Theology* 15, no. 1 (Spring–Summer 2003): 110.

[5]Among others, see Vincent Lloyd, *Black Natural Law* (New York: Oxford University Press, 2016); M. Shawn Copeland, *Enfleshing Freedom: Body,*

Race, and Being (Minneapolis: Fortress, 2010); Emilie Townes, *Womanist Ethics and the Cultural Production of Evil* (New York: Palgrave Macmillan, 2006); Amey Victoria Adkins-Jones, "A Theological Anthropology of Racism," in *T&T Clark Handbook of Theological Anthropology*, ed. Mary Ann Hinsdale and Stephen Okey (London: T&T Clark, 2021), 345–55.

[6]Wildung Harrison, "Power of Anger," 49.

[7]On anger at fear of loss, see Brittney Cooper, *Eloquent Rage: A Black Feminist Discovers Her Superpower* (New York: St. Martin's, 2018), 203.

[8]I side with Diana Fritz Cates, against Martha Nussbaum (and Thomas Aquinas): vengeance is not a necessary part of anger. See Martha Craven Nussbaum, "Transitional Anger," *Journal of the American Philosophical Association* 1, no. 1 (2015): 41–56; and Diana Fritz Cates, "You Deserve to Suffer for What You Did," *Journal of Religious Ethics* 46, no. 4 (2018): 771–82. See also William Mattison, "Virtuous Anger? From Questions of *Vindicatio* to the Habituation of Emotion," *Journal of the Society of Christian Ethics* 24, no. 1 (2004): 159–79; and Diana Fritz Cates, "Taking Women's Experience Seriously: Thomas Aquinas and Audre Lorde on Anger," in *Aquinas and Empowerment: Classical Ethics for Ordinary Lives*, ed. G. Simon Harak (Washington, DC: Georgetown University Press, 1996), 47–88.

[9]Wildung Harrison, "Power of Anger," 49; Audre Lorde, "The Uses of Anger: Women Responding to Racism," in *Sister Outsider: Essays and Speeches* (1984; Berkeley, CA: Crossing, 2007), 127; Xolani Kacela, "Towards a More Liberating Black Liberation Theology," *Black Theology* 3, no. 2 (2005): 202; Wesley Morris, "The Videos That Rocked America. The Song That Knows Our Rage," *New York Times,* June 3, 2020, www.nytimes.com; MacDonald and Symmonds, "Rioting as Flourishing?" 29; Andrew Prevot, "A Meditation on Divine Anger" (American Academy of Religion Annual Meeting, San Diego, CA, November 23–26, 2019).

[10]Wildung Harrison, "Power of Anger," 49; see also Cooper, *Eloquent Rage*, 35, 68–69, 274; and MacDonald and Symonds, "Rioting as Flourishing?" 36–40.

[11]Heather Cherone, "Lightfoot Pleads for Calm as Officials Prepare to Release Video of Fatal Police Shooting of Adam Toledo," *WTTW*, April 15, 2021, www.wttw.com.

[12]On the latter, see Sarah Sorial, "The Expression of Anger in the Public Sphere," *Journal of Social Philosophy* 48, no. 2 (Summer 2017): 124.

[13]María Lugones, "Hard-to-Handle Anger," in *Overcoming Racism and Sexism*, ed. Linda A. Bell and David Blumenfield (Lanham, MD: Rowman and Littlefield, 1995), 207–8.

[14]As Daniel Silvermint notes, "We're"—he seems to mean whites—"often too quick to label victim rage 'excessive,' and we have to examine the biases that lead us to do so." Daniel Silvermint, "Rage and Virtuous Resistance," *Journal of Political Philosophy* 25, no. 4 (2017): 471.

[15]August Wilson, "Ma Rainey's Black Bottom: A Play in Two Acts" (New York: New American Library, 1985).

[16]Cooper, *Eloquent Rage,* 35, 62.

[17]Audre Lorde, "Eye to Eye: Black Women, Hatred, and Anger," in *Sister*

Outsider: Essays and Speeches (1984; Berkeley, CA: Crossing, 2007), 145–75; Wildung Harrison, "Power of Anger," 44.

[18]Hanif Abdurraqib, "Moments of Shared Witnessing," *On Being,* April 29, 2021, www.onbeing.org.

[19]Morris, "The Videos That Rocked America."

[20]Cooper, *Eloquent Rage,* 5, 161. Emphasis added.

[21]Jakub Urbaniak, "Grooving with People's Rage: Public and Black Theology's Attempts at Revolutionizing African Love," *Black Theology Papers* 2, no. 1 (2016): 6. As Michael Jaycox has argued, the insistence that anger be a "transition" to coolly reasoned argument contains two related flaws: it assumes a liberal vision of incremental progress toward justice, and it therefore misses the fact that situations of structural injustice demand cognitive disruptions, not simply deeper analysis along familiar lines. See Michael P. Jaycox, "The Civic Virtues of Social Anger: A Critically Reconstructed Normative Ethic for Public Life," *Journal of the Society of Christian Ethics* 36, no. 1 (2016): 123–43; idem, "Nussbaum, Anger, and Racial Justice: On the Epistemological and Eschatological Limitations of White Liberalism," *Political Theology* 21, no. 5 (2020): 415–33.

[22]"Mike Wallace Interview with Martin Luther King Jr.," *CBS Reports,* September 27, 1966, http://www.cbsnews.com/news/mlk-a-riot-is-the-language-of-the-unheard/.

[23]Jelani Cobb made the same assessment of the Ferguson riots half a century later. Jermaine M. McDonald, "Ferguson and Baltimore according to Dr. King: How Competing Interpretations of King's Legacy Frame the Public Discourse on Black Lives Matter," *Journal of the Society of Christian Ethics* 36, no. 2 (2016): 141–58. See also Daniel J. Ott, "Nonviolence and the Nightmare: King and Black Self-Defense," *American Journal of Theology & Philosophy* 39, no. 1 (January 2018): 64–73.

[24]MacDonald and Symmonds, "Rioting as Flourishing?" 129. Although some highly placed persons make the case that they should use their power in unjust institutions from within, the privilege of this power can become a refuge from conflict, an excuse to wait for a "more opportune moment" or to capitulate through lopsided compromise. See also Massingale, "Anger and Human Transcendence," and Bryan Massingale, "Anger for the Sake of Justice: The Ethics of Black Rage," Catholic Theological Society of America, June 7, 1996.

[25]St. Thomas Aquinas, *Summa Theologica: Complete English Edition in Five Volumes,* trans. Fathers of the English Dominican Province (Westminster, MD: Christian Classics, 1981), I-II q. 55 a. 4. Hereinafter *ST.*

[26]*ST* II-II q. 158 a. 1.

[27]MacDonald and Symmonds, "Rioting as Flourishing," 29, quoting Macalester Bell, "Anger, Virtue, and Oppression," in *Feminist Ethics and Social and Political Philosophy: Theorizing the Non-Ideal,* ed. Lisa Tessman (New York: Springer, 2009), 177.

[28]Cooper, *Eloquent Rage,* 35, 274–75.

[29]E.g., *ST* II-II q. 158 a. 1.

[30]For example, Lisa Tessman, *Burdened Virtues: Virtue Ethics for Liberatory Struggles* (New York: Oxford University Press, 2005), 124.

[31]Morris, "The Videos that Rocked America."

[32]Lorde, "Eye to Eye"; Cooper, *Eloquent Rage,* 30–31, 169–70.

[33]Silvermint, "Rage and Virtuous Resistance," 470. For a middle position—violent revolution alongside nonviolent methods, and only when necessary, see Anna Floerke Scheid, *Just Revolution: A Christian Ethic of Political Resistance and Social Transformation* (New York: Lexington, 2015). I would not want to argue that behavior that prophetically mirrors the Reign of Justice cannot spark hope and fire the imagination to seek alternatives to violence.

[34]MacDonald and Symmonds, "Rioting as Flourishing?" 39–40.

[35]Cf. *ST* II-II q. 158 a. 1.

[36]Sorial argues that responsibility for correctly analyzing and targeting the causes of oppression belongs wholly to victims. See Sorial, "The Expression of Anger," 134, 137. I disagree. Even respecting epistemological privilege, it is unjust to charge the people with the least resources and the most vulnerability with carrying the burden of analysis alone. Thus, all victim protest deserves a robust hearing followed by solidaristic assistance.

[37]Morris, "The Videos That Rocked America," italics and ellipsis in original.

[38]Willie James Jennings, "Only a Criminal Can Change the World: Martin Luther King Jr. and The Moral Imperative of Disobedience" (Fordham University, March 24, 2021). Amia Srinivasan lays equal blame at the feet of Western philosophy; see "The Aptness of Anger," *Journal of Political Philosophy* 26, no. 2 (2018): 142. Srinivasan also implies that maximizing "the value of our total cognitive economies" should not be an exceptionless moral imperative (141).

[39]Srinivasan, "The Aptness of Anger," 142.

[40]Cooper, *Eloquent Rage,* 169.

[41]Ibid., 202–12.

[42]Laura E Alexander, "Human Rationality, Kinship Obligations, and Natural Law" (The Society of Christian Ethics Annual Meeting, online, January 8, 2021).

[43]On emotion's physicality, see Mattison, "Virtuous Anger," 161, 176.

[44]Wildung Harrison, "The Power of Anger," 50.

[45]Ibid., 47.

[46]Joy Ann McDougall, "The Return of Trinitarian Praxis? Moltmann on the Trinity and the Christian Life," *Journal of Religion* 83, no. 2 (2003): 198.

[47]Ibid., 192.

[48]Ibid., 202.

[49]*ST* II-II q. 47 a. 2.

[50]*ST* I-II q. 14 a. 2.

[51]Jeffrey J. Maciejewski, "Persuasion, Natural Rhetoric and the Gift of Counsel," *Heythrop Journal* 61, no. 1 (2020): 124.

[52]*ST* I-II q. 14 a. 3, italics added.

[53]Philip Lorish and Charles Mathewes, "Theology as Counsel: The Work of Oliver O'Donovan and Nigel Biggar," *Anglican Theological Review* 94, no. 4 (2012): 719.

[54]Lloyd, *Black Natural Law,* ix, xi.

[55]Kathryn Tanner, "In the Image of the Invisible," in *Apophatic Bodies:*

Negative Theology, Incarnation, and Relationality, ed. Chris Boesel and Catherine Keller (New York: Fordham University Press, 2009), 117. See also Karen Kilby, "Is an Apophatic Trinitarianism Possible?" *International Journal of Systematic Theology* 12, no. 1 (2010): 65–77.

[56]Tanner, "In the Image," 134.

[57]Ibid., 125, 123–24.

[58]"2020 National Popular Vote Tracker," *Cook Political Report,* www.cookpolitical.com.

[59]Mary Clare Jalonick, "What Insurrection? Growing Number in GOP Downplay Jan. 6," *AP News,* May 14, 2021, www.apnews.com.

[60]With thanks to Elsie Miranda (personal communication) and to Stan Chu Ilo, "America's Public Confession without Repentance" (Catholic Theological Society of America, online, March 18, 2021).

[61]The term originates in Horst W. J. Rittel and Melvin M. Webber, "Dilemmas in a General Theory of Planning," *Policy Sciences* 4 (1973): 155–69. It labels complex social policy problems that cannot be comprehensively defined and so cannot receive definitive, once-for-all solutions. Thanks to Stephanie A. Puen for this reference.

[62]Robert A. Pape, "What an Analysis of the January 6 Insurrection Tells Us," *Washington Post,* April 6, 2021, www.washingtonpost.com. Thanks to Karen Peterson-Iyer for this reference.

[63]Massingale, "Anger for the Sake of Justice," 12.

[64]Wildung Harrison, "The Power of Anger," 54.

Sin and Suffering Revisited

A Conceptual Exploration

Karen Kilby

What is the status of suffering in Christian theology? Is it, for instance, properly termed evil? There are some things normally described as suffering that we might not confidently label evils—the suffering of remorse or the pain of a symptom that alerts a person and enables them to take steps to deal with curable illness, or a loneliness that pushes one to seek more human contact. Indeed, Ian McFarland argues that we are too careless in our use of the term "evil" and should avoid the word in connection with suffering because it is only sin that we can be certain to be against God's will. Instances of suffering may be evil, McFarland suggests, but since we do not know enough about God's relation to particular creaturely situations, we can never in any given case *know* whether to call a specific instance of suffering evil or not.[1]

I will in the end come to a somewhat different conclusion from McFarland's, but his position helpfully underlines the fact that reflection on the status of suffering in Christian theology requires among other things some reflection on its relation to *sin*. To put it another way, his position underlines the fact that we might more easily *use* a phrase like "evil, sin, and suffering" than know exactly how we think the elements within the phrase relate to one another.

I begin by offering a preliminary map of some options for relating suffering and sin—options available in the Christian theological tradition and in contemporary discourse—before turning to consider how the direction of focus of this conference volume on dehumanizing realities such as racism, colonialism, poverty, and sex abuse can and ought to shape our thinking on this broad question. I hope my exploration of the sin-suffering relationship will lend support to the hypothesis lying behind the volume, that contemporary attention to such dehumanizing realities has something to teach the Christian theological tradition and that the Christian tradition in turn may also have something useful to bring to our struggle with them.

Before beginning, however, it is worth commenting briefly on the issue of abstraction. One might ask about the legitimacy of moving *from* the initial challenge, given with the conference, to reflect in relation to particular dehumanizing realities such as racism, colonialism, poverty, and sex abuse,[2] *to* a quite general discussion of categories of sin and suffering. Is such an abstraction morally problematic—a turning of the attention away from terrible realities that actually affect people so that one can devote it to the more comfortable puzzles involved in sorting out one's toolbox of bland and general concepts? Indeed, the slide away from the concrete might be seen not just as an evasion of what is difficult and challenging but as a form of complicity with a guilty status quo: by moving to an abstract plane where no one need feel responsible for anything in particular, one takes all the heat and the challenge out of a discussion. Or to put the same issue from another angle: In failing to explicitly root oneself in any particular context, in seeking to float above all particular contexts to the level of a more universal conversation, does one not quietly import the concerns and presuppositions of one's own, usually highly privileged, perspective? This is a long-familiar critique of certain styles of systematic theology.

I cannot specify in advance that what I explore is defensible before these sorts of challenges. Part of the aim of the essay is precisely to experiment with whether anything can in fact be said at such a high level of generality which might prove of use in grappling with concretely dehumanizing realities. If it can be—if there is anything of use to say—it will be only because it is at least to some degree already informed by more concrete kinds of theological work. What follows is I hope, in other words, an abstraction that depends on, rather than coming before, attention to the particular.

I

For much of the Western Christian tradition, especially the premodern tradition, suffering is above all seen as the consequence of sin. We are all guilty in Adam, and so there is no particular tension felt around the fact that we all live lives shaped by the consequence of the fall, lives subject to suffering and death. The unequal distribution of suffering in this life is not a significant focus of theological concern because the sin-suffering relationship is fundamentally framed at a global rather than an individual level: *all* are implicated in the fall, and all are shaped by original sin and its consequences, including the presence of suffering in life. In the premodern period, finally, attention tends to be much more on sin than on suffering: the root cause of all the problems is a matter of greater concern than the suffering which is one of its consequences.

In our current culture there are at least two widely available analogues to this premodern suffering-as-a-consequence of sin pattern, but they operate much closer to the level of the individual. A first is the pattern of thinking according to which in each case suffering must be the fault of the sufferer, who has failed to think positively enough or eat enough vegetables or exercise enough.[3] Although only a fairly small minority would proclaim explicitly as a general principle that if you suffer it is because you have sinned, there is a cultural current, an undertow, pulling in this direction. The second contemporary analogue to the premodern suffering-as-a-consequence-of-sin pattern is an I-sin-you-suffer pattern, where the wrongdoing of one individual causes the suffering of another. As with the I-sin-and-therefore-I-suffer pattern, there are of course times when this is a manifestly appropriate way to think—I throw the punch and it is your nose that bleeds, I utter the insult and it is you who feels the humiliation. But at least in a contemporary British context, quite often there seems a more general *need* to find a place to pin blame when public attention is drawn to some new and shocking suffering. Even when the suffering and destruction arise from earthquake or tsunami, it never seems to be more than a day before the focus of the news shifts toward finding an underlying "sin": someone is scandalously at fault for an inadequate early warning system or inadequate building regulations.

A third pattern comes into play if we turn to sin and suffering as typically found in contemporary philosophy of religion. Here, especially in discussions of theodicy, there is particular interest in suffering *not* linked to sin—in so-called natural evil. "Moral evil" on the view of many philosophers of religion is not so hard to reconcile with God's goodness since it can be explained by appeal to free will. Natural evil, including especially suffering, poses the difficult challenge. When "moral evil" does enter consideration, the concern is typically with the suffering and other harm it brings about rather than with the evil done, the "sin" itself. So whereas for the premodern Christian tradition, sin and suffering are joined and the theological interest is almost entirely on sin, for the modern theodicists, sin and suffering are typically isolated from one another as far as possible and the intellectual interest falls squarely on reckoning with the *suffering*.[4]

In Julian of Norwich, we find a fourth pattern: a striking intensification and an unexpected twist on the standard suffering-as-consequence-of-sin view. Sin itself *is* according to Julian the greatest suffering at least for the soul on its way to salvation—"the greatest scourge any chosen soul may be smitten with," "the most pain any soul can have, to turn from God to sin." Our sin thus draws not God's anger but God's compassion—he beholds "the sin as sorrow and pain," and the more the sin, Julian rather shockingly indicates, the greater the honors God wishes to heap on the soul for having had to endure the shame of it.[5]

The final pattern to mention is more familiar—it can be found quite widely in some strands of Christian thought and practice. In the recent Catholic tradition, it is notable in the theology of Hans Urs von Balthasar and in John Paul II's *Salvifici Dolores*: here sin is the problem to which suffering is the cure. The cure is not automatic or mechanical, but all suffering is pregnant with this possibility, to be united with the suffering of Christ for the redemption of the world. There is an association of suffering with the essence of love, with sacrifice, and ultimately with redemption—the resolution of the problem of sin. It is notable that where this is the case, the theological preoccupation with suffering can be as intense as is the preoccupation with sin, by contrast with what I am taking to be the mainstream premodern tradition.

To summarize, then, the premodern Western Christian tradition tends to see suffering as a consequence of sin at a global, universal level and places a much greater focus on sin than on suffering; contemporary everyday instincts often frame suffering also as a result of sin—of wrongdoing or failure—but at the individual level with again, perhaps, a principal focus on identifying and calling for change to this wrongdoing and failure; contemporary philosophers of religion preoccupied with theodicy are inclined to *separate* sin and suffering and concentrate on suffering; it is possible, if rarer, to think of sin *as* suffering, as we see in Julian; and finally, suffering can be associated with love and cast in the role of cure for sin, a component of redemption, perhaps even the key component.[6]

II

Against this background, it is interesting to consider how one might frame the dehumanizing realities to which this conference volume directs our attention. I begin by proposing three simple theses. These dehumanizing realities are each of them, first of all, the site of both sin and suffering: to name them is to bring before our minds simultaneously appalling sin and dreadful suffering. Second, they each name sin and suffering at what can be termed an intermediate level. They do of course affect individuals, but they operate collectively, beyond the individual, both in the wrongness done, the sinfulness, and in the wrongness suffered, the devastation they cause. And yet they do not have the absolutely general reach of original sin as conceived in the tradition. And third, in each the relationship between sin and suffering is one of complex entanglement.

Let me discuss each of these theses a little more fully. First, I am suggesting that we can appropriately talk about both sin and suffering in relation to such things as colonialism, racism, sex abuse, and poverty. The claim does not require much justification, certainly not in the case of colonialism, racism, and sex abuse. On some political and economic visions, poverty might not bring with it connotations of wrongdoing but be viewed as a sad consequence of the finitude of resources and the necessarily uneven outcomes of the best possible economic system. It is clearly beyond the scope of this essay to enter into debate with such views. The simpler solution is that that those who do not hear in the word "poverty" overtones of wrongdoing simply replace it with other terms that more clearly carry such connotations. References to poverty in later versions of the conference description were in fact expanded in such a way as to underscore elements of culpability: "exploitative capitalism," "systemic neglect of the poor."

Second, I am suggesting that in each of these cases sin and suffering are found paired *neither* at the individual level *nor* at the most universal level. It is possible that some of the evils under consideration—exploitative capitalism, racism, and colonialism—have so shaped and pervaded the world that no one is left unaffected, whether through suffering under these systems or through benefiting from and carrying responsibility for them. They are global in reach. But even if this is the case, these sin-suffering complexes do not have the kind of universality across time that original sin is held to do: we have not always been capitalists, and humanity was still, presumably, beset by sin before the emergence of colonialism.

That there is a level at which we properly speak about sin that is neither the level of the genuinely individual fault nor the absolutely universal original sin—at this middle level—is what is at play in the language of structural or social sin. However, whether we do in fact speak "properly" about sin at this level or only indirectly and in a sense improperly remains, particularly within the Catholic tradition, an unresolved question. There was disagreement in the late part of the twentieth century between Latin American liberation theologians and the authorities in Rome over precisely this issue.

Where liberation theologians wrote about structural sin, John Paul II eventually adopted the slightly weakened language of "structures of sin." Something like exploitative capitalism is not to be described directly as sin but as a structure that has resulted from many individually sinful acts and that in turn can influence individuals, making further sin easier and more tempting. Animating this resistance to a full-blown concept of structural sin was a worry about a loss of individual personal responsibility, the sense that the fundamental location of sin was in the personal relationship between the soul and God. Anything else could be described as sinful, in an extended and secondary sense, only to the degree that it could be traced out from and back to this center.

Conor Kelly has argued that the two sides have increasingly converged, with, on the one hand, magisterial documents allowing that structures of sin, once established, can be called evil and have a kind of agency that is independent of any individual actor and liberation theologians, on the other hand, making increasingly clear that reference to structural sin does not remove questions of individual responsibility.[7] In my view, however, there remains a significant in-principle difference given in the very fact that magisterial documents continue to block or avoid the use of the word sin directly in relation to structures or collectives.

The magisterial location of sin so squarely in the freely chosen acts of an individual blends comfortably with the suppositions of modern culture and perhaps for that reason is clearer and easier to grasp than the position of the liberation theologians. It also sits well, it should be acknowledged, with the tradition of individual auricular confession. The position of John Paul II and Joseph Ratzinger seems to sit less comfortably, however, with either Old and New Testament texts or traditional thought on original sin than does that of the liberation theologians.[8] There are of course *some* biblical texts in which sin is depicted as an individual phenomenon, but the case liberation theologians make—about "the sin of the world," about the tendency of both the prophets and Jesus tend to castigate whole groups, and about the fact that the crucifixion comes in the gospel narratives not just out of individual betrayals, like that of Judas, but as a result of political and religious, collective, communal structural forces—seems to me very persuasive. The biblical material does not on the whole line up very satisfyingly with the tidy location of sin in the individual alone of which John Paul II and Ratzinger write. And original sin *is* sin, according to, say, the Council of Trent, even though it is not something that I as an individual have chosen. So although there is perhaps a certain theological novelty, a development, in liberation theologians' naming as sin something that exists neither fundamentally at the level of the individual nor as an absolutely universal phenomenon, this development seems easier to reconcile with Scripture and tradition than the magisterial pushback against it, locating sin univocally in the free individual choice of each. Indeed, nearly all the obscurity and intellectual difficulties one might attribute to the concept of structural sin are already to be found in the concept of original sin.

One reason for favoring the position of the liberation theologians, then, is that it seems to exhibit a greater fidelity to the

Christian past than does the resistance to it by the magisterium. A second reason is the way it relates us to the present. To name these mid-level phenomena directly as sin is to give an urgency, a manifest ecclesial relevance and necessity, to our response to them, to the need for resistance, for change of heart and mind. It is to make it absolutely clear that these things are at the center of the Church's calling rather than an add-on consideration for those who happen to have a special interest in social justice. It is to direct our attention to the right level of reality—to the phenomenon itself and not to what is in the end a rather speculative account of its origins and outworkings somewhere else, at the level of individual wrongdoing. There is a worry on the side of magisterial voices that to speak of structural or social sin might be to let the individual sinner off the hook and lead to moral and spiritual complacency. But there is an even stronger possibility, it seems to me, that by resolutely centering attention in individual culpability, one may encourage people to distract themselves from the central issue. My focus when hearing about such a "structure of sin," to use John Paul II's phrase, might be just to search my conscience to make sure that I, at least, have not involved myself in creating this structure. I will then also need to be on guard in future against my own danger of falling into it, but otherwise I am free to put it out of my mind: only my own individual sin need ultimately concern me.[9]

The dehumanizing realities which give focus to this volume are all, then, I am suggesting, sites simultaneously of both sin and suffering; and in each of them we are confronted with sin and suffering combined at a certain middle level, neither individual nor absolutely general. My third proposal is that in each case there seems to be in these realities a complex *entanglement*, an interweaving, of sin and suffering. As a first approximation, admittedly, one might reach for the I-sin-you-suffer pattern, the "I-throw-the-punch-and-your-nose-bleeds" pattern, transposed to a collective level: the sin is attached to one group, the suffering sustained by another. Greedy capitalists and greedy consumers sin; people living in poverty, including those far away on the other side of the globe, suffer. White people are guilty of racism, Blacks and others suffer. But it is often the nature of structural or social sins that they also draw into themselves those whom they afflict. Women do not only suffer from but are often on one level or another infected by sexism. Exploitative capitalism not only degrades the living conditions of those in poverty on whom it falls most heavily but also distorts their desires and view of the world. Al McFadyen's powerful monograph *Bound to Sin* delineates in some detail the way pathologies such as sex abuse and the Nazi genocidal system work to co-opt the will of their victims, binding them in some way into the sin of which they are the victim.[10] So sin and suffering, in these dehumanizing realities, are not symmetrically distributed—we are not all equally guilty of or responsible for sexism, or racism, or capitalism—and yet they are also not neatly separable.

III

Can theological anthropology be informed by secular studies of these dehumanizing realities? The analysis I offered so far is at such a level of generality that there has not really been any particular learning from any particular secular study exhibited. What I propose to learn from instead, however, is the sheer volume of such secular attention, the sheer proliferation, complexity, and increasing predominance of work in the humanities which in some way concerns itself with or locates itself in relation to one of these dehumanizing realties, one of these sin-suffering complexes. Perhaps something to learn from this shift—it is a multifaceted and diffuse but nevertheless I think quite distinct generational change in the humanities—is that it has to be here, at this midpoint between the individual and the absolutely general, that theology even at its most abstract must take its bearing for thinking *both* about sin *and* about suffering. This is not the only way, the only point, at which to think about either sin or suffering, but it should be the central paradigm and the starting point for thought about both.

This, from one perspective, is very old news. I am doing little more, for instance, than extending a line of thought which can be found several decades ago in Jon Sobrino's *The Principle of Mercy*, in which Sobrino describes sin as an inherently analogous term, for which the *analogatum princeps*, the prime analogate, must be murder: "murdering the Son of God, and continuing to murder the sons and daughters of God in history."[11] Sobrino is clear that there is also sin and the need for forgiveness on the more familiar personal level, but this must not be mistaken for the paradigmatic case: when one thinks about sin, one takes one's bearing from what he calls historic or structural sin.

But, in fact, it is not *quite* enough simply to repeat Sobrino. Sobrino's analysis, and that of other first generation Latin American theologians, has been called into question by Latin American feminist theologians and by queer theologians, and their broader sociopolitical criticism includes raising doubts about precisely where the center of sin and suffering is imagined. Indeed, there are multiple theological proposals for exactly where to turn one's attention when thinking about sin and the suffering it causes, proposals at least as wide-ranging as the examples of dehumanizing realities listed in the description of this conference.[12] The multiple proposals are each compelling and challenging, and each urgently calls for their readers' or hearers' attention. And yet I suspect it is beyond the competence of any one academic theologian to give the due and necessary attention to each of them, much less to understand the ways in which they intersect and at times stand in conflict to one another, and much less still again to bring them into a synthesis.[13] Nevertheless, even in the absence of the possibility of a synthesis, we can learn from these many schools and strands and voices of theology, and the wider work with which they engage, that when we want to think about either sin or suffering, we must begin by thinking of these mid-level dehumanizing realities: we need to find the prime analogate of both sin *and* suffering here. It is possible, of course, to find separable, tidy, individual examples of sin to think with, and there are, certainly, forms of suffering not on the face of it attached to any larger system of sin—the grief of the widow who loses a spouse after a half century of marriage, the endurance of chronic pain, the suffering undergone by a person slowly dying through a progressively disabling disease and of the family member who nurses them through it. These experiences are not to be dismissed. But if we take seriously what the many voices of this scholarly generation teach us and the sheer weight, reach, and gravity of the evils to which they call us to attend, then we must view such cases of individual and separable suffering or sin as—in the actual world we live in—the unusual and exceptional rather than the standard cases. If we want to understand suffering, no matter how clear-cut such cases may seem, then, they are not where we should begin.

What difference does such a shift in attention make? It gives a particular perspective on the modern theodicy project, first, insofar as most theodicies seek a focus on a suffering separated as much as possible from sin. One doesn't think well, or truly, about human suffering in general if one insists on thinking about it apart from sin, and in particular apart from these mid-level sin-suffering complexes that weigh so heavily on so many and implicate so many.[14] Of course the philosopher of religion might respond that the goal of theodicies is not to think as well as possible about suffering in any general way but to think about the defense of God's existence and justice in the face of evil, and for these purposes certain kinds of test cases are particularly useful. This would be an acceptable response were the exploration of theodicy a fringe preoccupation of a few scholars. But that so many spend such effort, and induct new generations of students into focusing in the same way, on a debate that in effect misrepresents both suffering and evil and therefore misconstrues what is at stake in thinking of God's relation to a world marked by suffering and evil, is troubling.

In the sin-suffering typology with which I began, I mentioned a suffering-as-cure-for-sin pattern. Would rooting one's fundamental understanding of suffering in these entangled sin-suffering complexes, the dehumanizing realities of this conference volume, rule out of court all such concepts of redemptive suffering? That would be too much to claim. But it ought to at least slow down tendencies to sacralize or valorize suffering, to associate suffering first of all with a pure, intensified form of love. Above all we should associate suffering with sin, with being afflicted and damaged by a larger system of sin and likely drawn into its webs. If sometimes by God's grace, people manage to resist the wider webs even as they are afflicted by and suffer under them, then it is the resistance, the refusal to be drawn in and to cease to love even as one suffers, rather than the suffering itself, that speaks to us of the cross of Christ, of the sacred and the redemptive.

Such a reorientation would also lead us to resist a proposal like Ian McFarland's, that we must not name suffering as evil, because it is sin alone that we know to be against the will of God. If we expect to think about sin and suffering together, complexly entangled, then this cannot be right. Indeed, there are patterns of thought and structures of society that we precisely know *as* sin, not because we have such a complete knowledge of the history of their development that we can trace individual acts of resistance to God's will out of which they grew, but much more simply and directly because of the widespread suffering they bring about. And if we know them to be sin, to be against God, because of the harm they inflict, then it cannot make sense to remain agnostic about the status of that very harm. We cannot perhaps *always* say that suffering is an evil, but in what I am suggesting are the central, paradigmatic cases of suffering in our world, we certainly are constrained to view it that way. And so we can say, whatever exceptions there may be, typically, paradigmatically, suffering is evil.

IV

There is something, then, that the theologian, even when operating at a high level of abstraction, ought to learn about sin, about suffering, and about the relation of sin and suffering from the combined witnesses of many non-theological (and also theological) voices. Does this abstract level of theological analysis have anything to offer in return?

There is cause for hesitation here. The language of sin is off-putting, at least when used outside the context of diets, for many people, including many church people. It brings overtones of shame, of stain, of sexual condemnation, of a frightening God, and of an oppressive, condemning, perhaps hypocritical church. Ordinary Catholics are much more comfortable, in my experience, with the language of imperfection, messiness, and brokenness—except perhaps when mention of sin can be rattled off as part of a familiar liturgical prayer. If professional theologians are happier to speak about sin, it may be only because years of formal study have partially deconditioned them to the word's aversive qualities. So one cannot *lightly* suggest that there is something in the tradition of the language of sin to offer for wider consumption.

It is possible, then, that this tradition is too damaged by the way it has been used and received to offer anything of value. If we do not work on this assumption, however, is there anything useful the theological tradition brings to the table? A first candidate is the fact that in properly formed Christian theology one does not speak about sin apart from grace, nor about suffering without some testimony to hope, nor evil except in the context of a larger good. These are principles that can of course all too easily be abused—they can be turned into a minimization of sin, a refusal to attend to suffering, a general evasion of the darkness of the world. They are not, that is to say, *easy* principles to adhere to while also maintaining a "fidelity to the real," to borrow once again a phrase from Sobrino. Nevertheless, these principles—don't speak about sin apart from grace, don't speak about suffering without testimony to hope, don't speak about evil except in the context of a larger good—remain theologically necessary. Are they also politically practical? I would be overstepping my competence in political matters to make that claim too generally. At the very least, however, they seem to me to point to a helpful question one can ask across many contexts, a helpful question one can put to movements seeking to inspire change across a wide and disparate range of issues.

More substantially, the long tradition of wrestling with the concept of original sin and its relationship to the individual sinner may have something to contribute to an understanding of these sin-suffering complexes. Original sin ought not, to repeat a point made earlier, be identified with these mid-level phenomena, even though some of them can have such an extraordinarily and devastatingly wide and intergenerational reach. But there is a long history of reflecting theologically on what it means for an individual to find themselves enmeshed in an evil much greater than themselves, and I think this can be useful, especially for thinking about, say, the position of the straight person in relation to homophobia and heteronormativity; or the man in relation to sexism; or the person born into wealth, confidence, and security in relation to the class system; or the white person in relation to racism.

To be born into original sin is to be born with what one might call a double moral and spiritual problem: First, one is guilty of the sin itself, one is born into a culpable lack of original righteousness, the lack of a sanctifying grace which one *ought* to possess. One is born, so to speak, objectively sinful, objectively in the wrong state, before one has done anything at all. And second, there is concupiscence: one starts out wired, as it were, with an inclination to make the situation worse, to get it wrong in new ways as one lives one's own particular life, to sin further.

There is an analogous situation for the person born into the comfortable part of the global North, or for the white citizen of a society in the grip of anti-Black racism. However little they may know or care, they are born, first of all, into an objectively guilty situation and as a member of an objectively guilty group, into a situation that is—for instance—as materially luxurious as it is only because of past misdeeds by this group. And second, they are raised in a culture and situation that programs them with a kind of analogue to concupiscence, a passive, unreflective racism or consumerism, in the cases I am considering, which in turn makes them very likely, as they move through life, to make their own personal sinful contribution to the racism or the exploitation that already pervades and structures their society. Both an objective guilt and a corruption of the instincts are given in original sin, and something very like both an objective guilt and a corruption of the instincts seems to be involved in these social or structural sins.

There are several ways in which working with such analogies can be helpful. First, it can do something to counter two false reactions to which those who are more on the sinning than the suffering side of a particular sin-suffering complex, those whom one might call the structural sinners, are inclined. One is the desire to deny involvement in the evil, the inclination to try to persuade oneself—"I don't put women down, I don't sign up to white supremacy or make racist statements, I'm not a huge fat-cat capitalist corporation, surely I can't really be blamed for all this"—and together with that desire, the sanctimonious, defensive, and dangerous anger that arises when anyone suggests something to the contrary. The other is the compulsion, having recognized one's complicity, to escape it—the anxious conviction that there must be a route by which to return oneself to innocence, to moral purity. At least for those with Christian faith who go to church and weekly declare their sinfulness, it should, with the help of reflection on historical patterns of Christian belief, be possible to come to terms with this acknowledgment of ongoing involvement in and responsibility for a sinfulness that is bigger than me, a sin that I did not ask to be part of but which nevertheless makes me guilty. And also for those who are anyways declaring their sinfulness every Sunday if not in their daily prayer, it should be possible to live a life oriented not to innocence and exculpation but to *metanoia*, an ongoing, lifelong process of conversion of mind and heart.

Of course, one does not *need* to invoke the language of sin and suffering or the conceptuality of original sin in order to point to a path beyond an individualistic, exculpating blindness to various kinds of systemic injustice. But it can be one tool, one framework, for helping us think better, see better, even see the reasons for our own blindness, as well perhaps as helping us capture and give language to the recurring patterns that we encounter in this fundamentally good and grace-filled but so very afflicted world.

Notes

[1]Ian McFarland, "The Problem with Evil," *Theology Today* 74, no. 4 (2018): 321–39. McFarland only *explicitly* says that we should not name what is typically termed "natural evil," i.e., suffering not caused by sin, as evil. He never, however, makes clear what we should call suffering that *is* caused by sin, and at a key juncture he writes that evil cannot apply to states of affairs, only *actions* (335). This implies, then, that even in the case of suffering-caused-by-sin, it is not the state of affairs (your ongoing suffering) that can properly be termed evil but only what brought it into existence (my sin). That there is a kind of ambiguity on this issue is itself striking: there is little attention to the "evil" (if it is one) of sin-caused-suffering.

[2]I return repeatedly to these four examples simply because they were the four mentioned in my original invitation to speak at the conference and served as my touchstones as the paper emerged.

[3]For insight into such thought patterns, see Barbara Ehrenreich, *Smile or Die: How Positive Thinking Fooled America and the World* (New York: Granta, 2009).

[4]Something that makes the work of Marilyn McCord Adams stand out from many other philosophers of religion is the way she deliberately avoids this separation. See, for instance, her list of "horrendous evils" in "Horrendous Evils and the Goodness of God," in Marilyn McCord Adams and Robert Merihew Adams, *The Problem of Evil* (Oxford: Oxford University Press, 1990). For my own challenge to the notion that sin need not worry those wishing to provide theodicies, cf. "Sin, Evil and the Problem of Intelligibility," in *God, Evil and the Limits of Theology* (London: T&T Clark/ Bloomsbury, 2020) 85–98.

[5]Julian of Norwich, *Revelations of Divine Love*, trans. Elizabeth Spearing (London: Penguin, 1998), 39, 76.

[6]This is no doubt an incomplete map—I cannot claim that the positions I have laid exhaust all possibilities in Christian or contemporary secular culture. It is also a slightly messy, overlapping mapping: the perspectives I have sketched are not necessarily mutually exclusive, in that the same thinker may relate sin to suffering in more than one of these ways.

[7]Conor Kelly, "The Nature and Operation of Structural Sin: Additional Insights from Theology and Moral Psychology," *Theological Studies* 80, no. 2 (2019): 293–327. See also Kristin E. Heyer, "Social Sin and Immigration:

Good Fences Make Bad Neighbors," *Theological Studies* 71, no. 2 (2010): 410–36, for a clear and helpful account of social sin in liberation theology and John Paul II, which she draws into a "dialectical" relationship.

[8]It is interesting to note that John Paul II's apostolic exhortation *Reconciliatio et Paenitentia* mentions original sin only once, whereas "freedom" occurs twenty-four times and "individual," fifty-four.

[9]For a partly parallel, but more detailed, exploration of some of the issues around structural sin touched on here, cf. Charlotte Bray's forthcoming Durham University PhD thesis, provisionally titled "Sin and the Vulnerability of Embodied Life: Towards a Constructive Development of the Idea of Social Sin within the Catholic Tradition," especially chapters 1–3.

[10]Alistair McFadyen, *Bound to Sin: Abuse, Holocaust and the Christian Doctrine of Sin* (Cambridge: Cambridge University Press, 2009). Augustine's thought plays an important role in McFadyen's analysis. Although I have drawn on the Council of Trent for the sake of simplicity, there are also, I believe, Augustinian overtones to the position I have outlined.

[11]Jon Sobrino, *The Principle of Mercy: Taking the Crucified People from the Cross* (Maryknoll, NY: Orbis Books, 1994), 87.

[12]The conference theme reads: "There is abundant evidence that we live in a dehumanizing world: Colonialism. Inadequate access to healthcare. Exploitative capitalism. White supremacy. Cisnormativity. Xenophobia. Ecological devastation. Sexism. Political and ecclesial corruption. Disproportionate access to vital natural resources. Heteronormativity. Glorified individualism. The violence of war. The violence of our homes, our workplaces, and our church. Sexual assault. Sexual harassment. Sexual abuse. Mental health stigma. Sizeism. Ableism. The systemic neglect of the poor and other vulnerable populations."

[13]That no individual can do the intellectual work needed in order to be intellectually responsible—as a theologian or even simply as a believer—is an important theme in the work of Karl Rahner. Cf. "The Pluralism in Theology and the Unity of the Creed in the Church," *Theological Investigations,* vol. 11, 3–23; "The Faith of the Christian and the Doctrine of the Church," *Theological Investigations,* vol. 14, 24–46; and for my own brief discussion of this theme, *Karl Rahner: Theology and Philosophy* (London: Routledge, 2004), 85–89. What is described here adds an extra layer, with a distinctive kind of moral freighting, to the problem he identified.

[14]Theodicists are also often concerned with (non-human) animal suffering, but even in this case, given the preponderance of domesticated over wild animals in our contemporary world, and given the terrible conditions under which domesticated animals usually live and die, the intellectual separation of sin from suffering can seem problematic.

Francis's Theological Anthropology of Young Adults

Christus Vivit as Resource for Undergraduate Theological Educators

Cynthia L. Cameron

Christus Vivit, released in 2019, is Pope Francis's fourth apostolic exhortation and the culminating document of the 2018 meeting of the Synod of Bishops, which focused on youth and young adults. In this document, Francis lays out his vision for a Church that is renewing attention to its formation of and its ministry to young people. In a time when—at least in Europe and North America—many young people are disaffiliating from the Church, the pope is calling for the Church to seek renewed relevance in the lives of its young people.[1] Unlike most other official documents, this document is addressed specifically and first "to all Christian young people;" it is secondarily addressed to "the entire People of God, pastors and faithful alike, since all of us are challenged and urged to reflect both on the young and for the young."[2]

Revealed in Francis's reflections in this apostolic exhortation is a nascent theological anthropology of youth.[3] Although it was clearly not Francis's intention to lay out a systematic theological reflection on what it means to be an adolescent or young adult, *Christus Vivit* does give us some material to work with in the construction of such a theological anthropology. Thus, the purpose of this essay is to explore the resources this document provides to theologians and theological educators in the construction of a theological anthropology that takes adolescence and young adulthood seriously. After briefly describing the need for a theological anthropology of youth, I turn to the resources the Pope offers us in this document, the limitations of the document, and the implications for Catholic theological education.

The Absence of Young People in Theological Anthropology

Although age is often listed as a category of marginalization or discrimination, it is under-explored in systematic theology. Theologians will mention age as a category of difference, but few of them provide any systematic reflection on what it means for humans, as created by God, to age. Including age in our understandings of the kinds of experiences that inform our theological anthropologies becomes all the more important since age is never a stable category in a person's life.[4] The experiences of an infant, a toddler, a child, an adolescent, a young adult, a middle-aged adult, and an elderly person are all very different. In addition, this unstable category of age helps draw our attention to, for example, the intersections of gender, race, and class. What it means to be a Black female adolescent is not only different from what it means to be a white female adolescent; it can also be very different from what it means to be an older Latinx man or an adult Asian woman. Because of this, some of the key questions of Catholic theological anthropology take on new meaning when age is brought into the conversation, which provides a richness and nuance to our theological reflection on human experience.

While age is largely ignored in Catholic systematic theologies, young people are not entirely absent from the study of Christian spirituality and pastoral theology. First, there are a number of scholars who investigate the spiritual lives of young people. For example, Christian Smith and his collaborators, using survey data from and interviews with adolescents and young adults from around the United States, describe the faith-lives of these young people.[5] Although these resources provide a great deal of information about the faith practices of young people and some information about how young people understand their own faith, Smith does not attempt to provide a theological explanation of what it means to be an adolescent or young adult.

A second area of research includes those who consider ministry with youth and young adults. Theresa O'Keefe, for example, provides an example of a theologian and religious educator who is thinking theologically about ministry with young people. She argues that adults who work with adolescents are invited to form robust relationships with them, teaching adolescents how to be adults by demonstrating and describing the skills that are necessary for adulthood.[6] Although O'Keefe is attentive to the challenges and opportunities presented by adolescence and young adulthood, she is focused instead on the responsibilities of the adults with whom these young people are in relationship.

When authors do consider age as a relevant category for theological exploration, they tend to focus on children. For example, David Jensen's book *Graced Vulnerability* presents a theological understanding of what it means to be a child.[7] Jensen's argument—that any theology of childhood has to consider children as they currently are—is helpful for the task of incorporating age into our theological anthropological reflections. Our theologies tend to assume that the human person under consideration is a middle-aged adult; however, what we need is an approach that takes each stage of the life-span as equally representative of what it means to be a human person. In other words, the child or the adolescent or the young adult is a fully human person, not on their way to becoming a fully human person when they reach adulthood.

Jensen names another problem that arises when we consider age in our theological anthropologies: theology is written by middle-aged adults, mostly white, male, cisgender, middle-class, middle-aged adults. As Jensen notes in relation to a theological consideration of children, "The problem becomes even more acute once we recognize that those who typically define and assign difference tend to be those in power. Children, presumably, have little say in defining what a child is. . . . To understand children in God's image, moreover, is to reject the multiple attempts to mold children in *our* image."[8] The same caution is appropriate for theological considerations of young people; theological reflection on age runs the risk of reflecting the experiences of the middle-aged adult and not of young people. On the other hand, the immaturity that leads theologians to—intentionally or unintentionally—overlook adolescents also suggests that they are not yet developmentally mature enough to provide meaningful theological anthropological reflection on their own experiences of their adolescence.

Jensen, however, recognizes the significant challenge of writing for and about a group of people to which one no longer belongs, suggesting that, because adults are in relationship with children, they can speak authentically for children who are not yet capable of speaking for themselves.[9] Perhaps the same can be true for the consideration of adolescents and young adults in our theological anthropologies. Having passed through these life stages ourselves and being currently in a variety of formal ministerial relationships and informal friendships with young people provides us with a glimpse at their experiences of their own humanity.

Christus Vivit: A Resource for Theological Anthropology

To reiterate, although Francis's apostolic exhortation *Christus Vivit* is not intended to be an exploration of a theological anthropology that centers the experiences of young people, it does tell us a great deal about what Francis thinks about young people, which can give theologians a place to start in formulating a more capacious theological anthropology, one that takes seriously age in general and young people in particular. Here I want to highlight three key aspects of the operative theological anthropology that are revealed in this document: that youth is a legitimate life stage, worthy and important in its own right; that what it means to be a human person is grounded in friendship with Jesus; and that this anthropology is oriented toward human flourishing, both for young people and for all people.

First, Francis argues that being a young person is good in itself and that young people are not merely "not-yet-adults." He insists that "youth is not something to be analyzed in the abstract. Indeed, 'youth' does not exist: there exist only young people, each with the reality of his or her own life."[10] Being a young person is more than simply being in a period of transition between childhood and adulthood. In fact, being a young person is an experience of grace:

> God is the giver of youth and he is at work in the life of each young person. Youth is a blessed time for the young and a grace for the Church and for the world. It is joy, a song of

home and a blessing. Making the most of our youthful years entails seeing this season of life as worthwhile in itself, and not simply as a brief prelude to adulthood.[11]

The greatest gifts of adolescence and young adulthood, for Francis, are hopefulness and a future-orientation that seem characteristic of many young people. He calls on young people to dream big dreams and to look to the future with hope and joy. He says,

> Youth, as a phase in the development of the personality, is marked by dreams which gather momentum, by relationships which acquire more and more consistency and balance, by trials and experiments, and by choices which gradually build a life project. At this stage in life, the young are called to move forward without cutting themselves off from their roots, to build autonomy but not in solitude.[12]

Paradoxically, while Francis understands adolescence and young adulthood as oriented toward the future, this is not because being an adult is somehow better than being young. It is the very openness to the future that makes adolescence and young adulthood valuable in its own right.

Second, Francis's operative anthropology of young people is intimately connected to his understanding of the importance of friendship with Jesus. He sees a profound connection between the youthfulness of Jesus and the youthfulness of young people. The fact that Jesus died while still what we might call a young adult provides a point of contact between Jesus and young people that can develop into a profound friendship. After arguing that Jesus is both young and youthful, Francis calls young people to seek out a friendship with Jesus that can provide meaning and grounding to life: "No matter how much you live the experience of these years of your youth, you will never know their deepest and fullest meaning unless you encounter each day your best friend, the friend who is Jesus."[13] Recognizing that young people are oriented toward forming friendships and intimate relationships, Francis invites young people into the love of God as experienced in the friendship of Jesus. This is, he argues, a never-ending relationship that provides constancy, reliability, and confidence for the future.

And, third, Francis's operative theological anthropology as it concerns young people, is oriented toward human flourishing. Francis, of course, acknowledges that young people around the world face significant hardships and challenges. He names war; exploitation; marginalization; exclusion based on religious, ethnic, and economic status; and the commercialization of youthfulness as among the barriers to human flourishing experienced by young people. He draws particular attention to the potential dehumanization of young people in an increasingly digitalized culture, the impact of migration on young people, and the systems of abuse, including sexual abuse of young people, found both in the Church and in the world.

In the face of these and other challenges faced by young people, Francis insists that God is calling all humans, and particularly young people, to a life of flourishing and thriving, to a fulfilling life through friendship with God, "who loves you, wants you to be happy."[14] Francis invites young people—to borrow a phrase from St. Francis de Sales—to be who they are and to be that well, saying:

> You have to discover who you are and develop your own way of being holy, whatever others may say or think. Becoming a saint means becoming more fully yourself, becoming what the Lord wished to dream and create, and not a photocopy [of someone else]. Your life ought to be a prophetic stimulus to others and leave a mark on this world, the unique mark that only you can leave.[15]

Francis names fraternal relationships and service to the world as ways that young people can find this flourishing life. Since they are already oriented toward the formation of friendships, Francis invites young people to a communal life that recognizes the beauty and dignity of others and seeks their thriving. In this way, the bonds of friendship draw young people outside of themselves; Francis says,

> God loves the joy of young people. He wants them especially to share in the joy of fraternal communion, the sublime joy felt by those who share with others. . . . Fraternal love multiplies our ability to experience joy, since it makes us rejoice in the good of others. . . . May your youthful spon-

taneity increasingly find expression in fraternal love and a constant readiness to forgive, to be generous, and to build community.[16]

Service to the world is a particularly important part of flourishing for Francis. He commends the various ways that young people already commit themselves to the service of others—assisting the poor, working to end environmental degradation, fighting against oppression and marginalization. He calls them to continue these efforts to make the world a better place and "to offer a Christian response to the social and political troubles emerging in different parts of the world."[17] In these ways, young people are witnessing to a way of living that is full of joy, a sense of purpose, and love. "The best way to prepare a bright future is to experience the present as best we can, with commitment and generosity"; for Francis, a flourishing young person is one who is living the "*now* of God."[18]

While *Christus Vivit* tells us a great deal about Francis's operative theological anthropology of young people, there are still some limitations to it. Among them is that Francis is not really saying anything new. His focus on relationality and human flourishing are not innovative or revolutionary ways of thinking about the value of the human person in general. What makes his operative theological anthropology interesting, though, is his application of these ideas to adolescence and young adulthood as a life stage that is good in itself and not merely a stepping-stone to the good of adulthood. This is an invitation to theologians and religious educators to think theologically about adolescence and young adulthood.

That said, I do want to focus on one additional weakness in the document, one that has the potential to limit its reception by the very young people that Francis is reaching out to. Because Francis is speaking to at least three audiences—young people, those who minister to them, and the whole Church—there is an awkwardness to the document. Francis is often switching back and forth between addressing young people themselves and a clearly adult audience. This has the effect of implying that the young people are not fully a part of a conversation about them. This is compounded by the fact that the experiences of young people, when they are present, are mediated through the Synod's final document. In other words, when Francis talks about listening to young people, he is reflecting on voices relayed to him by the bishops, who were themselves relying primarily on surveys and conversations with those who minister to young people. Alongside this is a sense of Francis speaking to young people in much the same way that the ancient sage spoke to the young men in the book of Proverbs. Like Proverbs, it is the advice of an older adult for a young person who has no voice in the document. All of this seems to somewhat undercut Francis's message that adolescence and young adulthood are life stages that are in themselves valuable and that young people have a voice and a role in the Church.

Implications for Catholic Theological Education

Given Francis's contribution to our reflections on a theological anthropology of youth, it is important for those who teach and minister to young adults to consider the implications for Catholic colleges and universities. In particular, what are the implications for instructors' pedagogical commitments and practices in Catholic theological education? How can Francis's vision for a theological anthropology that understands adolescence and young adulthood as inherently good provide a foundation for thinking about what happens in the classrooms?

There are two understandings of "pedagogy" to consider. The first is pedagogy as a general approach to theological education. What is the general orientation of the instructor to the young people who are in the classrooms? Do instructors operate as if young people are inherently good as they already are, in ways that honor their relationality, and that demonstrate a desire for their flourishing?

Feminist educator bell hooks, in her book *Teaching Critical Thinking*, suggests that love can serve as a robust foundation for liberative pedagogies; this foundation is a commitment to love the young people in classrooms that resonates well with Francis's anthropological approach in *Christus Vivit*. hooks says that "when we teach with love, combining care, commitment, knowledge, responsibility, respect, and trust, we are often able to enter the classroom and go straight to the heart of the matter."[19] For hooks, good classroom pedagogy is rooted in love, which reflects the kind of theological anthropology that Francis describes: it assumes the fundamental goodness of young adults, it is highly relational, and it is focused on their flourishing. In other words, when Catholic theological educators take the time to establish loving relationships with their students—demonstrating to students, in ways that students can see and hear, that they love them as they already are—they are laying a foundation that will allow for the exploration of theological ideas that can have profound meaning for students. Conversation around weighty theological concepts such as love, grace, communion, friendship, and sacrifice have the potential to be more capacious and engaging when students already have a sense that their instructor values who they are and is interested in their lives and experiences. This kind of loving approach to pedagogy insists on robust student engagement and learning; for hooks, it is an approach that demands a great deal from students. She notes that "all meaningful love relations empower each person engaged in the mutual practice of partnership. Love between teacher and student makes recognition possible; it offers a place where the intersection of academic striving meets the overall striving on all our parts to be psychologically whole."[20]

A second aspect to thinking about pedagogy is a consideration of the day-to-day practices of syllabi, classroom management, instructional techniques, and assessment. Educational philosopher Elliot Eisner is helpful for thinking through what instructors do and fail to do to respect the full humanity of the young people in their courses. Eisner argues that in each school there are three curricula—the explicit, the implicit, and the null—and that each of these teaches something to students.[21] Or, more simply, teachers teach in three ways: in what they say, what they do, and what they don't do.

What do instructors *say* in their pedagogical approaches that affirms the goodness of young people, their relationality, and their flourishing? Do they tell students that they think that young people are good as they are, and do instructors say this out loud in ways that students can hear? Does the syllabus account for their ability to flourish as human beings, no matter what talents or challenges they bring to the learning experience? Do classroom practices and assessments give them the opportunity to form meaningful relationships in the classroom and give them the opportunity to reflect on their relationships outside of the classroom?

What do instructors *do* to affirm the goodness, the relationality, and the flourishing of the young people in our classes? How do instructors welcome students into the classroom and get the class started? How do they deal with students who struggle to understand readings or complete assessments? How do they demonstrate to students that they matter, that they are committed to the flourishing of students?

And, finally, what do instructors do that undercuts all of this? How do they fail to honor the goodness of young people, their relationality, and their flourishing? Do instructors continually interrogate their syllabus, reading lists, and pedagogical practices to ensure that classrooms are just, not just in terms of race and gender, but also in thinking about age and ageism?

In conclusion, Francis has provided educators and theologians with a helpful document to ground thoughtful consideration of young adults, to think theologically about young adulthood, and to recommit ourselves to their full flourishing as young adults within Catholic colleges and universities. Valuing young adulthood as a stage in life that is good in its own right provides theologians and theological educators with an expansive vision of who these young people are and not just who they may become.

Notes

[1] See Robert J. McCarty and John M. Vitek, *Going, Going, Gone: The Dynamics of Disaffiliation in Young Catholics* (Winona, MN: St. Mary's, 2017). The authors' description of disaffiliation is informed by a joint study by St. Mary's Press and the Center for Applied Research in the Apostolate (CARA) at Georgetown University.

[2] Pope Francis, post-synodal apostolic exhortation *Christus Vivit—To Young People and to the Entire People of God* (2018), www.vatican.va, 3. Hereinafter *CV*.

[3] In the document, Pope Francis defines "youth" as those people between the ages of 16 and 29 (*CV*, 68), which overlaps with what is often called mid-adolescence (approximately 14–17), late adolescence (approximately 18–21), and early adulthood (approximately 22–30). However, the dividing lines among the life-stages are ill-defined; for a useful summary of this issue, see Alexa C. Curtis, "Defining Adolescence," *Journal of Adolescent and Family Health*, 7, no. 2 (October 2015). For the purposes of this essay, "youth" will be understood as a fluid category that includes those between 16 and 29, with adolescence marking the earlier part of this age range (approximately 16–21) and young adulthood marking the later part (approximately 22–29).

[4] Unlike, for example, categories like gender, race, sexual orientation, and even socioeconomic class, which, while fluid, do not tend to change across the life-span.

[5]Christian Smith with Melinda Lundquist Denton, *Soul Searching: The Religious and Spiritual Lives of American Teenagers* (New York: Oxford University Press, 2005); Christian Smith with Patricia Snell, *Souls in Transition: The Religious and Spiritual Lives of Emerging Adults* (New York: Oxford University Press, 2009); Christian Smith with Kari Christoffersen, Hilary Davidson, and Patricia Snell Herzog, *Lost in Transition: The Dark Side of Emerging Adulthood* (New York: Oxford University Press, 2011); Kenda Creasy Dean, *Almost Christian: What the Faith of Our Teenagers Is Telling the American Church* (New York: Oxford University Press, 2010).

[6]Theresa A. O'Keefe, *Navigating toward Adulthood: A Theology of Ministry with Adolescents* (New York: Paulist, 2018).

[7]David H. Jensen, *Graced Vulnerability: A Theology of Childhood* (Cleveland, OH: Pilgrim, 2005), 44. Like other theologians who consider this lifestage, Jensen defines childhood as beginning in infancy and lasting until age 18. Those we might consider early- and mid-adolescents are included in his view; however, the bulk of his attention is given to pre-pubescent children.

[8]Ibid., 42–43.

[9]Ibid., xiv.

[10]CV 71.

[11]CV 135.

[12]CV 137.

[13]CV 150.

[14]CV 145.

[15]CV 162.

[16]CV 167.

[17]CV 174.

[18]CV 178.

[19]bell hooks, *Teaching Critical Thinking: Practical Wisdom* (New York: Routledge, 2010), 161. Educational philosopher Nel Noddings provides a similar approach in her work on cultivating an ethic of care in schools. See, for example: Nel Noddings, *The Challenge to Care in Schools: An Alternative Approach to Education*, 2nd ed. (New York: Teachers College Press, 2005).

[20]hooks, *Teaching Critical Thinking*, 162–63.

[21]Elliot Eisner, *The Educational Imagination: On the Design and Evaluation of School Programs*, 3rd ed. (New York: Pearson, 2001), 87–107.

Rahner's Embodied Subject

Carnal Phenomenology
and Rethinking Humanism "Otherwise"

Jack Louis Pappas

*Non seulement l'esprit parle à l'esprit, mais la chair
parle à la chair.*
—Paul Claudel[1]

The theology of Karl Rahner remains a consummate achieve-
ment of mid-twentieth-century Catholic thought. In the wake
of a long nineteenth century, defined by ecclesial hostility to the
variegated currents of philosophical modernity, it was primarily
Rahner's theology that cleared the path forward for a renewal of
Catholic intellectual life. Yet the significance of Rahner's *aggiorna-
mento* of the Catholic theological tradition has been increasingly
challenged in the wake of the Second Vatican Council. This is
indicative both of a seismic intellectual shift over the last several
decades and of a limitation of the reception of Rahner himself.
Insofar as Rahner is frequently identified as the paradigmatic
modern theologian, the "*ne plus ultra* of theological enlightenment," his correlation of transcendental philosophy with Catholic
theology has apparently been rendered passé—if not totally ob-
solete—by subsequent developments in continental philosophy.[2]
Indeed, given Rahner's apparent dependence on modernity's turn
to the subject and a corresponding idealist metaphysics, he is
sometimes interpreted as either failing to anticipate or adequately

confront "postmodern" efforts to deconstruct modern subjectivity and the metaphysical tradition.[3]

The most succinct summary of these critiques is perhaps offered by Rowan Williams, who writes, "Rahner remains firmly within the limits of a transcendentalist analysis of subjectivity; he belongs in that world of 'ontotheology' and Cartesian introspection from which Heidegger [and the traditions of phenomenology, hermeneutics, structuralism, and deconstruction following him] firmly turned away."[4] In other words, Rahner's reinscription of theological discourse in terms of an existential anthropology or fundamental ontology is taken to be indicative of an uncritical reliance on the presuppositions of post-Kantian subjectivism in general and its construction of an autonomous, self-determining account of the human being in particular. Echoing Rahner's long-time friend and sometime rival Hans Urs von Balthasar, Williams argues that Rahner's theology runs aground to the extent that it seeks to locate the conditions of possibility for the reception of Divine revelation in an *a priori* capacity of the human subject in the form of a "pre-apprehension" of Being [*Vorgriff auf esse*]. For Williams, Rahner's affirmation of an essential continuity between categorial, divine self-revelation and a universal transcendental *a priori* delimits theological discourse to a kind of abstraction, derived from an originary and indeterminate "formal possibility."[5] More, Rahner retains modern idealism's "cleavage"[6] between a pure transcendental ego and the empirical, concrete self, an opposition which threatens to negate our native "sense of belonging in a world [on account of] its obsession with subjectivity and the self-constitution of the subject."[7]

In response to these critiques, I explicate how Rahner's theological approach represents nothing short of a radical revision of transcendental subjectivity and of the conception of the human being as such. According to Rahner, the human being is nothing other than "the being which loses himself in God" and attains ultimate significance only in concrete union with Christ.[8] I demonstrate how Rahner's account of this openness represents a mode of a carnal phenomenology that endeavors to think otherwise than both modern humanism and postmodern antihumanism.

To further substantiate my claim that Rahner's distinctively counter-subjective—and ultimately Christocentric—mode of humanism is provided by way of a carnal phenomenology, I proceed in two stages. First, I explain how embodied perception is foundational to Rahner's view of the subject and its transcendentality by drawing parallels between his existential anthropology and the phenomenology of Maurice Merleau-Ponty. In so doing, I show how Rahner's anthropology offers the prospect for a revisionist humanism grounded in affectivity, relationality, and corporeal mediation in contrast to narrowly subjectivist and cognitivist constructions of the human being. Second, I briefly gesture toward how this carnal phenomenological reading of Rahner helps clarify the relationship between his view of the connection between *a priori* (transcendental) revelation and *a posteriori* (categorial) revelation in a manner that integrates his so-called "existential anthropology" within the broader horizon of an incarnational theology.

Carnal Phenomenology: Rahner with Merleau-Ponty

The term "carnal phenomenology" is, of course, not a term that Rahner himself utilizes. I employ this term anyhow in the spirit of retrieving several elements of his existential anthropology that tend to be occluded by his critical interpreters—namely, his construction of the transcendental subject in both his early work, as represented by *Geist in Welt* (*Spirit in the World*), and *Hörer des Wortes* (*Hearers of the Word*).

Despite his critics' claims to the contrary, Rahner's account of the subject and its transcendence must be thoroughly differentiated from either rationalist or idealist constructions of subjectivity, such as those of Descartes or Kant or Fichte.[9] Indeed, Rahner's approach conceives the transcendental subject in a way that is fundamentally incompatible with any form of subjectivity that gives priority to an abstract, self-positing ego that spontaneously imposes its own conditions of possibility or constitutes its other (including the empirical ego) as its object. Rahner stringently rejects any conception of the self that is abstracted from its dependence on intersubjective, historical, and concretely embodied existence. As indicated by the very title of *Geist in Welt*, he understands human transcendentality in terms of a primacy of desire, a self-exceeding dynamism [*Geist*] that is always oriented toward the other in a mode fundamentally predicated upon receptivity and exposure to the world [*Welt*].[10]

"The being of what intuits receptively," Rahner writes, "must be the being of another as such. Antecedent to any apprehension of a definite other, the knower itself must have already and always entered into otherness."[11] The human being is thus characterized by a "bivalence" in which alterity acts as the very precondition that mediates and constitutes subjectivity itself.[12] By revising the notion of subjectivity as an intertwining of the self with the world, Rahner re-conceives the modern turn to the subject by grounding it in a noncompetitive relationship between interiority and exteriority. There is no cleavage between the transcendental and the empirical but rather a kind of *a priori* coincidence of identity and otherness that Rahner takes to be an irreducible fact of human existence. He elaborates on this view further via his account of corporeality or "sensibility" [*Sens*].

According to Rahner, corporeality is grounded in the reciprocity between spirit and materiality, which he takes to be the underlying paradoxical structure of human existence. That is, the human being is at once kinetic and self-transcending by virtue of her temporality as well as also ineluctably finite and restricted according to the spatialized fragility of the body. "Sensibility means the givenness of being over to the other, to matter. So the sensible is always situated at that undivided midpoint between self-possession through separative setting-self over against every other [*Sichabsetzen*], and a total abandonment [*Verlorenheit*] to the other which would completely conceal the existent from itself."[13] This bivalent orientation is not a mere juxtaposition of two opposed quantities. Rather, it is a tension-in-unity, an interlaced polarity, whose vinculum and expression is the body itself. Spirit or "consciousness" [*Geist*] is not a static entity or "substance" but is instead characterized as a self-exteriorizing intention of given phenomena, a self-exceeding transcendence that knows itself as consciousness only by way of its restriction by the other. As Andrew Tallon comments, human self-transcendence *and* restriction reflect the double character of embodiment that is given in the simultaneity of openness and self-possession. "My body (i.e., embodiment as consciousness's first otherness) is a *pre-apprehension* [*Vorgriff*], a corporeal connatural anticipation of another. . . . [A]s emanation of spirit, sensibility makes consciousness present in space-time as affection [*Einfülung, Urempfindung*], then as cognition and volition."[14] This dynamic process, which

Rahner articulates as a "return-to-self" [*reditio in se ipsum*], is not simply a reflexive traversal from "interior" to "exterior" but an intertwining of intentionality with phenomenality of invisible with visible, and of consciousness with materiality.[15]

Consequently, Rahner takes difference to be constitutive of identity at every level. The cognitive-affective "self-presence" of spirit is achieved only relatively to the degree that the self is inherently defined by otherness, as much as presence is indexed by absence. Likewise, spirit is itself only to the extent that it is incarnated, just as the body is "spiritualized" only in its being vivified by the dynamic transcendence of the spirit which it expresses and incarnates.[16]

Precisely on account of this chiasmatic or intertwining matrix of human existence, Rahner's notion of subjectivity is as much a *friction* between self and other as it is a mode of reciprocity. The relation and recognition that the body founds and mediates is never achieved as a total transparency, or totality. Rather, it is always a chiaroscuro, a mediate-immediacy delimited by the opacity of the other that resists availability, appropriation, and exhaustive recognition. This tension should not be confused with a dualistic conflict between the spirit's appetitive self-exceeding and the intrinsic limitations of embodied facticity. Instead, it is a wholistic tension reflective of the irreducible chiasm of spirit and corporeality that constitutes the central paradox of human existence.[17] The paradox of the human being is given according to the fact of our mediation by difference. Although spirit knows itself only by returning to itself, this return is fulfilled and constituted by an otherness that is both the source of its ultimate desire as much as its frustration.

When translated into more explicitly phenomenological terrain, the basic features of Rahner's existential anthropology reveal striking similarities with the approach of Maurice Merleau-Ponty, who articulates a similarly revised account of the human subject and its transcendentality. In contrast to any Cartesian or idealist conception, Merleau-Ponty describes the "true cogito" [*cogito véritable*] in terms of a foundational *inherence* in the world.[18] For Merleau-Ponty as for Rahner, this inherence of the self in its environing world consists of an irreducible bivalence and reciprocity such that "the world is all in us and I am outside myself."[19] That is, the true cogito is given as a concrete *incarnation*, an embodied temporality that is always already enmeshed within a broader matrix of intersubjective and intercorporeal relationships, a being-present-within-the-world [*être-au-monde*]. This reciprocal and mediating relationship forecloses any possibility of a naked ontological account of the world or a pre-empirical "excarnate" apperceptive subject. Merleau-Ponty writes: "[The subject] only achieves his ipseity by actually being a body and by entering into the world through this body.... [M]y existence as subjectivity is identical with my existence as a body and with the existence of the world, and because, ultimately, the subject that I am, understood concretely, is inseparable from this particular body and this particular world."[20] If the human being is constitutively embedded within the milieu of otherness by virtue of the body, then it is always also ecstatic and oriented toward our own self-transcendence.

Like the reciprocal relationship between Rahner's notion of pre-apprehension and sensibility, Merleau-Ponty understands the subject as a coincidence of passive sensation and dynamic perceiving. The human being is at once a passive recipient of the world as well as an active agent who anticipates an ultimate horizon of meaning as enacted through spontaneity of perception. "To perceive is not to experience a multitude of impressions.... [I]t is to see an immanent sense *bursting forth* [*jaillir*] from a constellation of givens."[21] The bivalence of receptive sensation and intentional perception is co-mediated and "intertwined" [*entrelacé, chiasmus*] for Merleau-Ponty at an *a priori* level via the body. Although this notion of the co-mediating character of embodiment is first articulated in his *Phénoménologie de la perception*, Merleau-Ponty gives more expansive treatment to the concept of intertwining in his later work *Le Visible et l'invisible*.

There Merleau-Ponty writes that "my body as a visible thing is contained within the full spectacle. But my seeing body subtends this visible body, and all the visibles with it. There is a reciprocal interpenetration of one in the other."[22] The touching body is always also touched just as the beholding body is always also visible and as the hearing body is always also sonorous. The *coincidentia oppositorum* whereby the lived body and objective body are intertwined, Merleau-Ponty names "the flesh" [*la chair*]. Merleau-Ponty describes the flesh in a fashion that strongly echoes Rahner's conception of the self-mediating identity-in-difference of

incarnate Spirit's "return-to-itself." Incarnate subjectivity is neither
a total "fusion" nor an interminable "separation" between subject
and object (sensor and sensed). Rather, the flesh acts as a porous
border, a membrane that is penetrated—crossed—from either side
both by consciousness and the phenomenality of the world. As
such, perception for Merleau-Ponty is not a narrowly cognitive
"grasp" of entities but a foundational, affective embeddedness
in the world that is both receptive and active.[23] As an incarnate
subject, the human being is at once self-transcendent and always
already situated in relation to the other. Moreover, and again like
Rahner, Merleau-Ponty's view of the entangled relation between
self and world is understood as a possible occasion of friction
and even rupture, not merely in terms of sheer continuity.[24] That
is, Merleau-Ponty does not deny that our exposure to the other is
as much an occasion of possible trauma as it is a vehicle of possible transcendence. But, in either case, the human being cannot
be extricated from the mediating horizon of the flesh.

From Carnal Phenomenology
to Incarnational Theology

When placed in parallel to Merleau-Ponty's account of the flesh,
a picture of Rahner's existential anthropology and theology begins
to emerge that is markedly different from the narrowly cognitivist interpretations offered by his critics. The stakes of this carnal
phenomenological interpretation are most explicit when applied
to Rahner's notion of pre-apprehension [Vorgriff], which acts as a
certain bridge between his existential anthropology and dogmatic
theology. For Rahner, the dynamic orientation of the human being
toward an infinite horizon acts both as the condition of possibility
for the apprehension of any finite phenomenon, as well as for our
ultimate reception of concrete historical revelation.[25] Taken in a
narrowly philosophical sense, it is precisely here that Rahner affirms an unbounded account of human subjectivity in an explicitly
idealist mode. By contrast, a carnal phenomenological reading
suggests that pre-apprehension does not so much indicate a pre-
reflective act of cognitive appropriation as it names the affective
openness of corporeal sense toward that which exceeds its ability
conceptually to delimit or cognize. In theological terms, Rahner's
emphasis on pre-apprehension is often taken to be illustrative

of his reduction of Divine revelation to the innate structure of human subjectivity and his broader elevation of transcendental revelation over categorial revelation.

A carnal phenomenological reading, however, foregrounds an underlying reciprocity between transcendental and categorial revelation as mediated via the body which is itself always already assumed in Christ's Incarnation:

> The fundamental assertion of Christology is that God became *flesh*, became matter. . . . [The Word] of God himself establishes this corporeal part of the world as his own reality, both creating and accepting it at the same time. Hence, he establishes it as what is different from himself in such a way that this very materiality expresses *him* and allows him to be present in this world.[26]

As such, for Rahner, the body can be interpreted as *both* the created condition of possibility for our ultimate reception of revelation *and* the revelatory self-expression of the Divine Word as ultimately assumed in the eternal and irrevocable reality of the hypostatic union. Rahner anchors Christology in a reciprocal bi-directional movement that mirrors the very intertwining of the flesh itself. To the extent that the self-exceeding orientation of human pre-apprehension is nothing less than God's own self-communication, our anticipatory openness is thus at once conditioned and ultimately fulfilled by God.[27] Building on the formula of the Council of Chalcedon, Rahner affirms that in Christ God's self-emptying love is both given and received by humanity because, in his very person, humanity and divinity are indissolubly united in the event of the Word's being made flesh. Christ's *descent* into corporeality and finitude is always at the same time the consummation of humanity's self-transcending *ascent* to God.

Inasmuch as the flesh acts as the porous medium of our self-transcendence, it is always also implicitly the very locus of God's concrete self-communication. This corporeal self-disclosure of God reflects not only the very fact of its being created through the Divine Word, but—and more radically—also the fact that the Word eternally assumes this very flesh, concretizing his identification with human existence and rendering it explicit as divine-human flesh. Moreover, Rahner understands the creation of the flesh and its assumption as one and the same act. The Word simultaneously *assumes by creating* and *creates by assuming*: "We can understand creation and Incarnation as two moments and two phases of *one* process of God's self-giving and self-expression, although it is an intrinsically differentiated process. . . . [T]he creative Word which establishes the world establishes this world to begin with as the materiality which is to become his own, or to become the environment of his own materiality."[28] The whole of embodied human existence is consequently an expression of the Divine Word such that God's very self is disclosed to us not by an overcoming of our corporeality and finitude, but immanently through its carnal self-transcendence.

Conclusion: Rethinking Humanism

Rahner's distinctive foregrounding of subjectivity and his anthropological reorientation of theological discourse does not, as his critics allege, represent a concession (or even a collaboration) with modern humanism's constructions of solipsistic rationality, agency, and autonomy. For Rahner, any humanism that affirms humanity to be its own self-authoring master can only ultimately denigrate what is most uniquely human. For if the human being is precisely that being "which loses himself in God" and whose *concretissimum* is the incarnate Word manifested in Christ, then the unique dignity of humanity can be understood only *negatively* in terms of an openness and exposure to the other that cannot be mastered or placed at our disposal.[29] Both Rahner's account of the subject and the humanism that it enacts are therefore thoroughly theocentric and Christologically indexed. Rahner writes: "Christianity renders every concrete humanism contingent, dispensable in favor of another, future oriented humanism, by situating everyone within God's open future. In its conviction of human freedom, rooted in and oriented towards God, Christianity opens up the permanent possibility . . . of man's dependence on and relation to the intractable and incomprehensible one, which calls him into question."[30] The mode of subjectivity that such a humanism affirms is not that of an excarnate and all-constitutive subject. Rather, it is an infinite orientation toward an anterior alterity given in the decentered vulnerability of the enfleshed body. This carnal exposure and openness thus allows for a paradoxical affirmation of reciprocity between oneself and another such that our fulfillment is only given in excess of what we natively possess—even to the extent that this receptivity itself becomes the concrete manifestation of the Divine Word.

In a world increasingly riven by exploitation and dehumanizing violence, Rahner's carnal phenomenology suggests that an authentic Christian humanism remains capable of envisioning humanity in terms that resist objectification or the identification of the human being as a Promethean subject beyond the reach of material vulnerability and constraints of history. Such a vision of the human being thus lends itself to a commitment to solidarity and a radical openness to the other as the real and mediating expression of God's saving action within the world and within the flesh. The broader significance of Rahner's thought then cannot be mistaken for a kind of theological enactment of the Cartesian and Kantian turn toward the subject or as a speculative flight from the world. On the contrary, Rahner's turn toward the self represents a radical intervention in theological discourse that redirects us toward the demands of concrete life and summons us to consider the human being in its suffering and poverty, its finitude and woundedness, as much as its irreducible particularity as the foremost summons to encountering God's self-disclosure.

Notes

[1]Paul Claudel, "La Sensation du divin," in *Présence et Prophétie* (Fribourg, Switzerland: Egloff, 1942), 49–130, 61. Translated into English, Claudel writes, "Not only does spirit speak to spirit, but flesh speaks to flesh."

[2]Joseph O'Leary, *Questioning Back: The Overcoming of Metaphysics in the Tradition* (Minneapolis: Seabury, 1985), 97.

[3]See Rowan Williams, "Balthasar, Rahner and the Apprehension of Being," in *Wrestling with Angels: Conversations in Modern Theology*, ed. John Riches (Grand Rapids, MI: Eerdmans, 2007), 86–105; John Milbank, *The Word Made Strange: Theology, Language, Culture* (Hoboken, NJ: Wiley-Blackwell, 1997), 15; Jean-Luc Marion, "The Possible and Revelation," in *The Visible and the Revealed*, trans. and ed. Christina M. Gschwandtner (New York: Fordham University Press, 2008), 11–12; and Jean-Yves Lacoste, *Experience & The Absolute: Disputed Questions on the Humanity of Man*, trans. Mark Raftery-Skehan (New York: Fordham University Press, 2004), 200n9. For the most part, these critiques repeat an initial line of criticism made by Hans Urs von Balthasar, who alleged that Rahner ultimately reduced Christianity to a monolithic foundation in transcendental philosophy that emphasized the dynamism of subjectivity at the expense of objective revelation. See Hans Urs

von Balthasar, *Theo-Drama IV: The Action,* trans. Graham Harrison (San Francisco: Ignatius, 1994), 274.

[4]See Williams, "Balthasar, Rahner and the Apprehension of Being," 98.

[5]Ibid., 90.

[6]Ibid., 93–94.

[7]Ibid., 94.

[8]Ibid.

[9]Harald Holz, *Transzendentalphilosophie und Metaphysik: Studie über Tendenzen in der heutigen philosophischen Grundlagenproblematik* (Mainz, Germany: Matthias-Grünewald-Verlag, 1966), 130–35.

[10]Karl Rahner, *Spirit in the World,* trans. William Dych (New York: Continuum, 1994), 92–97.

[11]Ibid., 79.

[12]Thomas Sheehan, *Karl Rahner: The Philosophical Foundations* (Athens: Ohio University Press, 1990). Sheehan explicates this bivalence at length in the following passage: "The bivalence of sensible receptivity and intellectual spontaneity finds its unity in man as the spirit who becomes and must become, sensibility in order to be spirit, in man, that is who remains the potentiality for a self-presence which is ever and constitutively in a state of relative self-absence." See p. 196.

[13]Rahner, *Spirit in the World,* 117.

[14]Andrew Tallon, Introduction to Karl Rahner, *Hearer of the Word,* trans. Joseph Donceel (New York: Continuum, 1994), xvi.

[15]Rahner, *Spirit in the World,* 226–27.

[16]Rahner, *Hearer of the Word,* 53.

[17]As suggested by Robert Doud, there is a strong correlation between Rahner's view of human corporeality and finitude with the fact of human concupiscence. See Robert Doud, "Sensibility in Rahner & Merleau-Ponty," *The Thomist* 44, no. 3 (1980): 376. This interpretation is substantiated by Rahner's explicit engagement with the question of concupiscence in his essay "The Theological Concept of Concupiscence," in *Theological Investigations,* vol. 1: *God, Christ, Mary, and the Church,* trans. Cornelius Ernst (Baltimore: Helicon, 1961), 347–82.

[18]Maurice Merleau-Ponty, *Phenomenology of Perception,* trans. Donald A. Landes (London: Routledge, 2012), xvi.

[19]Ibid., 392.

[20]Ibid., 431.

[21]Ibid., 23.

[22]Maurice Merleau-Ponty, *The Visible & the Invisible,* trans. Alphonso Lingis (Evanston, IL: Northwestern University Press, 1968), 138.

[23]Ibid., 146.

[24]Merleau-Ponty offers an extensive engagement with instances of traumatized disintegration from normative perception via an analysis of aphasia and sexual trauma. In these liminal instances of apparent rupture with the milieu of perception, Merleau-Ponty notes that these symptoms nonetheless affirm an undeniable perdurance of our underlying entanglement with the sensible. That is, these symptoms express (signify) a withdrawal from the porous coexistence of the world whereby I have "locked myself up" and

have quite literally lost touch with both myself and the world. However, even when I am shut within myself, I am never completely cut off from the world because, though I may be withdrawn from it, it is never withdrawn from me. I am always already in relation and oriented toward the world as permeated by double-sensation of my incarnate being. It is on these grounds that Merleau-Ponty identifies the nature of therapy as the "reopening" of the body. See Merleau-Ponty, *Phenomenology of Perception*, 159–68.

[25]Karl Rahner, *Foundations of Christian Faith*, trans. William V. Dych (New York: Crossroad, 1978), 128–33.

[26]Ibid., 197.

[27]Ibid., 198.

[28]Ibid.

[29]Rahner, "Christian Humanism," *Theological Investigations*, vol. 9, 245.

[30]Ibid.

How Theological Anthropology Might Inform the Church's Self-Understanding

Martin Madar

Theological anthropology and ecclesiology have a lot in common. They both reflect on human existence. The former investigates what it means to be human in light of God's revelation. The latter reflects on how communities of believers ought to live out their call to be the disciples of Jesus. Despite this overlap, theological anthropology became a meaningful dialogue partner of ecclesiology only in the twentieth century. The reason for this is understandable in light of the historical development of Catholic ecclesiology.[1]

From the inception of formal ecclesiological writings in the fourteenth century, the context of crisis was a key determining factor of both the content and style of Catholic ecclesiology.[2] First, it was the conflict over the relationship of the temporal and spiritual powers, then the conflict over the role and authority of the council vis-à-vis the pope. Soon after it was the crisis produced by the Protestant Reformation, and then came the Enlightenment and Modernity. As a result, ecclesiology came to focus on the institutional dimension of the church, particularly on articulations of its authority.[3]

While the juridical and legalistic approaches to ecclesiology never denied that the church is fundamentally a group of people, their emphasis on the institutional and hierarchical dimensions of the church saw little if any need at all for theologians to attend comprehensively to the actual people who make the church and to the process of ecclesiogenesis. Ecclesiology was by and large a "hierarchology," as Yves Congar aptly put it.[4] To attend to the reality of the church as a human society, this juridical approach to ecclesiology employed some social and political theory, but theological anthropology was absent. To incorporate theological anthropology, theologians would have needed to be interested in exploring the concrete reality of the church as communities of believers.

Catholic ecclesiology began to undergo change slowly in the nineteenth century, and then it went through a burst of renewal in the first half of the twentieth century that culminated in Vatican II. By returning to the language of Scripture, the church Fathers, and the liturgy, theologians retrieved various insights from the ecclesiological tradition of the first millennium that exposed the church's interior dimension and brought some balance to the one-sidedness of the institutional approach.

The Second Vatican Council ratified this move and effected a shift in Catholic ecclesiology. The shift consisted essentially of moving away from an overly institutional and juridical view of the church to an ecclesiology that brings out the church's transcendent dimension. The development was certainly a gain for ecclesiology since it now accounts better for the breadth of the Christian theological tradition. In several places, the council itself engaged the insights of theological anthropology. For instance, an understanding of the human person as *capax Dei* underlies the council's view of the church as people of God who receive God's word together.[5] This contrasts with a juridical understanding of the church in which only the ordained receive God's word. One can also find a robust account of the human person in the council's *Pastoral Constitution on the Church in the Modern World (Gaudium et Spes).*[6] It offers an elaborate portrait of the contemporary human being with whom the church ought to be in dialogue. The portrait had bearing on how the council envisioned the church's mission in and dialogue with the world.

Since Vatican II, the insights of theological anthropology have influenced the treatment of various topics in contemporary ecclesiology. For instance, theologies of ministry are typically grounded in theological anthropology.[7] The treatment of women's ordination by feminist theologians usually includes reflections on the human person as *imago Dei* and on the issue of gender complementarity.[8] Understanding of the church by Latinx theologians is often rooted in insights emerging from theological anthropology.[9]

It should also be noted that theologians working in the area of theological anthropology have demonstrated that their work has implications for ecclesiology. For instance, M. Shawn Copeland and Susan Ross have shown that their treatment of body and embodiment in relation to sex, gender, and race has implications for the understanding of the image of the church as the body of Christ.[10] Reflections of Latinx theologians on popular religiosity among US Hispanics, in particular on such notions as *lo cotidiano* or *nosotros*, shed light on the church as an event of accompaniment.[11]

Although one can point out several examples where fruitful collaboration between ecclesiology and theological anthropology already exists or where theological anthropology is implicit in Catholic ecclesiology, the dialogue between ecclesiology and theological anthropology could be strengthened. In what follows, I discuss why it is important that these two theological disciplines become deeper partners in dialogue.

Theological Anthropology
and the Church's Self-Understanding

One significant limitation of much of contemporary ecclesiology is its idealizing tendency. This is particularly true of various communion ecclesiologies. The church is described in a lofty theological language such as the bride of Christ or communion, but it is often unclear whether such language describes any actual, historical community of the faithful. An observation of Neil Ormerod captures the situation well. He states:

> If one were to read many current books on ecclesiology the word [church] would probably evoke a highly idealized vision of church, one which relates not to any particular historical period or even denominational community but to a sort of timeless "universal" church to which we would all like to belong if we could find it, but which sadly does not exist in this earthly realm.[12]

As these words of Ormerod suggest, idealization of the church is theologically problematic, for it falsely gives the impression that the church is a supra-historical reality existing apart from the communities of believers we encounter in history. In this regard, the question raised by Joseph Komonchak gets to the core of the issue. He asks: "Are there any predications made about the Church ... that do not require to be verified in some concrete community?"[13] Komonchak answers the question with an unequivocal "no." I believe Komonchak is correct in insisting that the church on earth always designates some assembly of the faithful.

And this is where one might envision fruitful interaction between theological anthropology and ecclesiology, namely, in bridging the gap between the highly theological language, which came to dominate ecclesiology after Vatican II, and the concrete reality of the church as it is realized in communities of believers. For that to happen, ecclesiologists would need to zoom in on the women and men who every day give birth to the church and maintain it in being. They are the church. There is no church apart from them. It is important to inquire into their lives of faith, hope, and love. In this task, ecclesiologists should engage the rich tradition of theological reflection on what it means to be human in light of the gospel to help them describe the church in its concreteness.

Several decades ago, ecclesiologists made the correct move to shift the almost-exclusive focus of ecclesiology from the institutional dimension of the church to its theological and spiritual dimension. But the pendulum swung too far in the new direction. The focus on the institutional aspect of the church was replaced with a focus on its transcendent aspect. In either case, the connection with the people who are the church was neglected. Articulating that connection should be a priority for ecclesiologists today. Failing to do that, ecclesiology will continue to give the impression that it is a discourse about a mythical creature hovering somewhere above in a supra-historical realm having little to do with the communities of believers we encounter in history.

The idea that ecclesiology should explore the human dimension of the church is not new. It has been gaining traction in recent decades, especially in connection with the role that the social sciences can play in illumining our understanding of the human and social dimension of the church. While such work is in its infancy, the idea that theologians ought to pay close attention to the human and social reality of the church has become part of the ecclesiological mainstream.

I believe that when it comes to exploring the human aspect of the church, theological anthropology has something distinctive to contribute—something that escapes the grasp of the social sciences. For methodological reasons, social scientists leave out references to the transcendent in their explanations of human and social reality. They attempt to understand the human and the social as thoroughly as they can in purely natural terms, that is, in terms that do not invoke faith, theologically speaking. Theological anthropology, on the other hand, offers insights into the human condition that are based on the experience of an encounter with God. From that perspective, without being in competition with the social sciences, theological anthropology has something distinctive to say about what it means to be human in its individual and communal manifestation. Taken together, the insights of the social sciences and theological anthropology would offer a broader view of the church's concrete reality.

Moreover, dialogue between theological anthropology and ecclesiology may also stir our imagination resulting in some new images or metaphors of the church. What I have in mind is something akin to Elizabeth Johnson's project in *She Who Is*, in which she argues for the need to construct new language about God that would reflect the experiences of women and be a counterweight to the language about God that comes from the experiences of men.[14] In our case, the new language would reflect better the reality of the church on the ground than does much of the traditional language about the church. If we are honest, knowing the church as it really is, who resonates with the images of the church as the bride of Christ or temple of the Holy Spirit? I would like to be part of such a church, but I doubt that it exists on this side of the eschaton.

One image of the church that came to mind as I was reflecting on how theological anthropology might inform ecclesiology is the image of the church as *people stumbling in holiness*. The image is rooted in a fundamental conviction of Catholic anthropology, namely, that we are loved sinners who are called to be holy. The image also sums up in a most elementary way the basic insight of the doctrines of sin and grace.[15]

The expression "stumbling in holiness" is appropriated from the title of Brian Flanagan's recent book, in which he masterfully treats the topic of the church's holiness and sinfulness.[16] That the church is "holy" is one of the most basic statements about the church in the creeds. One also hears it proclaimed at every Eucharistic liturgy of the Roman Rite when prompted by the celebrant, the congregation says, "May the Lord accept the sacrifice at your hands . . . for our good and the good of all his holy Church."[17]

Holiness is the church's gift and its task. The church is holy on the account of what God has done for it; namely, God has endowed the church with gifts that allow it to be a sacrament of salvation. Among such gifts are "the word of God found in Scripture, the rule of faith found in the creeds, the sacraments, and the teaching and governing ministries of the church."[18] As a task, holiness of the church refers to the idea that the church participates in the life and love of God.

In this task, however, the church often falls short in varying degrees. Holiness thus describes the church's reality only partially. The church is also sinful. A considerable challenge for ecclesiologists is to hold these two truths about the church together at the same time without resolving the tension in favor of one or the other side of the equation.[19] Often, the tension is resolved by distinguishing between the church and its members, arguing that the church remains holy even though its members are sinful. Such a framework is problematic, however, for it leads to "an ecclesiological mistake, that of positing an idealized, ahistorical entity called the church distinct from the gathered assemblies of the faithful moving through history."[20]

The image of the church as people stumbling in holiness is significant theologically and pastorally. Theologically, it successfully maintains the tension between the church's holiness and sinfulness. Of crucial importance are the verb "stumble" and the preposition "in." Saying that the church "stumbles" in holiness recognizes that the church's participation in God's life and love is not without failings. At the same time, the choice of "in" instead of "into" affirms the "already and not yet" of the church's holiness. In other words, holiness of the church is not entirely an eschatological reality but something that marks the church's historical existence. Since it does not distinguish the church that is holy and its members who are sinful, the image of the church as people stumbling in holiness avoids idealizing the church. Both holiness and sinfulness are predicated about the faithful who live their Christian lives throughout history.

At a time when the Catholic Church all over the world faces various crises, most of which are of its own making, the image of the church as people stumbling in holiness is also pertinent pastorally. It represents the necessary first step in confronting the reality of the church's failing to live up to its call. Instead of undue defensiveness, the first step in eventual healing ought to be honesty. Acknowledging that the church stumbles in holiness is not only a condition *sine qua non* of the church's continual renewal,[21] it also represents a posture of humility befitting the disciples of Jesus.[22]

Another image of the church that came to mind as I was reflecting on how theological anthropology might inform ecclesiology is that of the church as a *wounded healer*. This image combines and holds in tension two beliefs about the church. First, the word "healer" names what the church ought to be. It describes its purpose. According to a standard tenet of ecclesiology, the church mediates salvation. In this regard, the Second Vatican Council taught that the church is like a sacrament, by which the council meant that the church is "an effective and graced sign before the world of God's saving love."[23] Insofar as the church is true to its calling, it makes present the salvific experience of a community.

When I think about people both generally and specifically, and when seeing them through the lens of theological anthropology, one conviction stands out: we are all hurting and need healing. To experience salvation would to a large extent involve healing. For the church, to mediate salvation would mean to mediate healing to a world that is hurting. The church ought to be an event of healing in human history.

Second, the word "wounded" in the image of a wounded healer describes the church as it really is. It is a group of people that is wounded by its own failures that are often systemic in nature. The doctrines of sin and grace teach us that our woundedness is in different degrees a permanent characteristic of human existence in history. The image of a wounded healer thus describes a paradox of the church's existence. Its mission of healing involves attending to its own wounds and brokenness and accepting these as part of its life of stumbling in holiness. Modifying slightly the words of Henri Nouwen from his book titled *The Wounded Healer*, the church can be seen as a healing community not because its wounds are cured and pains alleviated once for all, but because they are openings for a new vision.[24] At the heart of this vision of the church as a wounded healer is the compassion with which God wants to embrace the whole of creation.

Conclusion

The last one hundred years were remarkably favorable to Catholic ecclesiology. This discipline, which attempts a theological understanding of the church, went through a renewal, long overdue, unleashing new vigor and creativity to the field. After several centuries during which the idea of the church as an institution and society dominated the field, theologians recovered the transcendent and spiritual dimension of the church. This broadened the scope of Catholic ecclesiology and set the discipline on the trajectory of recovering greater balance where once was one-sidedness. What is needed at present is that theologians attend to the idealizing tendency of much of contemporary ecclesiology, which obscures the connection between the statements about the church and the actual churches as they exist in the communities of believers. Crucial in this will be keeping in mind that predications about the church always refer to some group of the faithful, not to some church hovering above and existing apart from the men and women committed to the gospel. Since the church is fundamentally a group of people and theological anthropology reflects on what it means to be human in light of God's revelation, ecclesiologists should enter into a deeper dialogue with theological anthropology to help them describe the church in its concreteness. Together with the social sciences, theological anthropology can offer a broader view of the church's concrete reality. A deeper dialogue with theological anthropology might also lead to constructing of new images of the church that would reflect better its concrete reality.

Notes

[1]This essay focuses on Catholic ecclesiology. For stylistic reasons, whenever the word "ecclesiology" is used by itself, Catholic ecclesiology is in mind.

[2]By formal ecclesiological writings I mean the writings that deal expressly with the topic of the church and approach it no longer within other fields (e.g., Christology, soteriology, or sacraments), as it had been until then.

[3]For a detailed account of the development of Catholic ecclesiology, see

Angel Anton, *El misterio de la iglesia: Evolucion historica de las ideas ecle-siologicas*, 2 vols. (Madrid: Biblioteca de autores Cristianos, 1986).

[4]Yves Congar, *Lay People in the Church*, rev. ed., trans. Donald Attwater (Westminster, MD: Newman, 1965), 45.

[5]See Second Vatican Council, "Dogmatic Constitution on Divine Reve-lation *(Dei Verbum)*" (1965), www.vatican.va, nos. 1–10.

[6]See Second Vatican Council, "The Pastoral Constitution on the Church in the Modern World *(Gaudium et Spes)*" (1964), www.vatican.va, nos. 4–39.

[7]See, for instance, Edward Schillebeeckx, *The Church with a Human Face: A New and Expanded Theology of Ministry* (New York: Crossroad, 1985); Edward P. Hahnenberg, *Ministries: A Relational Approach* (New York: Crossroad, 2003).

[8]See, for instance, Lisa Sowle Cahill, "Feminist Theology and a Participa-tory Church," in *Common Calling: The Laity & Governance in the Catholic Church*, ed. Stephen J. Pope (Washington, DC: Georgetown University Press, 2004), 127–49; Mary Ann Hinsdale, "A Feminist Reflection on Postconciliar Catholic Ecclesiology," in *A Church with Open Doors: Catholic Ecclesiology for the Third Millennium*, ed. Richard R. Gaillardetz and Edward P. Hah-nenberg (Collegeville, MN: Liturgical, 2015), 112–37.

[9]See, for instance, Roberto S. Goizueta, "*Corpus Verum*: Toward a Bor-derland Ecclesiology," in *Building Bridges, Doing Justice: Constructing a Latino/a Ecumenical Theology*, ed. Orlando O. Espín (Maryknoll, NY: Orbis Books, 2009), 143–66; Natalia Imperatori-Lee, *Cuéntame: Narrative in the Ecclesial Present* (Maryknoll, NY: Orbis Books, 2018).

[10]See, for instance, M. Shawn Copeland, *Enfleshing Freedom: Body, Race, and Being* (Minneapolis: Fortress, 2010); Susan A. Ross, "The Beauty of Embodiment: Body and Sexuality," in *Anthropology: Seeking Light and Beauty* (Collegeville, MN: Liturgical, 2012), 85–107.

[11]See Roberto S. Goizueta, *Caminemos con Jesús: Toward a Hispanic/Latino Theology of Accompaniment* (Maryknoll, NY: Orbis Books, 1995); María Pilar Aquino, "Theological Method in US Latino/a Theology: Toward an Intercultural Theology for the Third Millennium," in *From the Heart of Our People*, ed. Orlando O. Espín and Miguel H. Díaz (Maryknoll, NY: Orbis Books, 1999), 6–48.

[12]Neil Ormerod, "Ecclesiology and the Social Sciences," in *The Routledge Companion to the Christian Church*, ed. Gerard Mannion and Lewis S. Mudge (New York: Routledge, 2008), 639.

[13]Joseph A. Komonchak, "The Epistemology of Reception," *Jurist* 57 (1997): 187.

[14]See Elizabeth A. Johnson, *She Who Is: The Mystery of God in Feminist Theological Discourse* (New York: Crossroad, 1992).

[15]For a contemporary treatment of these concepts see, for instance, Daniel P. Horan, *Catholicity & Emerging Personhood: A Contemporary Theological Anthropology* (Maryknoll, NY: Orbis Books, 2019), 123–42, 189–236.

[16]See Brian P. Flanagan, *Stumbling in Holiness: Sin and Sanctity in the Church* (Collegeville, MN: Liturgical, 2018).

[17]*The Roman Missal*, study ed., 3rd typ. ed. (Collegeville, MN: Liturgical, 2011), 530.

[18]Flanagan, *Stumbling in Holiness*, 87.

[19]For a detailed treatment of the church's holiness and sinfulness, see Jeanmarie Gribaudo, *A Holy Yet Sinful Church: Three Twentieth-Century Moments in a Developing Theology* (Collegeville, MN: Liturgical, 2015).

[20]Flanagan, *Stumbling in Holiness*, 151.

[21]See Second Vatican Council, "Decree on Ecumenism (*Unitatis Redintegratio*)" (1964), www.vatican.va, no. 6.

[22]See Lk 18:9–14.

[23]Richard R. Gaillardetz, *The Church in the Making: Lumen Gentium, Christus Dominum, Orientalium Ecclesiarum* (New York: Paulist, 2006), 43.

[24]Henri J. M. Nouwen, *The Wounded Healer: Ministry in Contemporary Society* (New York: Image Books, 1972), 100.

PART II

CONTENDING

WITH CHRISTIAN CONTRIBUTIONS

TO DEHUMANIZATION

White Christian Privilege and the Decolonization of Comparative Theology

Tracy Sayuki Tiemeier

The "turn to the subject," one of the hallmarks of modern theology, has an ambivalent history and legacy. Although the emphasis on subjectivity has meant the valuing of human experience, it has also reified the Western White[1] Christian subject as the hidden norm of human being. Fundamentally, the "self" required an "other" through which, and against which, it would form. This self was Western, Christian, and White, while the other was non-Western, non-White, and non-Christian.[2] The "turn to the subject," then, was no neutral enterprise, and White Christian hegemony in Western academic theological thought and practice endured.

Just as modern Christian theology was embedded in a wider Western hegemonic context, so was comparative theology. Hugh Nicholson, drawing on Tomoko Masuzawa,[3] argues that the objective and scientific approach of nineteenth-century comparative theology actually presumed Christian normativity.[4] Early comparative theology and the later theology of religions, which sought a solution to the so-called "problem" of the religious other, therefore were not in opposition to hegemonic modern Western White Christian theology but rather were in continuity with it.[5]

The "new" comparative theology of today presents itself as a non-hegemonic alternative to the theology of religions or the universalizing comparative theology of the past.[6] Although Nicholson complicates this claim, he argues that the new comparative theology can resist hegemony through its explicitly constructive dimension.[7] By foregrounding and being upfront about the scholar's political and religious situatedness, interests, and goals, the new comparative theology can resist totalizing narratives that subsume the religious other into a Western White Christian framework.[8]

But much more than a simple recognition of one's religious and social location is required. Catherine Cornille highlights the role of epistemological and theological humility, for example.[9] She also recognizes the problem of Christian dominance in the creating, framing, and theorizing of comparative theology, and she acknowledges the need for the growing numbers of comparative theologians from outside of Christianity.[10] Additionally, Cornille notes the ways Christian comparative theologians have tried to grant priority to the other in comparative theology.[11] With mitigation strategies, the hope is that comparative theology can be a truly non-hegemonic theology.

Increasingly, though, *I* am losing hope. This is due, in part, to what Khyati Joshi's recent book on White Christian privilege exposes: the extent to which White Christianity is bound up with US national identity (and by extension the American academy).[12] Her work is a sorely needed intervention, and it offers a sobering assessment for any Christian theologian coming from, trained in, or working in a US context.[13] As Joshi explains, White Christians can be confident that their practices and perspectives will be known and respected in all areas of American life. Indeed, they control these spaces. Even their desire to "make others feel included" will betray their privilege, reinforce otherness, and maintain White Christian power.

The same can be said for comparative theology. White Christian comparative theologians can be confident that their major thinkers, doctrines, and practices will be granted theological significance. White Christian theological thinkers and categories define the academic field and control its spaces. Joshua Samuel points out that Western Christian comparative theologians imagine falsely that they have created a new way of theologizing—with boundaries and borders they maintain.[14] If the comparative theological self is normally White and Christian, the "religious other" is not. As a result, Western academic comparative theology reinforces White Christian supremacy rather than subverting it. A full-scale decolonization of the field is necessary.

To imagine the decolonization of comparative theology, I turn to An Yountae's decolonial theory of religion. Not unlike Joshi, An is concerned with the ways Christian hegemony persists.[15] The image of the abyss is the center of An's construction of a decolonial theology that resists the forces of neocolonialism.

The abyss is an expression of the self's *via negativa* in relation to the (divine) other. In Western mystical traditions, this abyss is the indeterminate, unknowing space between creature and creator, finitude and infinitude.[16] The mystical abyss is a space of the self's passage both in kenotic self-dissolution and in ecstatic self-fulfillment as the self unifies with the divine.[17] Hegel's dialectical abyss, on the other hand, removes the transcendent God from the abyss. As in the mystical journey, however, the dialectical journey also proceeds by way of a kind of self-negation that leads paradoxically to self-realization. The encounter of self with an other leads to anxiety, vulnerability, and loss before the other.[18] The self then recognizes itself in the other, allowing for reconciliation and a dynamic, dialectical self. Despite Hegel's problematic Euro-Christian-centrism, An wants to highlight the political and ethical priority of the other revealed through the dialectical abyss.[19]

The abyss is also central to the poetic imaginary of a number of Afro-Caribbean decolonial thinkers. French-Martinican theorist Édouard Glissant (d. 2011), for example, writes of the abyss of the Middle Passage. In this space, on the slave ship, there is the literal abyss of the Atlantic Ocean. Many were lost in that oceanic abyss. There were others though, as Glissant writes, whose "ordeal did not die . . . the panic of the new land, the haunting of the former land, finally the alliance with the imposed land, suffered and redeemed."[20] The colonial abyss is a movement of self in its erasure and dissolution and in its metamorphosis through coloniality. This metamorphosis is creolization, the emergence of a collective Caribbean consciousness.[21]

Whereas the impossibility of naming the nameless divine has led some thinkers into theopoetics, the impossibility of speaking the unspeakable trauma of the Middle Passage has led decolonial thinkers like Édouard Glissant to "counterpoetics" or "forced poetics."[22] Bodies, histories, selves, and even the divine have fallen into the abyss.[23] Forced poetics is the process of picking up the pieces, re-collecting them, re-forming them, and finding new ways of being together and reconstructing the divine through the trauma of history.[24]

Theologizing in the colonial abyss must be founded on respect and equality without erasing difference, ignoring power differentials, or falling into "the trap of imperialism."[25] An proposes a cosmopolitical theology. Unlike cosmopolitanism, which presumes a oneness of the cosmos that already exists, cosmopolitics is a verb, a co-creative and ongoing process.[26] Cosmopolitics is a constant movement of deconstruction and reconstruction, of passage in the colonial abyss that commits to picking up the pieces together and building justice through relational solidarity.[27] But this cannot happen without real confrontation with the violence of coloniality, past and present.[28] A decolonial cosmopolitical theology must commit to a full accounting of the ongoing violence of coloniality.[29]

A decolonial cosmopolitical theology is a theology of ruin and exile, a theology from below, a theology of struggle, a theology of self-dispossession and re-collective self-emergence, and a theology of solidarity committed to the dismantling of systems of power.[30] It affirms the power of displaced, fragmented people to rebuild themselves, the cosmos, and the divine: "The unnamable name of the divine then denotes the very condition of abyssal ruin from which we construct a decolonized cosmopolitan future and a new, creolized name of God."[31]

An's call for a radical shift in theology offers us ways of envisioning and reenvisioning the decolonization of comparative theology. For Édouard Glissant, the image of a slave ship in the Middle Passage expresses the absolute loss and communal trauma in which and through which enslaved peoples moved to the unknown future and birthed a new people. Recentering on the colonial abyss, I ask: Where is comparative theology? Western academic comparative theology did not, and does not, stand with the enslaved who are chained in the slave ship; it is instead standing on the decks with the slavers, its own identity forged on the backs and bodies of enslaved, colonized peoples.

But as much as the field is implicated through the image of a slave ship in the oceanic abyss, the attention An pays to forced (theo)poetics also offers a starting point for the decolonization process in comparative theology. The theopoetic process of creolization was and is a process of relational solidarity and communal becoming in the colonial abyss. This process was also comparative and multireligious. The emergence of creole religions testifies to the collective theological and religious actions of people caught in the colonial abyss. This is the comparative theology of the colonized, creolized peoples working actively to reconstruct their creolized God. Academic comparative theology has hope if it is willing to confront its colonial history and ongoing coloniality, self-divest and abandon its colonial self to the abyss, align with the comparative cosmopolitical theology of colonized, creolized peoples, and commit to new ways of being in the world that prioritize relational solidarity and justice.

Khyati Joshi's constructive suggestions offer us a way to imagine what this self-abandonment and realignment to cosmopolitical justice might mean for Western academic theology. Joshi's first suggestion is to become "proximate." Following Bryan Stevenson, who argues that people must "get proximate" to what they seek to change, Joshi insists that it is not enough to talk about other religions. One must learn proactively about religions as they are entangled in the intersecting issues and concerns crossing religious communities. One must then build relationships with persons and communities to which they will be accountable.[32]

Getting proximate in comparative theology requires more than religious literacy or even interreligious friendship. The danger of interreligious friendship is that the friend becomes a hermeneutical tool, or the "some of my best friends are . . . " defense.[33] Getting proximate means building relationships with individuals *and* their communities without expecting them to do the educating. It requires prioritizing the well-being and flourishing of these communities. This is what An means by relational solidarity. More than pledging good will, writing about justice, or using others to further oneself, one must align their whole being with persons and communities in their struggles for justice.

Joshi also argues that there must be a change in language. For Joshi, changing language requires, first, shifting public policy debates away from Christian concerns and, second, learning proactively about religions other than Christianity without using Christian categories to define those religions.[34] Comparative theology as a whole has tried to highlight the necessity of articulating the religion of comparison on its own terms. However, Christian comparative theologians still tend to prioritize their own categories and concerns.[35] In the end, they recenter themselves in the theological comparison. Instead, they and the Western academy must work actively to decenter White Christian language, categories, and concerns, and make space for the rich comparative theologizing already occurring in the colonial abyss.

Related to the issue of language is the need to change our questions. This requires recognizing that assumptions of Christian normativity often underlie questions posed to religions other than Christianity.[36] Changing the questions also requires resisting asking abstract theological, textual, or ritual questions. The emphasis instead should be on lived religion.[37] This is a tough one for comparative theology, and theology in general, as texts, abstraction, and normativity have been hallmarks of what has been considered theological in the Western academy.[38] Comparative theologizing in the colonial abyss begins with the death of ontotheology and the birth of a people through the cosmopolitical struggles of the oppressed.

In addition to language and questions, Joshi argues that there must be a change in focus. This means to shift perspective, to question one's bias and privilege, and to ask how something looks from other vantage points, particularly marginalized ones.[39] Though comparative theology highlights the significance of other vantage points, it has not always been mindful of bias or privilege. It has also reinforced systems of power in religious traditions through its choices of authoritative sources. Privileging marginalized traditions and sources on all sides of the comparison allows for a more nuanced alignment and discussion of cosmopolitical struggle. This also requires a more complex picture of coloniality. Clara A. B. Joseph's postcolonial history of India and St. Thomas Christianity highlights the ways the construction of Christianity as White and Western reinforces a problematic assumption of the East as non-Christian.[40] Comparative theologies that highlight Western Christian sources reinforce this binary assumption. The result is that they may also reinforce the idea that Christians from formerly colonized contexts were passive in their Christianity, and therefore victims of history, not active subjects of Christian theologizing, and not worthy of being an authoritative source for comparative theology.

For Christians who want to be in relational solidarity with marginalized religious communities, there is a strong tendency to stress common humanity and similarities between religions. Joshi insists that this foundational assumption must change. Changing foundational assumptions requires knowing, talking about, and appreciating differences.[41] One of the strengths of comparative theology is particularity and difference. Francis X. Clooney's resistance to constructive conclusions is a testament to difference.[42] Resisting a secondary constructive move also resists the strong White Christian impulse to consume and instrumentalize others. Am I calling for a moratorium on Christian constructive comparative theology?[43] Not necessarily. However, I would say that White Christian comparative theologians need to focus on listening rather than speaking, centering others instead of recentering themselves.

Finally, Joshi argues that Christians must change the paradigm. Shifting from a Christian normative paradigm does not mean shifting to a homogenized, seemingly secular and more inclusive paradigm, which only covers over Christian normativity and privilege.[44] Instead, the paradigm must be real multireligious flourishing.[45] In comparative theology, the paradigm must shift to multireligious flourishing and justice as well, which requires decolonial cosmopolitical theology. White Christian comparative theologians and the Western academy must first contend with their own coloniality. They must be proactive and brutally self-critical. They must be honest about their power, privilege, and contexts. They must center voices other than their own and be in relational solidarity with those already engaged in the comparative, multireligious re-collection and reconstruction of themselves in the cosmopolitical struggle for justice. This includes the academy. White Western Christian comparative theologians must be willing to promote others above themselves. To give up speaking and publishing spots in favor of marginalized voices. To use their power and privilege to work for a full realignment of the field.

As a final point, I want to note briefly what this means for Western Christian comparative theologians like myself whose work brings in South Asian religions. First, there must be a full account of the ways Western Christian scholars have ignored or enabled persistent problems of power and oppression in India due to their well-meaning but unsuccessful attempts to resist Western stereotypes and demonizations of India. Comparative studies that examine historical texts try to demonstrate the complexity and significance of South Asian philosophizing and theologizing. But they often fail to situate these texts in ongoing traditions of interpretation or hold themselves accountable to those living traditions.[46] This ultimately contributes to the Orientalist fantasy of a rich South Asian past that has devolved into superstition and primitivism.

Second, there must be renewed focus on Dalit and Adivasi concerns as well as other marginalized and oppressed persons of all genders. There is sometimes the desire to find representatives or central theologians in South Asian religions in order to demonstrate a theological and even scholarly parity. Overemphasizing schools of thought, recognizable authorities, or textual traditions may help highlight complex theological approaches that Westerners will recognize and value, but this continues the colonial construction of South Asian religions through Christian categories. Instead, what are we missing about Christianity by ignoring the memoirs of Assamese Christian poet Temsula Ao or Dalit Roman Catholic writer Bama?[47] What are we missing about Hinduism if we aren't listening to the Hijra (third gender) practices and activism of A. Revathi, or the taboo-breaking narrative of writer Kamala Das Surayya's Hindu Nair upbringing, or the memoir of Dalit feminist Hindu-turned-Buddhist activist Urmila Pawar?[48] We must focus on real people in their real lives, with religion and class and gender and nation all bound up inextricably together. This also may mean rejecting the binary set-up of two traditions in much of comparative theology—which belies the multireligious character of many people's lives, especially marginalized ones—and which my students insist on interpreting oppositionally, repeatedly calling my class "Christianity vs. Hinduism" instead of "Hinduism and Christianity."

Third, there needs to be a realignment of the field to decolonial liberation and relational solidarity. Passage in, through, and back to the colonial abyss requires a constant process of theological dispossession, loss of self, and rebirth to a creolized unknown that refuses to ignore the colonial ruins and its trauma. A Western Christian comparative theology of South Asian traditions must commit to a new starting point that begins and ends with religious "others" (in South Asian religious traditions, including Christianity). It sees as its twin goals solidarity with those others and the flourishing and justice of those others. It values sources beyond texts as theologically significant, from popular vows to pilgrimage to home traditions to folklore and more. Finally, its primary audience can no longer be the academy; instead, its audience has to be the religious communities with which it seeks to be in solidarity and to which it must be accountable.

In the end, the comparative theology of the Western academy is a neocolonial discipline and must commit proactively to its decolonization. Its decolonization requires resituating it in the colonial abyss, moving below deck and into the ruins of history. Here, there already is a flourishing comparative theology from below. The cosmopolitical and multireligious struggle of the creolized masses does not ossify religious systems and boundaries; indeed, creolized religions re-collect whatever traditions and practices from its collective identity enable decolonial modes of being, theologizing, and struggling for justice. Comparative theology need not essentialize religion in its process. But in the passage in and through the colonial abyss, academic and White and Christian-aligned comparative theology must divest of itself and join with cosmopolitical struggles for justice.

Notes

[1]There is a robust conversation about capitalization when discussing race. Capitalizing the B in Black is becoming more and more common as a way to show respect, recognize Black as a shared cultural identity, and/or highlight the sociopolitical construction of the racial designation for people of African descent. However, capitalizing the W in White is more contested, as there are other issues at play beyond capitalizing terms for sociopolitically constructed identities. Some argue, for example, that not only does White not signify a shared cultural identity, capitalizing the word reinforces supremacist groups who seek to assert one. While recognizing that the choice of capitalization is complex, I choose to capitalize both Black and White. Inasmuch as Black carries meaning as a cultural identity, so does White (even though White people may not consciously recognize shared cultural markers). Moreover, neither Black nor White are neutral terms. They were and are forged together through the forces of Western imperialism. See Kwame Anthony Appiah, "The Case for Capitalizing the *B* in Black," *Atlantic*, June 18, 2020, www. theatlantic.com; *New York Times*, July 5, 2020, www.nytimes.com; Kristen Mack and John Palfrey, "Capitalizing Black and White: Grammatical Justice and Equality," *MacArthur Foundation*, August 26, 2020, www.macfound.org.

[2]*Race: A Theological Account* (New York: Oxford University Press, 2008), 81.

[3]Tomoko Masuzawa, *The Invention of World Religions: Or, How European Universalism Was Preserved in the Language of Pluralism* (Chicago: University of Chicago Press, 2005).

[4]Hugh Nicholson, *Comparative Theology and the Problem of Religious*

Rivalry (New York: Oxford University Press, 2011), 22–24.

[5]Ibid., 26–28.

[6]Ibid., 29.

[7]Ibid., 33–41.

[8]Ibid., 41–42. Paul Hedges, on the other hand, argues both that there is more complexity in the old comparative theology than Nicholson suggests and that there is some important and positive continuity between new comparative theology, theology of religions, and old comparative theology. Christianity itself was and is formed through an interreligious environment, and comparative theology—old and new—recognizes the significance and value of "the religious Other." Even so, Hedges agrees with Nicholson that the constructive, contextual element of the new comparative theology is important for a non-hegemonic comparative theology. Hedges, "The Old and New Comparative Theologies: Discourses on Religion, the Theology of Religions, Orientalism and the Boundaries of Traditions," *Religions* 3 (2012): 1120–37.

[9]Catherine Cornille, *Meaning and Method in Comparative Theology* (Hoboken, NJ: Wiley Blackwell, 2020), 105.

[10]Ibid., 107–8.

[11]Ibid., 106.

[12]Khyati Y. Joshi, *White Christian Privilege: The Illusion of Religious Equality in America* (New York: New York University Press, 2020), 1.

[13]There are, of course, growing bodies of academic work on White privilege and Christian privilege in America. Joshi's work, however, is important for highlighting the extent to which both are intertwined and are embedded in America's very foundation. See Margaret A. Hagerman, *White Kids: Growing Up with Privilege in a Racially Divided America*, reprint ed. (New York: New York University Press, 2020); Paula S. Rothenberg, *White Privilege: Essential Readings on the Other Side of Racism*, 5th ed. (New York: Worth, 2015); Lewis Z. Schlosser, "Christian Privilege: Breaking a Sacred Taboo," *Journal of Multicultural Counseling and Development* 31 (January 2003): 44–51; Warren J. Blumenfeld, "Christian Privilege and the Promotion of 'Secular' and Not-So 'Secular' Mainline Christianity in Public Schooling and in the Larger Society," *Equity & Excellence in Education* 39, no. 3 (2006): 195–210; Tricia Seifert, "Understanding Christian Privilege: Managing the Tensions of Spiritual Plurality," *About Campus* 12, no. 2 (May–June 2007): 10–17.

[14]Joshua Samuel, *Untouchable Bodies, Resistance, and Liberation: A Comparative Theology of Divine Possessions* (Boston: Brill, 2020), 36.

[15]An Yountae, *The Decolonial Abyss: Mysticism and Cosmopolitics from the Ruins* (New York: Fordham University Press, 2016), 5.

[16]Ibid., 9.

[17]Ibid., 9–10.

[18]Ibid., 57.

[19]Ibid., 80–82.

[20]Édouard Glissant, *Poetics of Relation*, trans. Betsy Wing (Ann Arbor: University of Michigan Press, 1997), 7.

[21]An, *The Decolonial Abyss*, 101–7.

[22]Ibid., 130.

[23]Ibid., 135.

[24]Ibid., 129.
[25]Ibid., 136.
[26]Ibid., 137.
[27]Ibid., 138.
[28]Ibid., 137.
[29]Ibid.
[30]Ibid., 138.
[31]Ibid., 139.
[32]Joshi, *White Christian Privilege*, 210–11.
[33]Even my own attempts, which include co-authorship, fall into this problem. See James L. Fredericks and Tracy Sayuki Tiemeier, eds., *Interreligious Friendship after Nostra Aetate* (New York: Palgrave Macmillan, 2015).
[34]Joshi, *White Christian Privilege*, 214–15.
[35]A notable exception is Michelle Voss Roberts. See Voss Roberts, *Body Parts: A Theological Anthropology* (Minneapolis: Fortress, 2017); Voss Roberts, *Tastes of the Divine: Hindu and Christian Theologies of Emotion* (New York: Fordham University Press, 2014).
[36]Joshi, *White Christian Privilege*, 215.
[37]Ibid.
[38]Samuel, *Untouchable Bodies, Resistance, and Liberation*, 34–37.
[39]Joshi, *White Christian Privilege*, 216–17.
[40]Clara A. B. Joseph, *Christianity in India: The Anti-Colonial Turn* (New York: Routledge, 2019).
[41]Joshi, *White Christian Privilege*, 220.
[42]Clooney theorizes this most helpfully in two of his earlier works: Clooney, *Seeing Through Texts: Doing Theology Among the Śrīvaiṣṇavas of South India* (Albany: State University of New York Press, 1996); and Clooney, *Divine Mother, Blessed Mother: Hindu Goddesses and the Virgin Mary* (New York: Oxford University Press, 2004).
[43]Say, for example, like James L. Fredericks's "moratorium" on theology of religions. See James L. Fredericks, *Faith among Faiths: Christianity and Non-Christian Religions* (Mahwah, NJ: Paulist, 1999).
[44]Joshi, *White Christian Privilege*, 222.
[45]Ibid., 223.
[46]Although Reid Locklin has insisted on grounding his own study of Advaita Vedānta at the feet of contemporary Advaita teachers and theologians, far too few White Christian theologians have done this. See Locklin, "A Century of Advaita Mission: Tracing a Lineage and Opening a Conversation," *Journal of Ecumenical Studies* 52, no. 4 (2017): 488–526. See also Reid B. Locklin, *Liturgy of Liberation: A Christian Commentary on Shankara's Upadeśasāhasrī* (Leuven: Peeters, 2011).
[47]Temsula Ao, *Once upon a Life: Burnt Curry and Bloody Rags: A Memoir* (New Delhi: Zubaan, 2013); Bama, *Karukku*, trans. Lakshmi Holmström, 2nd ed. (New Delhi: Oxford University Press, 2012).
[48]A. Revathi, *The Truth about Me: A Hijra Life Story*, trans. V. Geetha (Gurgaon, India: Penguin, 2010); Kamala Das, *My Story,* 2009 ed. (Noida, India: HarperCollins, 2009); Urmila Pawar, *The Weave of My Life: A Dalit Woman's Memoirs*, trans. Maya Pandit (New York: Columbia University Press, 2009).

Brief Notes on Christian Fascism

Derek Brown

On January 6, 2021, a group of Trump supporters stormed the United States Capitol building in an apparent attempt to disrupt and stop the certification of Joe Biden's victory of the presidential election. As we now know, the group consisted of people from varying economic classes (from the unemployed to multimillionaire tech CEOs), ideological affiliations (from outright white nationalists to deceived centrists who earnestly believed that the election was stolen), and political histories (more than a few former Obama voters were arrested, and one was killed). As we also know, the vast majority of those arrested were white (95 percent) and male (85 percent). These latter statistics, combined with geographic data, have led to good research that suggests many rioters were motivated by a reaction to a relative decrease in their counties' white population.[1]

Yet neither racial nor economic motives alone seem capable of explaining the event. For one, Trump, in both elections but especially in 2020, actually outperformed Mitt Romney with Black Americans.[2] Yet Romney's whiter and wealthier constituency did not storm the capitol after his loss. Racism and xenophobia, especially articulated through an adherence to the far right "Great Replacement Theory," might be a contributor to someone's willingness to storm the Capitol, but it is clearly not a sufficient condition.[3]

My argument in this essay is that analysis and critique of the rise of the right in America, marked especially by the events of January 6, must account for the specifically Christian fascist component of the new right. Doing so is important because, as I will argue, the strategies best suited to resist Christian fascism are not necessarily the strategies with which the American "resistance" movement is familiar: antiracism, worker co-ops, calls for equality, anti-discrimination laws, voter rights, unionization. All of these are worthwhile projects, but none alone addresses the specific challenges brought by Christian fascism. In the final analysis, traditional liberal and left-liberal responses to fascism fall short because of their failure to address the core fascist values of inclusion and unity. A revolutionary response would have to do so.

Fascism and Christian Fascism

Perhaps the relative lack of engagement with the Christian fascist element of the new right can be explained by the difficulty of discussing fascism as such. For one, the term has no commonly accepted definition. Nor does it always refer to the same sphere of activity: Fascist, as an adjective, can describe aesthetic, economic, racial, nationalist, and even libidinal regimes and structures, among others. Likewise, the term suffers from semiotic indeterminacy: "fascist" is sometimes a descriptive and sometimes a prescriptive term. This tension between the descriptive and prescriptive is of course latent in any definitional attempt but takes on higher resonance for those on the left who would never want to describe someone or something as "fascist" in a value-neutral way. The historical record reflects these indeterminacies: even self-described fascists do not agree on the ideological content of the program.[4] Finally, we are here concerned not just with "fascism" in the abstract but with Christian fascism in particular: although all fascisms might contain a mythical element, the introduction of Christianity into fascism brings about a theocratic dimension that can and does lead to fundamentalist and reactionary violence.[5]

Despite these difficulties, and perhaps because of them, Christian fascism demands further study. This is for some of the reasons already mentioned: the violence of January 6 and the ongoing violence of the Christian fascist–supported occupation of Palestine, which is worthy of deeper and more stringent critique than I can offer here, provide evidence of the reactionary violence of which Christian fascists are not only capable but are in some ways destined to commit. But beyond this obvious violence, Christian fascism remains an important site of inquiry because its resistance challenges many received liberal notions of good praxis. As I will argue in more detail shortly, liberal values of inclusion—so heavily relied upon in contemporary liberatory and anti-discrimination discourses—are not only insufficient for resisting fascism but are in many ways guilty of unintentionally countersigning a fascist political formalism. Finally, and most provocatively, I hold that it is important to study and critique Christian fascism because, from a purely practical and *realpolitik* perspective, Christian fascists are *doing something right*. In a postmodern age incredulous toward metanarratives and in a secularizing age skeptical of any perceived mythicism or enchantment, Christian fascism stands as one of the few mythical metanarratives capable of organizing and galvanizing a large and committed activist branch—committed even to death.

For these reasons many have recognized the need to study and critique fascism in general and Christian fascism in particular. Of theologians, Dorothee Soelle is perhaps the most well-known critic of Christian fascism. Specifically, Soelle is critical of what she terms "Christo-fascism," by which she refers to the sort of Christian fascism that reduces politics to personal morality, especially a morality concerned with sexual and family ethics.[6] Chris Hedges draws heavily from and countersigns Soelle's argument but adds that Christian fascists read this morality in a merito-cratic way reminiscent of Max Weber's analysis of the Protestant work ethic. In this way, the rich and powerful are interpreted as practitioners of good morality and so winners of God's favor. As Hedges helpfully notes, this meritocratic morality leads to a deep suspicion of public goods and services: A so-called reliance on the state becomes a sign of personal immorality; political defense of the welfare state, to say nothing of the socialist state, a sign of the anti-Christ.[7] Operating more as psychoanalysts than theologians, Erich Fromm and Slavoj Žižek each interprets Christian fascism through the lens of libidinal economy: Fromm argues that the sadomasochistic fascist takes pleasure both in having an authority figure to whom he shows reverence and in exercising authority over those whom the fascist regards as somehow inferior.[8] Žižek is interested especially in the masochistic element, which he thinks is especially marked in Christian fascism: for Žižek, the Christian fascist articulates an ascetic rejection of pleasure (which is often an ideological and resentful response to poor material conditions) that itself becomes the biggest source of pleasure in the fascist's life.[9] Finally, and each at least partly inspired by a spirit of Jewish messianism, Walter Benjamin and Jacques Derrida each interpret Christian fascism as idolizing the present: Benjamin worries that the fascist aestheticization of politics precludes the possibility of revolution,[10] and Derrida argues that the fascist valorization of an in-group of "friends" occludes the possibility of the revolutionary inbreaking of others.[11]

Each of these approaches contributes to a rich understanding, interpretation, and description of fascism in general or Christian fascism in particular. But in order to construct a more prescriptive analysis—what should we do about Christian fascists?—I want to specify and limit the scope of analysis. For this, I will offer a brief study of the twentieth-century Christian fascist Carl Schmitt. Schmitt, the "crown jurist of the Third Reich," was a committed Catholic and Nazi who produced juridical work that defended, among other horrors, the Enabling Act of 1933, which granted Adolf Hitler dictatorial power.[12] Although outside of a few obscure advocates there is no reason to think that the contemporary Christian fascist movement has been directly influenced by Schmitt, he remains important to study because of his insight into the specificity of Christian fascist government.[13]

The Political Theology of Christian Fascism

Schmitt's argument, in brief, is the following: The sovereign is the one who decides both when a state of exception—an event for which there is no legal precedent—occurs and what to do about it.[14] In the case of the aforementioned Enabling Act of 1933, Schmitt opined that the Reichstag Fire, and the alleged impending communist threat that it represented, constituted an exceptional and existential threat to the sovereignty of the Weimar Republic. In turn, and as Schmitt's legal theory suggests would happen, Hitler and his cabinet were granted sovereign, dictatorial power to respond to the crisis. Or, rather, Hitler and his cabinet's sovereign ability to respond to the threat was recognized by the republic. According to Schmitt, any attempt to deny this reality of sovereignty is misguided naïveté at best or misleading power politics at worst. For example, the alleged constitutionalism of

America—according to John Adams, America is a nation ruled not
by "men" but by "laws"—can only ever obscure the true reality
of the situation: America is not ruled by laws but by a few very
particular people, and an appeal to laws over people only serves
to shelter these true sovereigns.

The Christian fascist element becomes apparent when Schmitt
declares that this formal structure of governance—there is one
sovereign, and this sovereign both does have and should have
the power to both declare the existence of a state of emergency
and to decide what to do about it—*is the Christian form of
government*. That is, Schmitt argues—and seems to genuinely
believe—that Adolph Hitler's dictatorship is in accordance with
the divine teaching of Christian monotheism: as God created out
of nothingness and decides the truth of creation from both a transcendent external perspective and from within creation, so Hitler
will create the Third Reich and decide likewise. In this perspective,
the alternatives to sovereign dictatorship—democracy, liberalism,
parliamentarianism, socialism, and so on—are signs of atheistic
immanence: it is only sovereign dictatorship that recognizes and
respects the alleged theological fact of political transcendence.

Implied within this Christian fascist structure is a high valorization of the unity of "the people": all those who accept the
"truth" of this transcendent sovereignty are, through their very
acceptance, part of the fascist collective. These are, as Schmitt
calls them, "friends." Those who resist this formal structure present existential challenges to this allegedly Christian truth and
so are, as Schmitt calls them, "enemies." The people, the *volk*,
are identified through their shared assent to the sovereign dicta-
tor and through their shared enmity toward those who do not
recognize the sovereign's power. As this structure of sovereignty
is allegedly Christian, Schmitt's enemies are both political and
religious opponents. Schmitt has articulated a violent religious
fundamentalism. As this structure of allegedly Christian sovereignty has manifested itself in Germany, Schmitt has articulated
not only a Christian fundamentalism but one that is intrinsically
identified with an ethnocentric nationalism. To summarize this
argument, for Schmitt, unity, transcendent law, and order should
be defended both because they are goods in and of themselves
and because they are, in particular, *Christian* goods. Likewise, attempts at revolution from within or critique from outside should

be resisted both because revolutionary disorder is a bad in and of itself (it is allegedly un-Christian) and because revolution and disorder against the particular transcendent sovereign—for Schmitt, Hitler; for the January 6 rioters, Trump—must, by definition, be attempts at revolutionizing and overthrowing the divine order.

The Liberal Critique

Typically, and largely because of Chantal Mouffe's influential interpretation, this Christian fascist argument is read as primarily antagonistic to liberalism.[15] Indeed, Schmitt provides plenty of reason to suggest this interpretation: Schmitt, for example, famously describes the figure of "the liberal" as the one who answers Pilate's question "Christ or Barabbas?" with "a proposal to adjourn or appoint a commission of investigation."[16] Moreover, the content of Schmitt's program seems to suggest a full-blown attack on liberal values. Schmitt is a racist, a nationalist, an anti-Semite, and a religious fundamentalist. He envisions a pure state of pure politics for a pure Christian-German people and is willing, he says, to "physically destroy" anyone who gets in the way.[17] It is difficult to imagine a more illiberal program, and we would all certainly choose the liberal value of equality over the fascist value of ontological inequality.

However, my argument is that one should be wary of reducing a critique of Schmitt—and Christian fascism in general—to a defense of liberal values. While tolerance is clearly preferable to intolerance, and while equality is obviously a more admirable goal than inequality, it is also the case that the liberal critique of fascism risks unintentionally reinscribing some of the most subtly pernicious aspects of fascist thought. Consider the well-intended liberal response to Donald Trump's Muslim ban. This response was typified in a poster, designed by Shepard Fairey of Obama "hope" poster fame, of a cartoon Muslim woman donning an American flag hijab. The intent here is clear: where Trump sows division and hatred, the liberal emphasizes inclusion and hospitality. Can one imagine a similar response to Schmitt's Nazi anti-Semitism? The analogue would be a cartoon Jewish man with a German flag yarmulke on his head. The example reveals the absurdity of the liberal gesture not only because it denies the hatred directed from Nazi Germany toward Jews, but also because it imposes a totalitarian sameness onto the Jewish community.

Liberal critiques of fascism that emphasize inclusion argue that the problem with fascism is its exclusionary nature. This critique asks and argues about the answers to the questions: Who counts? Who is in and who is out? Who constitutes "We the People"? The problem with such a fight is that this fight over "who counts" is precisely the fight that Schmitt and modern Christian fascists want to have. If this inclusionary concern is the primary critique offered by liberals, then neither liberalism nor fascism disagree that unity is a value worth pursuing. In other words, the liberal and the fascist share a prescriptive disagreement over the material constitution of "the people"—and these disagreements are important, and the liberal is right to critique the racism and xenophobia of the fascist—but they more or less agree that "the people" is a worthwhile ideal to pursue and defend.

An Anti-Fascist Theology beyond Liberalism

I suggest an alternative approach: Rather than argue for a more inclusive "the people"—whether German, American, or any other—I suggest emphasizing and aggravating the ruptures inherent within any fictive unity termed a "people." In other words, I am suggesting a different interpretation of "difference." Whereas the liberal looks to valorize differences—for example the difference between Christians and Muslims, between whites and Blacks, between men and women, and so on—for the sake of a larger, multicultural, and more inclusive in-group, my suggested approach interprets difference through the hermeneutic lens of inequality and exploitation: not the difference between cultures but the exploitative and oppressive differences between owner and employee, between prison guard and prisoner, between landlord and renter, between soldier and civilian, between protester and police officer, between the International Monetary Fund and indebted states, and so on. These differences are not to be valorized, but intensified, organized off of, and eventually overcome.

That such an approach is a viable strategy for combating fascism is implied by Schmitt's private writings. While in his officially published texts Schmitt tends to critique liberalism, his private correspondences and journals reveal that Schmitt was most troubled by the figures of "The Jew" and "The Communist."[18] This should be unsurprising, as it was primarily Jews and Soviets, not liberals, who were targeted by the Nazis. It is in these private writings that Schmitt reveals that "The Jew" and "The Communist"—and the two are near synonyms for Schmitt—present a more material challenge to fascism than does "The Liberal," precisely because Jews and communists reject the formal valorization of unity shared by both the liberal and the fascist. The diasporic Jew, for example, resists identification with the political nation-state. This rejected identification challenges the fascist valorization of unity: and so the Jew must be either relegated to Zionism (and so made to fit a nationalist frame) or subjected to genocide (and this choice between Zionism and Judeocide explains the perhaps surprising alliance between the Nazi and the German-Zionist-Jewish elites, as witnessed by the 1933 Haavara Agreement).[19] Meanwhile, the communist emphasizes the class distinctions and power inequalities within a nation-state (and within the global capitalist order more generally). In doing so, the communist emphasizes division within the "*volk*," giving up the lie of intra-German or intra-American unity. This threat of domestic disturbance is why Schmitt's critique of Lenin was not the usual one concerning gulags, violence, and so on, but was instead the surprising charge that Marxist-Leninism was *too democratic*: Communism, Schmitt recognized, presented the possibility of a complete revolution of the transcendent sovereign model of political authority to which all Christian fascisms adhere.[20]

This Jew-Communist dyad disrupts and resists the valorization of ideal political belonging that is shared, albeit to differing degrees of inclusivity and exclusivity, by both fascist and liberal. The question posed by the Jew-Communist is not who belongs to the ideal unity, "the people," but is instead: What ruptures, oppressions, and exploitations inherent in *any* political unity are elided by both liberal and fascist valorizations of belonging? In this way, the international cosmopolitanism signified by the diasporic Jew and the political-economic critique of capitalism and imperialism signified and articulated by the communist present more radical and revolutionary challenges to Christian fascism than does liberalism, which remains attached to the ideal not of revolution but unity.

An anti-fascist political theology should opt for revolutionary and emancipatory praxis over liberal praxis: The answer to the

Christian fascist's idolization of purity and unity is not a liberal expansion of purity and unity but an emancipatory commitment to disruptive revolution. The anti-fascist response to the fascist idolization of order is not an idolization of a kinder liberal order but a commitment to a creative disordering of all exploitative and oppressive structures. For example, an anti-fascist political theology would respond to white nationalism by noting and organizing off of the class exploitation and gender oppression found within the so-called "white community." A promotion of the liberal values of compassion, equity, empathy, and so on are likely to fall on the Christian fascist's deaf ears—not least of all because the Christian fascist does understand himself as expressing compassion and empathy and as supportive of a sort of denuded equity inscribed within a carefully delimited in-group. The anti-fascist response for which I am advocating would not increase the scope and size of this in-group but would look to critique and materially deconstruct its identitarian form. The properly anti-fascist response to a fascist in-group is not to grow it but to smash it. As Schmitt tacitly knew, and as contemporary Christian fascists who fear "globalist socialists" also understand, it is the internationalism implied by the diasporic Jew and the communist's critique of capital that best promote the disruption and overcoming of the fascist fetish construct of "the people."

Finally, such an anti-fascist valorization of disjuncture is perhaps the best way to understand Jesus's words in Matthew 10:34, where we learn that Jesus did not come to bring "peace" but a "sword." From within this framework, we can understand that this disruptive sword is not antithetical to the peace, justice, and love that Jesus so clearly does promote: there is no true peace under this global capitalist order, fascist or not, and so a commitment to nonviolent love and justice might require an apparently "violent" revolution of the status quo. More than liberalism, it is this threat of revolution that most threatens the fascist program. After all, the Trump promise was to "make America great again"—a commitment to the past that promises the Christian fascist that the inbreaking of a more just future can be held off. Only a revolutionary program that forces and welcomes an emancipatory future will finally free us from the fascist/liberal grammar of inclusion. At the same time, and as none other than Ernesto "Che" Guevara noted, it is only the revolutionary's faithful love for justice that can bring this emancipated future into being. This revolutionary love for the oppressed and exploited does not look to better include them—include us—into the American empire but to set them free. As Che said: "At the risk of seeming ridiculous, let me say that the true revolutionary is guided by a great feeling of love. It is impossible to think of a genuine revolutionary lacking this quality."[21] My point here—which was Jesus's point with the sword, which was Che's point as well—is that this love calls not for more inclusion, not for an arithmetical model of "liberation" where we look to add more and more to "the people," but instead calls for an anti-fascist disruption and disjuncture. It is only with such an internationalist and anti-capitalist commitment, that is, only with a revolutionary love, that we might hope to experience the emancipatory force of what Walter Benjamin, among others, calls the messiah.

Notes

[1]Robert Pape and Keven Ruby, "The Face of American Insurrection: Right Wing Organizations Evolving into a Violent Mass Movement," *Chicago Project on Security and Threats.* January 28, 2021, https://d3qi0qp55mx5f5. cloudfront.net/cpost/i/docs/americas_insurrectionists_online_2021_01_29. pdf?mtime=1611966204. An overview of the research can be accessed here: https://cpost.uchicago.edu/research/domestic_extremism/.

[2]Asitha Nagesh, "US election 2020: Why Trump Gained Support among Minorities," *BBC News,* November, 22, 2020, www.bbc.com.

[3]Thomas Chatterton Williams, "The French Origins of 'You Will Not Replace Us,'" *New Yorker,* November 27, 2017, www.newyorker.com. Of course, Trump's relative popularity with both Black voters and white supremacists—relative to previous Republicans—might also suggest that the relationship between white supremacy and so-called "Black issues" might not be as straightforward as liberal race reductionists might suggest.

[4]For an introductory overview of these difficulties, see Kevin Passmore, *Fascism: A Very Short Introduction* (New York: Oxford University Press, 2014).

[5]Typically, this mythical element of fascism leads to an understanding of fascism as a "political religion." See, for example, Luca La Rovere's "Interpretations of Fascism as a Political Religion in Post-Fascist Italy," *Politics, Religion, and Ideology* 15, no. 1 (2014): 23–44. As I will argue, something of the specificity of Christian fascism is lost in an appeal to this formally abstract "religion."

[6]Dorothee Soelle, *The Window of Vulnerability: A Political Spirituality,* trans. Linda M. Maloney (Minneapolis: Fortress, 1990); Dorothee Soelle, *Beyond Mere Obedience* (Cleveland: Pilgrim, 1982).

[7]Chris Hedges, *American Fascists: The Christian Right and the War on America* (New York: Free Press, 2008). Hedges is especially helpful in arguing for the convergence of religious and secular responses to Christian fascism and so arguing against Christian methodological imperialism (as might happen with John Milbank's "radical orthodoxy").

[8]Erich Fromm, *Escape from Freedom* (New York: Holt Paperbacks, 1994).

[9]Slavoj Žižek, *The Sublime Object of Ideology* (Brooklyn, NY: Verso, 2009).

[10]Walter Benjamin, "The Work of Art in the Age of Mechanical Reproduction," in *Illuminations*, trans. Harry Zohn (New York: Mariner, 2019), 166–95.

[11]Jacques Derrida, *The Politics of Friendship*, trans. George Collins (Brooklyn, NY: Verso, 2006).

[12]For an introduction to Schmitt's life and thought, see Gopal Balakrishnan, *The Enemy: An Intellectual Portrait of Carl Schmitt* (Brooklyn, NY: Verso Books, 2002).

[13]Josh Vandiver, "The Radical Roots of the Alt-Right," *Gale Primary Sources*, 2018, https://www.gale.com/binaries/content/assets/gale-us-en/primary-sources/intl-gps/intl-gps-essays/full-ghn-contextual-essays/gps_essay_plex_vandiver1_website_v2.pdf.

[14]Most of the following synthesizes Carl Schmitt's arguments in *The Concept of the Political*, trans. George Schwab (Chicago: University of Chicago Press, 2007); *Political Theology: Four Chapters on the Concept of Sovereignty*, trans. George Schwab (Chicago: University of Chicago Press, 2006); and *Dictatorship* (Boston: Polity, 2013).

[15]Mouffe's engagement with Schmitt spans her career but is most clearly articulated in her *On the Political* (New York: Routledge, 2011).

[16]Schmitt, *Political Theology*, 62.

[17]See Schmitt, *The Concept of the Political*, 49.

[18]Carl Schmitt, *Glossarium: Aufzeichnungen aus den Jahren 1947 bis 1958,* ed. Gerd Giesler and Martin Tielke (Berlin: Duncker & Humblot, 2015).

[19]See Francis Nicosia, *The Third Reich and the Palestine Question* (Piscataway, NJ: Transaction, 2000).

[20]For an overview of this critique, see Jason Edwards, *The Radical Attitude and Modern Political Theory* (New York: Palgrave Macmillan, 2007), 154–82.

[21]Ernesto Guevara, "Socialism and Man in Cuba," from *The Che Guevara Reader*, 2nd exp. edition, ed. David Deutschmann (Victoria, Australia: Ocean, 2005).

Sexual Harassment
in Our Theological Training

Donna Freitas's Consent: A Memoir of Unwanted Attention *narrates how Freitas negotiated a predator priest-professor during her theological studies. This panel engages* Consent *to analyze and respond to this dehumanizing aspect of the institutions that train theologians.*

Sexual Trauma, the Production
of Women, and the Academy

Julia Feder

Given the centrality of conversation about trauma in the media and in the academy, many of us now know that "trauma" refers to a kind of suffering that disintegrates the sufferer and continues to do so long after the immediate threat of violence has passed. Donna Freitas's memoir *Consent* narrates this kind of suffering. As Freitas describes,

I have two sets of memories—one, which is exclusively devoted to this man and all that happened with him, and the other, which is exclusively devoted to everything else that happened in my life during grad school and since. One set is dark and ugly and sickening, and the other is bright and happy and thrilling. The darker set is dangerous; it lies in wait, hidden, lurking, until the moment when the happier side of me least expects, has almost forgotten, it is there, and suddenly it lashes out with the force and violence of a knife slashing through everything else that I am, everything that I've become, wounding me all over again.[1]

In many ways, Freitas's writing is itself an act of traumatic healing—i.e., an attempt to describe her disintegration and, thus, to stitch an integrated life back together. Trauma scholars have recognized both the benefits and limitations of such an act of resistance. Narration remakes what has been lost in a new way, seeks to repair the primary site of woundedness—the fractured individual—and, thus, prepares her to again (or perhaps for the first time) to offer her whole self in relational self-donation—wounded and strong, sinner and sinned-against, confident and self-doubting. But because narration cannot erase the harm that has occurred, many trauma scholars resist talking about "healing" at all because they do not wish to suggest that traumatic violence is something that can be "cured."[2] Yet I think that we might able to talk about "healing" if we conceive of "healing" in its present participle form—as an ongoing process that is often nonlinear. Freitas's narrative highlights this well, resisting any sharp distinction between victim and survivor. As she writes, "I am a survivor, but I also am, and always will be, a victim."[3] In claiming this dual identity, she paradoxically insists on a radical kind of integration—one that need not wait for a cure that will not come or a healing that will not arrive. There is no fairy-tale ending; there remains a tension that will be resolved only eschatologically. I think that this is actually more hopeful than its alternative. If healing must wait until suffering is over, there is not much reason to live in hope. This is all the more critical because scholars are just beginning to note that some of the ways that traumatic violence is traumatic is because it confirms what marginalized people already know: the world is not safe. The identities and behaviors of women and other nondominant individuals are continually shaped by the threat of violence. For those of us who cannot escape marginality, we cannot hope for healing that consists in a triumph over suffering in this life. We must hope for healing in the midst of continued suffering and precarity.

As I read Freitas's memoir, I was shaken by her discussion of dress and sexual agency. Though this is not a large component of her narrative, it is a consistent one. Before her abuse, Freitas explains,

I loved boots, high-heeled boots, and wore them as often as I could. I loved the way the boys turned their heads, admiringly, as I walked by. I could never have enough of their attention, I was never satiated by it, and I dressed as much for them as I did for me. . . . I was proud of my attention-grabbing looks and outfits and confidence, and I was happy in my sexual prowess. I was stupid with power. I would be punished for it.[4]

As I noticed this thread in her narrative it felt (intuitively) to me to be a risky one—namely, to write in a public way about an often unacknowledged kind of tension that simmers below the surface for many of us boot-lovers beginning at twelve or thirteen years old. On the one hand, prior to her abuse, she understood herself as a whole subject—confident, expressive of her enthusiasm and her desires, expecting care from others and able to give care in return. But, on the other hand, her abuse took its power from narratives already internalized from a young age about female lack of agency, clerical power, and professorial power and amplified fears that she had been "asking for it" all along.[5] She admits,

There is a part of me now, a part I can't shake or darken enough so I no longer see it, that believes I *was* eventually punished for my behavior, for exploring beyond the boundaries young women were allowed, for wandering into what was typically the territory of young men; for the way I moved through life, sexual and sensuous and playful. It is one of those suspicions that cut me into two. One woman, proud of the freedom she felt and how she used that freedom. The other, sure that punishment is always lurking just around the corner for women like her. And my punishment happened to be him. He was the man God sent, that the world sent, that the patriarchy sent to take the giddy light that burned inside of me and snuff it out.[6]

In a way, Freitas was both a victim and a survivor even before a discrete violation had occurred. As philosopher Ann Cahill argues, the fear of rape organizes women's lives determining how and when and where they move, how they socialize, and how they dress. With this sustained threat in the background of everyday life, when sexual violence does happen, it is often experienced as a *fulfilled* threat, surprising only insofar as it was a fear already imagined but one that the victim *thought* she had sufficiently warded off through "daily protective practices" performed like spells—wearing the right clothing, staying inside at the right times, refraining from taking up too much space or attention, and acting sufficiently innocent in order to gain protective allies.[7] Cahill claims, "The prevalence of rape and the threat of rape literally forms aspects of feminine bodily comportment. Rape not only happens to women; it is a fundamental moment in the production of women *qua* women."[8] To be formed by the threat of rape looks like being overwhelmingly warm, but unable to remove an outer layer for fear of how it would be interpreted. To be excited, but to be trained to restrain it for fear of how it would be misunderstood. To be interested in getting to know others, but to be forced to be quiet because "interest" can only be interpreted one kind of way in women. Freitas writes,

> I smiled often that first semester, though not just at him. I could never hide my happiness in the classroom, in reading philosophical theory, in asking questions. Why would I have ever thought to hide the rapture on my face when I showed up to his seminar or when I walked in the door of his office? I was grateful to be there. I was lucky, still. The smile on my face, that intellectual insatiability gnawing its way through my insides, I consented to them with gusto. They were the physical, visible manifestations of all that I was feeling. That smile was, still is, to blame for so much of what came next, I think. The exuberance that was always spilling from my person. It was an outright invitation for him, for anyone, really, to look my way.[9]

In a culture that was somehow clearer than ours about women's sexual safety and agency, blaming abuse by a powerful professor and priest on intellectual enthusiasm or even sexual interest in peers would never make sense. But, these narratives of self-blame are able to get a foothold because our cultural context is one in which to be a woman is to be formed by the threat of rape. To be a woman who expresses her sexual agency or who relishes the pleasure of her body is a transgression that will and must be punished.

As Freitas notes in her book, no amount of education or intentional program of consciousness-raising would have likely dissuaded her perpetrator from his abusive behavior.[10] He did, in fact, write an essay arguing that his exploitative obsession with her was a way for him to grow closer to God—evidence of his willingness to go to great lengths to rationalize his abusive actions. Freitas's perpetrator is probably not an exceptional case. Most abusive individuals do not do what they do because they have *not yet* been intellectually convinced that their behavior is harmful. Most abusive individuals act abusively because they believe (with good cause, in most instances) that they will not be held accountable for their actions.

The shape of academic theology discourages accountability for sexually exploitative behavior in several ways. I want to point out just a couple of those: first, jobs are limited; second, success in the field depends on a one-on-one relationship with a dissertation advisor. When jobs are few and far between, doctoral students are increasingly vulnerable to exploitative relationships of all kinds (sexual or otherwise). As Freitas puts it, "When it happens to you and you are young and powerless, and the person who is making it happen holds your dream in his hands, fragile and beautiful and glowing with hope, there is a lot you will do to try to ensure that he doesn't use those hands to crush it."[11]

Graduate programs should be responsible for outlining what an appropriate student-teacher relationship looks like early on in a student's career and they must be responsible for clearly communicating how students can report boundary violations and what the consequences will be for faculty who transgress boundaries. Training like this can not only help victims to notice when they've been victimized, but they can also help to preemptively signal to potential perpetrators that exploitative behavior will not be tolerated. When professional behavior is clearly defined, this also can help to alleviate some of the anxiety that men report surrounding the prospect of mentoring women after #MeToo.[12] If we know what appropriate boundaries are, we can freely give of ourselves within those boundaries with minimal second-guessing. And, of course, we (as faculty members) need to have the courage to enforce the consequences that we agree upon even when the perpetrator is a friend or someone whose work has been important or even unfairly targeted in other respects (i.e., progressive stars in the field who have been subject to unfair criticism by the bishops). We need to be prepared to defend such colleagues on issues that matter but to enforce consequences when these colleagues commit acts of violence or abuse.

Perhaps, measures that schools like Yale are now instituting in the wake of a collapsing job market might also be useful in alleviating the vulnerability to abuse that traditional advising has created: "team-based advising" or "advising systems" that cross program boundaries.[13] If an advisor acts exploitatively, a student may feel freer to reach out for help if she knows that this advisor is not the only one responsible for training and advocating for her. Freitas describes the harm that was committed against her as twofold: both her perpetrator and her university are culpable. As she puts it, "One man held the wrecking ball at just the right angle, then a group of administrators swung that wrecking ball with all the force it had straight into me."[14] We can do a lot more to exercise our power to protect students within our institutions by speaking openly about the dangers of abuse and inviting more people into the mentoring process.

Consent, Sex, Gender, and Power

Julie Hanlon Rubio

I read Donna Freitas's extraordinary memoir in a year in which I have been thinking a lot about clergy sexual abuse. With my colleague Paul Schutz and social scientists at Santa Clara University, I am in the middle of a two-year study investigating clericalism as a root cause of abuse.[15] We have come to understand clericalism as a structure in the Catholic Church in which sex, gender, and power come together. We hypothesize that sex, gender, and power incentivize and enable sexual violence. They are always in the room when sexual violence is happening and being excused, but in church contexts, they are entangled in a system that isolates and privileges clergy.

These issues are not abstract for me. Because I have spent the last twenty-two years working in Jesuit institutions, I feel responsible. Many of my current students are Jesuit scholastics or priests. When the Jesuits released lists of credibly accused priests, the Midwest Province list included a now deceased Jesuit who was a former colleague and family friend. This past year, when a Jesuit educational institution announced the resignation of a high-ranking administrator due to misconduct or boundary violations, I was encouraged to see a willingness to take responsibility but more convinced that this crisis is ongoing.[16] In grouping these issues together, I do not mean to suggest their equivalence. However, following many experts in the field, I use sexual violence as a broad term to cover forced physical sexual activity, unwanted sexual touch and communication, harassment, grooming, or stalking of children and adults.[17] Though it is important to distinguish levels of violation, it is also crucial to see the connections among them and to note that in all cases people are harmed. Freitas's detailed account of sexual violence helps us understand how clericalism functions through its essential elements of gender, sex, and power to enable abuse, keep abuse from becoming public, protect clergy perpetrators, and leave victim-survivors vulnerable.

Gender is perhaps the element we talk about least in conversations on clergy sexual abuse. This is surprising because the one thing all Catholic clergy perpetrators have in common is their gender. Current research shows that priests are no more likely to abuse than pastors, teachers, coaches, or family members. According to criminologist Karen Terry, no one factor, including being a victim of abuse, can explain why some priests become perpetrators and others do not.[18] Yet, as Rebecca Solnit points out, "Violence doesn't have a race, a class, a religion, or a nationality, but it does have a gender."[19] The overwhelming majority of perpetrators are men.[20] In and outside of Catholic contexts, men target women, men, and children over whom they have power, especially in male-dominated, hierarchical spaces.

In *Consent*, Freitas aptly describes the male-dominated environment of theology graduate school in the 1990s. Lay students and faculty are newcomers to a world saturated with maleness—seminarians, priest professors, reading lists of male theologians. As a lay woman, a young woman, an academic woman who dresses well, she stands out. When the priest professor she understood to be a mentor begins to stalk her, she interrogates *her* gender expression— the clothes she wore and the intellectual enthusiasm she showed. Behaviors any disinterested observer would associate with being a good student, the clericalist culture incentivizes her to interpret as gendered, and therefore potentially sexual and implicating.

For Freitas, the priest professor both is and is not a man. As a priest, he must be male, and yet he is also somehow stripped of gender, dressed in a black robe, not allowed to marry or provide for anyone. Freitas says she did not think of him as a man.[21] Participants in our clericalism study, too, had a hard time connecting gender and priesthood. A priest seems to give up gender when he puts on clerical clothes. Yet the behavior of the priest professor follows the male role in a dating script gone horribly wrong. Performing a toxic masculinity, he sends letter after letter until they create a huge pile in Freitas's apartment; calls and visits unceasingly at multiple locations having somehow gotten ahold of her personal information; waits for her around every corner; manipulates her in conversation, never taking no for an answer. He pursues her without any regard for her will. He "refused my no," she says.[22] He "simply *could not see me*."[23] A friend, a mother of two sons, worried about false accusations of date rape, recently asked me, what are men supposed to do if it *seems like* women are saying yes? How are they supposed to know? That's it, I replied. If they can't hear the "No," of a woman, man, or child, something is wrong. Regardless of their intentions, male performance of masculinity can blind men—including male priests—to the vulnerable humans in front of them.

Like gender, sex plays a role in sexual violence, just not the role many believe it plays. There is no good data linking homosexuality or celibacy to abuse. True pedophiles are rare; the vast majority of perpetrators are heterosexual, non-celibate men.[24] However, problematic sexual ideas and inclinations still contribute to sexual violence. Outside clerical contexts, as both Freitas and Jason King have documented, males lead in hook-up culture, enjoying status in this arena, while women are often shamed because of their participation and disappointed by the lack of emotional connection, and are all too often victims of date rape or "bad sex."[25] In church spaces, "sexual integration" indicates coherence between one's vocation and one's desires for sex and intimacy.[26] A sexually integrated celibate acknowledges his desires and pursues self-care and healthy friendships with appropriate boundaries. We might also apply the term to perpetrators of sexual violence. In sexually imposing themselves on victims without emotion or care, they reveal a lack of sexual integration. In both cases, perpetrators fail to respect the norms of what Margaret Farley calls "just love."[27] They fail to do justice in sexual relations. Instead of practicing vulnerability, they do harm by following their own distorted desires without regard to others.[28]

Sex also plays a role for victim-survivors. In Freitas's story, her happy dating life stands in contrast to interactions with the priest professor who for her is "not even a sexual being."[29] This is why, at first, she eagerly accepts his invitations to go to the theater or dinner. This is like going out on the town with grandpa.[30] Only gradually, the lines blur. Later, when he badgers her to see him, these encounters seem more like "dates" to be avoided, though not completely. Freitas's narrative showcases the way victim-survivors of clergy sexual abuse are often confused about what is going on. The priest cannot be making sexual overtures because he is celibate, "by definition, safe."[31] She is either crazy for thinking there is anything inappropriate going on, or she is guilty for seducing the most unsexual of beings. Social work professor Diana Garland's definitive study of women abused by their pastors highlights a widespread inability to believe anything sexual could be happening because ministers are not allowed to be sexual with people in their congregation.[32] Though sex is not the whole story, sexual violence and the silencing of victims is made more possible by confusion about sex.

Of course, power is also a part of the context enabling sexual violence. The priest professor in Freitas's narrative holds many kinds of power—male, professor, academic keeper of the keys to her professional future, beloved, and, of course, Father. All of these aspects of power embolden him to continue pursuing her, even to the point of absurdity, as he inserts himself in the life of her family, corresponding with her mother who is fighting cancer, and using these letters as texts in a class on suffering. The literature on sexual violence suggests that sometimes perpetrators use their power to enact violence, sometimes perpetrators who feel powerless find power through violence, and sometimes neediness and power coexist. In this case, a needy-yet-powerful male, priest professor acts violently and compels complicity with clericalism.[33] People in the university who should have helped instead conspire to protect Father. Incredibly, his only punishment was a sabbatical.[34]

For victim-survivors, power shapes the feeling of being trapped—of having no options, because who would believe them if they spoke up anyway?[35] Silence and lies to self and others seem the only real options. Freitas explains that she could not trust herself over all that she has been taught to trust—church, academy, priest.[36] She could not name the abuse.[37] The perpetrators' power was so great that he could not be avoided in her profession—our profession. So she gave up her dream of becoming a professor.

But must we, as Freitas seems to suggest near the end of her book, see him either as a "a calculating monster" or "a kindly man" diminished by a flawed institution?[38] In my view, neither alternative is sufficient. It is important to acknowledge that anyone could be victimized by a "monster," someone so cunning and lacking in compassion that nothing could stop him. But I worry that when we call perpetrators "monsters," we perpetuate the idea that they are unusual rather than ordinary, acting alone rather than enabled by structural clericalism. Ordinary perpetrators act and go on with their lives, go on in our profession, because of these structures. Responding well to the story Freitas has so courageously given us requires us to see that, yes, this man, this priest professor, acted monstrously. But it also requires us to understand why he did so and to assess if he would and could still do so today. It requires us to interrogate notions of sex, gender, and power that incentivize sexual violence, restrict the options of those who are victimized, and enable cover-up and escape from consequences, in and outside of the church, then and now.

Theological Education
and the Danger of Mentoring

Jason King

I'm Dan—at least, I'm the person named "Dan" in Donna's memoir *Consent*. Looking back on the moment in graduate school when Donna told me about the stalking she was suffering, I get anxious. I know it could have gone differently. There was nothing in our graduate school that encouraged supporting people going through what Donna was going through, and there were lots of incentives to stay quiet about or deny her experience. I make this point to note the issue I want to focus on. The system—the system of graduate school theological education—tends to exclude essential parts of our humanity and so make us vulnerable to abuse. I get at this issue by focusing on the role of the mentor.

Systems develop to address persistent and complex problems.[39] A developed system is relatively stable, having institutional elements that perpetuate the work as people move in and out of the system.[40] Despite this skeletal description, it is sufficient for understanding key elements of the US system of theological education. It is a system geared toward the problem of teaching students what is needed for preserving and advancing theology. Its elements include acquiring skills at writing, researching, and languages, content across a range of subfields, frameworks to understand thinkers and movements, and a specialization and subspecialization within the field. These aspects of learning are supported by institutional elements that dictate classes to be taken, tests to be passed, and research projects that can be pursued and that include chairs, deans, and provosts to enforce these policies.

This system also requires a dissertation director. The director is meant to guide students through the completion and defense of their research project. Directors often do more though, serving as mentors. They are crucial for increasing students' chances of completing programs (especially for women and minorities), being employed, earning higher incomes, navigating organizational structures, feeling satisfied with the work, and having a sense of self-worth.[41] These benefits arise from a relationship that extends beyond academic performance into personal, social, and formative aspects.[42] However, the system of theological education only includes the academic component and moves the rest of mentoring outside of the system. In this liminal space, there is no ethics governing mentors' actions, and so the requirement for a director comes with tremendous risk.

By focusing on teaching and learning, the system of graduate theological education moves most of students' humanity into a liminal space. Some financial concerns—like funding or job prospects—can be discussed, friendships and romances hardly ever. We have to learn an academic language which often creates barriers to expressing who we are. On arriving at graduate school, I learned to recognize my Appalachian dialect and began to say "cement" and not "CE-ment" and to avoid words like "y'all" and "cricks." In "Mentoring (In)Hospitable Places," Susan Abraham recounts an all too familiar story of having to fight dismissal, questioning of her abilities, and befuddlement at her concerns in order to voice experiences and insights as a lay theologian from India.[43]

Donna's story highlights how the role of the mentor is also in this liminal space. While graduate students need directors, the relationship is governed by few protocols, almost all of which are limited to teaching and learning. It would have been easier for the system to penalize Fr. L for failing to turn in grades rather than for sexual harassment or assault. There are no assessments of directors, no evaluation of the work they do outside of the classroom, no peer review of their mentoring, and no psychological testing to ensure that they are not narcissists or predators. It leaves students, who must have a director, vulnerable to exploitation.[44] Mentors can cause students to "quell" their identity or culture, force students to fight for their perspective and risk losing support, or create false selves to protect their real selves from exploitation. The last option echoes the "two sets of memories"[45] Donna developed to survive.

It is also possible to flip this around and see the problem. Female professors, professors of color, LGBTQ+ professors often take up extra work mentoring students—especially female students, students of color, and LGBTQ+ students—but are not credited for this extra work as they progress toward tenure.[46] In other words, caring or not caring for students, supporting or victimizing students: The system does not recognize any of these as important. They are outside the system.

Moving the relationship of students and their mentor from its amoral, liminal space into the system is difficult. Institutional structures make a system durable and stable, but they also make it resistant to change. As a friend and fellow graduate student, I could not change the system to help Donna. Dr. H, the chair of the department, was thoroughly enmeshed in the system. He was responsible for schedules, faculty, funding, and students. He believed Donna, sent her to human resources, spoke with Father L, and rearranged Donna's program. All of this, and Dr. H could not stop Father L. He even realized how limited he was by finally telling Donna, "[I]t's time . . . [y]ou need a lawyer. You need a lawyer now. You must get one."[47] Moreover, the dynamism of the institutional structures creates an incentive for people to doubt themselves rather than the activities of their professors. Donna called into question her enthusiasm, dress, language, and visits to Father L's office before questioning the professor's intrusions into her personal files or her family life. The dynamics of graduate theological education was to exclude aspects of Donna's life that did not pertain to academic training, aspects like friends, allies, personality, and stalking.

In excluding parts of Donna's humanity, the system also generates internal mechanisms for defending itself. The provost was one, staring silently at Donna for making him aware of what was occurring, with "no compassion, no sign that [her] grief, [her] fear, [her] despair, moved him, not even a tiny bit."[48] Rather than nakedly blocking Donna's challenge to the system, the human resources employee Tootsie lied and delayed, trying to prevent any actions from being taken. Both fit comfortably within and were supported by the system, and this positioning moves them to prefer preserving the system more than compassion for a human being.

While not part of Donna's story, the system can also generate a scapegoat mechanism to defend itself. When I was serving as chair of my department, I became aware of a professor priest who was asking female students how they pleasured their boyfriends. When I reported the incident, the school moved to protect him. Those above me said, "It was all a misunderstanding," "He's just a provocative teacher," "Students are too sensitive these days," and "He has been saying these things for years, so why is it a problem now?" Only when multiple students came forward and lawsuits were threatened did the school finally act. It decided not to renew his contract for the coming semester. Having expelled the problem though, no other action was taken, no new policy emerged, and no apology was offered.

As a result of all these defense mechanisms, we should marvel at the existence of a book like *Consent*. To take on the system of theological education, a person would have to tell a personal story, like a memoir, to counter the system's narrow academic focus. It would have to come from someone inside the system who experienced its machinations but also from someone outside the system to be able to oppose them. It would also need to be from someone with enough courage and power to withstand the oppositional force the system will deploy. It is amazing that Donna's story exists, and, as such, it is incumbent on us to use it to make things better.

As Donna's story makes clear, work has barely begun to alter graduate school education to account for the relationship between students and mentors. To start to address this problem, I want to speak about an ethics of being a mentor. While an ethics might seem abstract, I think it can alter the system of graduate theological education in two important ways. First, defining an ethics recognizes the importance of the mentoring relationship, acknowledging that it is real and powerful. An ethics points to the need for constraints that move people to do the work well and enables others to recognize when wrongs are perpetrated. Second, once defined, an ethics can become part of the system of graduate theological education. It can become an institutional element that moves the relationship out of liminal space and into the system where aspects of mentoring beyond academics can be effectively addressed.

What would an ethics of being a mentor look like? Drawing from the scholarship, I mention just a few key features. Mentors should listen to and help students develop their own voice, one not measured by how well it echoes or pleases their mentors. The mentor should work to ensure their students become part of the academic community, conversant in the field but also conversant with others working in the field.[49] There should be clear boundaries about the relationship, especially sexual boundaries.[50] The mentor should be vetted not only for professional competency but also for professional behavior. There should be a peer review of mentors to ensure these standards are met. Principles like justice, beneficence, and non-maleficence should guide these activities.[51]

Obviously, there is more. But even with these few expectations, think about how graduate education would change. Think of the ways it would limit mentors' power and the ability for students to recognize and respond to breaches. It would humanize the system because it would recognize that students and the relationship with their mentors is more than just the transmission of knowledge. It would mean a system where, to borrow a metaphor from Donna, victimized students would no longer have to cut their tongues out to survive.

Toward a Theology of the Survivor

Donna Freitas

The task of responding to analyses of my memoir is daunting, like coming out of the closet to my old profession about something

I was taught to be ashamed of by that profession—the fact that I am a victim of abuse. Over the course of this past year, I have also been telling certain former colleagues about this memoir and this fact about my past. In doing so, I have been met with a range of responses, sometimes with silence and rejection, which reinforces the shame I have learned to feel and this sense that I should continue to remain silent about what happened to me during graduate school. But sometimes I am met with compassion too. I am offered space and openness, and for that, I am grateful.

And of course, in this same vein, I am extremely grateful for the compassion, thoughtfulness, and openness of Jason, Julia, and Julie, for all that they've said in their essays and also for unburdening me of sharing details about what happened to me by sharing the gist of it yourselves. To Jason especially, for putting this panel together—Jason who has revealed himself to be Dan from my memoir, which made me laugh when I read this, and to whom I will forever be grateful. Jason has walked with me in this part of my life for over twenty years. I love that Jason has begun to tackle "an ethics of being a mentor." If only that existed back when we were in graduate school. Over the course of this year, I've been starting to tackle what I've been calling a "theology of the survivor," which I'll share a little bit about it here, in addition to my reflections on the memoir.

But I'll warn you that I plan to make you uncomfortable.

At the end of Julie's remarks, she said, "Ordinary perpetrators act and go on with their lives, go on in our profession because of these structures. . . . This man, this priest professor, acted monstrously and, incredibly, avoided consequences. But it also requires us to understand why he did so and to assess if he would and could still do so today." I want to pick up where Julie left off. Ordinary victims go on with their lives too. I am one of those. And I offer you the story of an ordinary victim in my memoir.

But there is a way in which, because of the memoir, I—and the rest of us—can see *me* as a character in a book, frozen in the particular time of graduate school that my memoir tells. It is true, too, that through the memoir, I turned what happened to me into an object for everyone's analysis—yours and my own.

But, I am *still a person*—not just a character. Someone lived the story in that memoir. I am still living that story and its consequences. I want to face this profession with the implications of my being *that character*, but in real life. My memoir tells the story of *theology* and theological schools—what happens to someone who is aspiring to become a theologian when she is abused within her professional training. It tells the story of what theologians and religion scholars did or didn't do in response. Today, I would like to talk about what theology and theologians *still* aren't doing in response—yes to me, but to everyone else who is a victim too. I want to face you with the *afterlife* of that story in the memoir, an afterlife which is also mine.

We can, and are, confronting clergy sexual abuse in the context of theology, but I worry that we continue to do this as though the victims are like characters in books, frozen in time, in their moments of abuse. Their experiences serve as little more than springboards for us to use to discuss priests, the hierarchy, and institutions—but not the victims, the survivors, themselves. Fairly invisible, they remain sidewalks for all of us, and we happily step on them, step across them, to avoid their cracks.

We—academics, theologians—often use our analytical skills and resources, our jargon, to dry out our conversations, to wring them of emotion. We dehumanize the conversation. We peel it away from particular people who are victims, survivors, because if we do not do this, the conversation, our writing about it, and our *feelings* about it might get messy. We do not like mess. We do not like it when things are dripping, oozing, icky, like the human body itself. So, we purify them. We purify our profession. We love purity in this field.

I want us to look at that. And I want you to look at *me* and see the casualty that I am—a specific, particular casualty of this profession *because* I was abused. I am the ooze. I am the mess this profession made and tries to cover over. We continue to talk about clergy abuse as though it's OVER THERE. But it's not. IT'S RIGHT HERE. I am the subject of clergy abuse, and I am right here.

Too often, we look away from someone like me, a survivor. We do not want to see or hear me. We would rather look at *him*, to analyze *him* and the why of his behavior—because he seems so different than we are. He is the monster, but *we* are not monsters. So, we other him so we don't have to associate ourselves with someone like him. We look at him as though he, alone, is the one responsible for what happened to *me*. But he is *not* alone, as Jason argued. My abuser is the product of a system. A system that you are a part and product of now, and that I was, too, before I left it. The system is *yours*. You maintain it. You perpetuate it.

But if we focus on the survivors *alongside* the abusers and the institutions, we are forced to ask a new set of questions. A much harder and more uncomfortable set of questions. Our questions no longer solely point to him or them, they point to *us*.

How did *I* not know this was going on within my chosen profession? How did *I* not see what was happening? Is there anything *I* could have done to help? Am *I* complicit? Is my chosen field complicit or, worse, responsible? Is the field itself capable of abuse and harm? Could it be that I somehow contributed to an experience of ongoing abuse or silencing? What is to be done about this, and what is my responsibility to do something?

Survivors point us back to ourselves and ask us to look inward, as opposed to over there to him, to them. They force us to directly confront hurt, vulnerability, shame, scandal, silence and secrecy. Survivors ask us to sit with these things even if we do not like it and it is uncomfortable. Survivors face us with the hardest of practical, theological questions: Are we willing to be the Good Samaritan? Are we *willing* to shift our eyes to see them, suffering and hurt and wishing people would stop walking by like they don't exist?

For Simone Weil and Dorothee Soelle, *creative attention*, the willingness to *see*, is the bedrock of healing and justice. The willingness to look is where the restoration of a person's humanity begins. In the not turning away, dignity is restored. It is too easy for us to spotlight the abusers and the abuse. It is much harder to spotlight the survivors. When we keep our attention on survivors, this forces us to look around—at one another. We have to be here, now, with the survivor herself.

I can tell you for sure that, within this field of theology, I lost my dignity. I was dehumanized. I was silenced. I was isolated. It was only in leaving this field that I was able to restore that dignity and humanity and find community within a profession again. It was only outside of this profession that I was able to find my voice again and use it to speak.

We cannot keep heaping survival on the survivors alone. If we do not all participate in the solution, in the survival; if the survival isn't collective; if we don't invite survival to exist out in the open, in public, within our profession then we are part of the problem. We are implicated in the abuse, in perpetuating it. We are bystanders to it.

So, what is your responsibility, then, to deal with this systemic problem? What is your responsibility, then, to someone like me? I know my saying these things must make you uncomfortable. But I have been uncomfortable among you for years. As so many others like me are uncomfortable too, for so many different kinds of reasons—systemic racism, sexual assault and harassment, the ways we make it verboten for people to discuss mental health issues in a professional setting. I think it is okay for me and my words to make you uncomfortable. For me to lay this at your feet as though it is yours too—because it *is* yours too. It has been mine for so long, I have carried it alone, and now I am giving it to you.

I am not pretending to be special. My story is just one story. But because I am no longer financially or professionally dependent on theology—and only because of this—I am able to speak honestly about that story. My safety lies in my independence. Every single one of you can decide to red flag me, decide I am a complainer, a troublemaker, overly emotional and uncomfortably angry, and that would be fine because I do not need you to approve of me anymore. I am independent of all of you.

But what does that mean for those among us who are still dependent? How and when will they find their voices to speak? How and when will we empower them to do so? How and when will we protect them so they might do so, if they want to? Without punishing them, ostracizing them, not tenuring them, not hiring them for doing so?

I want to be seen for the whole of who I am. The whole includes what happened in graduate school and all that came later. The whole includes ongoing silencing and abuse, as I tried to make my way in this profession. The whole includes my leaving the profession in order to survive. The whole also includes a tremendous amount of good things and professional success as well. The whole includes a tremendous amount of ongoing research and scholarship, much of which is still used in the scholarship and teaching of this profession that is theology.

My story, the memoir, is a doorway, I have realized, to this wholeness for which I long: my own wholeness as a theologian. By writing the memoir, I have offered my secret to the world and to you. But also through it, I show the world who I have become beyond the abuse. The memoir itself points to the whole of who I am—someone who was victimized, who lost a career, but someone who has also become a force in a different career. I took the ugliest thing that has ever happened to me, and I turned it into a literary work of which I am tremendously proud. And I have given you all a primary source of a victim not only of clerical sexual abuse but of clergy sexual abuse within the profession that is theology. I have given you all a story of survival despite theology and its theologians, despite this profession that turned its back.

But this whole also includes a wound that I still carry, that still festers, that still hurts despite all the other good that's happened in my life. This whole includes that I am not the person I wanted to become—a professor. This kind of wounding is the story of so many people for so many different reasons within and outside of this profession. I am no longer a member of this profession *because in order to survive and thrive and flourish I had to leave it*. My story is *also your story now too*. I am handing it over to you. It comes with a lot of lot of implications for yourselves and for this profession that is yours. I wonder what you'll do with it?

Notes

[1] Donna Freitas, *Consent: A Memoir of Unwanted Attention* (New York: Little, Brown, 2019), 20.

[2] Kim Anderson and Catherine Hiersteiner, "Recovering from Childhood Sexual Abuse: Is a 'Storybook Ending' Possible?" *American Journal of Family Therapy* 36, no. 5 (2008): 415–18.

[3] Freitas, *Consent*, 17.

[4] Ibid., 55.

[5] Ibid., 60.

[6] Ibid., 82–83.

[7] Ann Cahill, *Rethinking Rape* (Ithaca, NY: Cornell University Press, 2001), 121.

[8] Ibid., 126.

[9] Freitas, *Consent*, 39–40.

[10] Ibid., 301.

[11] Ibid., 22.

[12] Rob Bailey-Millado, "Men Are Afraid to Mentor Women After #MeToo and It Hurts Us All: Study," *New York Post*, May 17, 2019, www.nypost.com.

[13] Leonard Cassuto, "Can Yale Reform Its Humanities Doctoral Programs?" *The Chronicle of Higher Education*, May 14, 2021, www.chronicle.com.

[14] Freitas, *Consent*, 308.

[15] "Taking Responsibility: Jesuit Educational Institutions Confront the

Causes and Legacy of Clergy Sexual Abuse," Fordham University, www.fordham.edu.

[16]Liam Stack, "Head of Elite Catholic School Is Fired over Sexual Misconduct Charges," *New York Times*, April 12, 2021, www.nytimes.com.

[17]See "Types of Sexual Violence," *RAINN*, www.rainn.org.

[18]Karen J. Terry, *Sexual Offenses and Offenders* (Belmont, CA: Wadsworth, 2012).

[19]Rebecca Solnit, *Men Explain Things to Me* (Chicago: Haymarket, 2015).

[20]Anne Cossins, *Masculinities, Sexualities, and Child Sexual Abuse* (New York: Springer, 2000), 11.

[21]Freitas, *Consent*, 188.

[22]Ibid., 172, 100–101.

[23]Ibid., 161.

[24]Terry, *Sexual Offenses and Offenders*, 168–72.

[25]Donna Freitas, *Sex and the Soul: Juggling Sexuality, Spirituality, Romance, and Religion on College Campuses*, updated ed. (New York: Oxford University Press, 2015); Jason King, *Faith with Benefits: Hook-up Culture on Catholic College Campuses* (New York: Oxford University Press, 2017).

[26]Gerdenio Sonny Manuel, *Living Celibacy: Healthy Pathways for Priests* (Mahwah, NJ: Paulist, 2013).

[27]Margaret A. Farley, *Just Love: A Framework for Christian Sexual Ethics* (New York: Continuum, 2008).

[28]See James F. Keenan, "Vulnerability and Hierarchicalism," *Asian Horizons* 14, no. 2 (2020): 319–32.

[29]Freitas, *Consent*, 42.

[30]Ibid., 44.

[31]Ibid., 89. See also 96, 106, 109.

[32]Dianna Garland, " 'Don't Call It an Affair,' Understanding and Preventing Clergy Sexual Misconduct with Adults," in *Clergy Sexual Abuse: Social Science Perspectives*, ed. Claire M. Renzetti and Sandra Yocum (Boston: Northeastern University Press, 2013), 118–43.

[33]Freitas, *Consent*, 87.

[34]Ibid., 271.

[35]Ibid., 144, 152.

[36]Ibid., 183.

[37]Ibid., 205.

[38]Ibid., 317.

[39]See David Peter Stroh, *Systems Thinking for Social Change* (White River Junction, VT: Chelsea Green, 2015).

[40]See Daniel Finn, "Social Structures," in *Moral Agency within Social Structures*, ed. Daniel Finn (Washington, DC: Georgetown University Press, 2020).

[41]Peter Wilson, "Core Virtues for the Practice of Mentoring," *Journal of Psychology and Theology* 29, no. 2 (2001): 122.

[42]Lecretia Yaghjian, "Hidden Treasures in Theological Education," *Teaching Theology and Religion* 16, no. 3 (2013): 224.

[43]Susan Abraham, "Mentoring (In)Hospitable Places," *Journal of Feminist Studies in Religion* 33, no. 1 (2017): 119–25.

[44]Carol Lakey Hess, "Echo's Lament: Teaching, Mentoring, and the

Danger of Narcissistic Pedagogy," *Teaching Theology and Religion* 6, no. 3 (2003): 130–33.

[45]Freitas, *Consent*, 20.

[46]Lisa Hanasono et al., "Secret Service: Revealing Gender Biases in the Visibility and Value of Faculty Service," *Journal of Diversity in Higher Education* 12, no. 1 (2019): 85–98.

[47]Freitas, *Consent*, 268.

[48]Ibid., 267.

[49]See Patrick Altena, Chris Hermans, and Peer Scheepers, "Dependent Autonomy: Toward A Contextualised and Dialogical Aim for Moral Education," *Journal of Empirical Theology* 17, no. 2 (2004): 172–96.

[50]See Darryl Stephens and Patricia Beattie Jung, "A Comprehensive, Holistic, and Integrated Approach to Professional Sexual Ethics in Theological Education," *Theological Education* 50, no. 1 (2015): 59–60.

[51]See Wilson, "Core Virtues for the Practice of Mentoring," 126–27.

The Stones That Have Been Rejected

Contributions of Queer Educators in Catholic Schools

Ish Ruiz

According to New Ways Ministry, there are over one hundred documented cases of queer people and allies who have been dismissed from Catholic institutions, many of which are Catholic schools, because of their queer identity or for supporting people who are queer.[1] Catholic school leaders[2] who dismiss queer educators justify their actions by arguing that these educators are unsuitable ministers in Catholic schools because they behave in ways that are contrary to Catholic magisterial doctrine on sexual morality and allegedly could cause confusion that scandalizes the students. In several documented cases, dismissed queer Catholic school educators, many of whom also identify as Catholic, had meaningfully served their communities for many years (and were often open with their colleagues about their queer identity) before they were terminated. For these reasons, the dismissals of queer educators present a significant question: Who is a suitable minister at a Catholic school?

I argue that queer educators in Catholic schools can be suitable ministers despite their queer identity. More important, I assert that these educators offer indispensable gifts to Catholic education because of their queer identity. These stones that have often been rejected are indeed a cornerstone of their school communities (Ps 118:22). Their dismissals outrage many members of their school communities because, in addition to reflecting a view of Catholicism that is incongruent with an understanding of Christ's radically inclusive love, they deprive educational communities of valuable contributing members who touch the lives of the students and advance the central goals of Catholic education in significant ways.

This essay has three sections. The first reflects on what makes a good minister in a Catholic school; the second explores the testimonies of queer educators in Catholic schools; and the third concludes with a brief summary and reflection on why Catholic schools should retain queer educators even if these individuals dissent from magisterial teaching on sexual morality.

What Makes a Suitable Minister at a Catholic School?

The Catholic Church is evolving in its definition of "minister." The *Catechism of the Catholic Church* states that a minister is a person who participates in the baptismal royal, prophetic, and priestly mission of the Catholic Church.[3] The United States Conference of Catholic Bishops (USCCB) also notes this trifold office as the source of the ministerial call lay people share with the ordained. As such, this general function of "ministry" is extended to the lay faithful who, through the various Catholic institutions and apostolates, participate in the overall mission of the Church.[4]

The USCCB published a document in 2005 titled *Co-Workers in the Vineyard of the Lord: A Resource for Guiding the Development of Lay Ecclesial Ministry*, in which it offers some theological foundations to better understand the role of lay ministers in the Church. The US bishops build on the trifold offices conferred by the baptismal call of all Catholics[5] to explain the particular call of lay ecclesial ministers:

> The further call of some persons to lay ecclesial ministry adds a special grace by which the Holy Spirit "makes them fit and ready to undertake various tasks and offices for the renewal and building up of the church." Lay ecclesial ministry flows from an explicit faith commitment and is animated by the love of God and neighbor. It also entails an explicit relationship of mutual accountability to and collaboration with the Church hierarchy. By virtue of their

call, lay ecclesial ministers take on a new relationship to the mission of the Church and to the other ministers who work to accomplish it. Therefore, they must be persons who are known for genuine love of the whole Catholic Church.[6]

The document also calls for proper formation of those who pursue the call to lay ecclesial ministry. Notably, the US bishops also set several expectations for the suitability of ministry, among which is adherence to magisterial doctrine on sexual morality. When discussing indications for suitability, the bishops indicate that ministers must demonstrate that their "dispositions for ministry are practiced within the beliefs and disciplines of the Catholic faith. (It is important, for example, that marriages be canonically regular.)"[7] Furthermore, the bishops list "chaste living as a single, celibate, or married person" as a condition of psychological and social suitability.[8] At the same time, the bishops also acknowledge the diversity present within ministry and the broader Church as well as the importance of seeing ministry as a call from Christ.[9] This call, according to Edward P. Hahnenberg, is a specific commitment to God's call enacted in concrete ways through education, family relocation, and significant planning.[10] Richard Gaillardetz observes that this commitment creates in the lay person a new reality: a life of vocation.[11] In sum, I synthesize the following definition for lay ecclesial ministry: through baptism, discernment, formation, and commitment, lay ecclesial ministers are lay persons who respond to God's call to a life of specific vocation that is an extension of Christ's offices of priest, prophet, and king in order to serve and transform the world in light of the Gospel.

Curiously, in 2019, a US Catholic school argued (successfully) before the US Supreme Court that the designation of "minister" should legally extend to all employees in Catholic institutions whether they are Catholic or not. This institution claimed that, through their work, non-Catholic teachers are somehow charged with the transmission of Catholicism to the students.[12] Catholic leaders throughout the nation have supported the universalization of the term "minister" through the stipulated reclassification of school employees as ministers in their employment contracts. This is an area of significant theological inconsistency: considering that *Co-workers in the Vineyard* grounds the ministerial call in the baptismal reality of all believers, it would be inappropriate to say non-baptized employees are ministers. Clearly, this is a legal maneuver on behalf of Catholic leaders to exempt themselves from having to abide by non-discrimination policies in the legal sphere. However, integrity demands that Catholic leaders engage the public square in accordance with their own Catholic theological principles. Therefore, if the US Catholic magisterium is participating in American jurisprudence by declaring that non-Catholic educators can be ministers for Catholic schools in order to deprive them of non-discrimination protections, they are contradicting their own theology. Such legal efforts cause confusion on the theological definition of who can be a minister in a Catholic school. Furthermore, it adds another problematic dimension to lay ecclesial ministry: people will lose their legal non-discrimination rights if they accept a job at a Catholic school. Such actions cause harm to the vocation of Catholic school educators.

However, after acknowledging this significant inconsistency in how US bishops have defined "minister," I am still interested in arguing that queer employees in Catholic schools can be suitable "ministers." Regardless of whether that designation should be limited to religion teachers and campus ministers or all baptized employees—or as some bishops would argue, all employees irrespective of baptism (though I disagree)—there are a lot of Catholic queer people exercising a Catholic vocational call to ministry.

To understand the role of Catholic school ministers, in particular, I turn to the mission of Catholic schools. The USCCB's publication, *To Teach as Jesus Did*, proposed a trifold purpose of Catholic education. According to the US bishops, "[Catholic school] programs must strive *to teach doctrine fully, foster community*, and *prepare students for Christian service*."[13] With regard to the teaching of the doctrine, the bishops explained that schools need to qualify teachers to transmit the content of the Catholic tradition.[14] With regard to community, the document states, "Community is an especially critical need today largely because natural communities of the past have been weakened by many influences."[15] With regard to service, bishops establish that "service of the public interest is a notable quality of the Catholic and other non-public schools in America."[16] In view of this, I assert that Catholic school ministers are suitable ministers if they adequately contribute to that trifold purpose of Catholic schools through their work.

Crucially, the trifold purpose of Catholic school ministers can be evaluated with two different approaches: the distinguishability approach and the catholicity approach. The distinguishability approach in the United States has been advanced by Melanie Morey and John Piderit in their book *Catholic Higher Education: A Culture in Crisis*. Morey and Piderit argue that to protect the Catholic culture of a school, employees of the institution must serve as actors who promote the inheritability and the distinguishability of the Catholic tradition.[17] While inheritability addresses the institution's ability to transmit the Catholic faith, the distinguishability component attempts to present the Catholic worldview as a countercultural, distinctive element of the school when compared with the broader society in an attempt to generate deeper commitment.[18] According to Morey and Piderit, "The more distinct the community or culture, the greater the commitment it can command and sustain."[19] This creates a separation between what is in accordance with Catholic values and what is not, along with an urgency to promote what is in accordance with it. Significantly, they recommend hiring employees that will promote this mission of distinguishability as well as an exaltation of Catholic symbols that will promote a distinctive Catholic culture in the school.[20]

The second view, the catholicity approach, is largely proposed by Thomas Groome, whose kerygmatic philosophy of Catholic education identifies core components of Catholicism as central to the Catholic identity of the school.[21] Contrary to the distinguishability approach, Groome explains that the catholicity approach considers several core concepts to be guiding principles that can manifest themselves through pluralistic ways:

> I call [my educational] philosophy "Catholic" because although it is suggested by core convictions of Catholic Christianity, it can have general appeal and be persuasive apart from confessional Christian faith. It reflects catholicity as in the etymology of the term *kata holos*—"welcoming everyone." When such catholicity is the intent the particularity of Christianity can contribute most richly to the universal enterprise of education.[22]

Groome acknowledges the importance of core tenets of the Catholic faith but is seeking to place these core principles in conversation and collaboration with the larger culture. He cautions the Catholic school against *sectarianism*, by which he means "a bigoted and intolerant exaltation of one's own group that absolutizes the true and the good in its members, encouraging prejudice against anyone who has alternative identity—especially immediate neighbors."[23]

I favor the catholicity approach as it is more reminiscent of a universal church true to its name as "Catholic." The distinguishability approach sounds too much like a smaller, purer Catholic tradition that would be hard if not impossible to transmit to students. My thoughts are captured in the words of Regina Bechtle: "In a world where divisiveness grows ever more toxic and civility is in short supply in both political and ecclesial discourse, a 'both and' spirituality that integrates love of God and love of neighbor, that seeks to create coalitions and build bridges, will surely better serve today's lay ecclesial minister than a mindset wedded to rigid dichotomies and dualistic thinking."[24] Adopting this catholicity approach, through which schools focus on Catholic principles and acknowledge the universality and diversity of the Catholic faith, Catholic schools might make room for suitable queer ministers who reflect a diversified experience of Catholicism in the school community while also advancing the trifold purpose of Catholic education: doctrine, community, and service.

If These Stones Could Speak: Listening to Queer Educators' Testimonies

Literature on the experience of queer educators in Catholic schools is scarce, which is unsurprising given the risks this population faces and the need to hide their identity. Nevertheless, what exists reveals how queer Catholic school educators have served as witnesses in the transmission of the Catholic faith, building of community, and service to the common good according to the research.[25]

First, queer educators in Catholic schools, even if they engage in sexual behavior that is alternative to magisterial doctrine, can still serve as suitable witnesses for the transmission of the Catholic faith. An important indicator of this reality is the significant number of queer ministers who teach religion or work in campus ministry. Of the respondents to the 2018 survey that I

conducted with Bleasdale and Stockbridge, 77 percent of participants identified as religious studies teachers or campus ministers.
One participant noted, "Having LGBTQ+ religion teachers is very
important. I have seen firsthand how the lack of our presence,
accompanied with negative words, policies and treatment, often
turns off the spiritual and religious dimensions of the students'
lives."[26] This is crucial information: though unacknowledged,
queer educators have already helped build the Catholic culture
of Catholic schools.[27]

James Everitt's research specifically focused on gay and lesbian
teachers who identified as Catholic. Some of the participants
expressed awareness of their students' spiritual needs and were
ready to meet them.[28] These educators were well versed in Catholic
magisterial doctrine[29] and understood their role as witnesses for
their students. Everitt observes, "Working within Catholic schools
was a choice made freely by the participants in response to their
love for the Church and their hope that their own witness to the
Christian life would have an impact on their students. They were
intentional about their commitment to Catholic education, and
their love for their vocation within the Catholic education community was clear."[30] Three of the teachers in Kevin Stockbridge's
research were religious studies teachers who engaged with their
students in dialogue about the many teachings of the Catholic
Church. They reflected about how they teach students about the
Catholic faith through the lens of justice.[31]

In addition to the religious studies classroom, the witness
of queer educators with regard to Catholic doctrine is evident
in how they engaged the sacraments and prayer as a means to
affirm their own Catholic and queer identities. A participant in
Everitt's research remarked, "[My] understanding of my identity
has always been through the sacraments. It's always been my
relationship with Christ and with the sacraments that make me
a Catholic. So for me, Catholic identity in my prayer life has
always been secure."[32]

Overall, the queer educators saw themselves as unique assets
in the school's effort to evangelize the students. One participant
in Everitt's study expressed,

> I think if we get credit for anything [it's for] helping young
> people navigate their own faith. I mean, I think about the

missionary effort of the Church to evangelize people . . . that, to me, is evangelization right there . . . [being] able to share with a young person our own faith struggles in a way that is going to affirm them in their own faith struggles? If toasters were given out for reaffirming young people in the Catholic faith, I think [queer teachers would] have a lot of toasters.[33]

Another participant added, "We give meat to the Gospel, not in a sort of 'fluffy' way, but again, the 'rubber hitting the road' of it being painful or a struggle to continue to be a witness in the best sense of the word. If our Church were to recognize us for being the healers and the evangelizers that we are, wow."[34]

These queer educators, who often feel ostracized by the Church, are still freely choosing to stay as members of the Church. This makes them incredibly effective as ministers because they can impart unique insights to students that are apathetic or unsure about being Catholic. Students who are drifting away from the Church (which is an increasing number of students, according to the research) could benefit from hearing about, learning from, and engaging Catholics who have good reason to leave the Church yet choose to stay.[35] These *unlikely ministers* can model for the students what it means to disagree but still remain part of the Catholic community. As one of Everitt's interviewees explained, "Why do I stay? Because this is my family . . . and I might disagree with family members. I might disagree with experiences that have taken place in the past, but I'm not going to walk away from my family."[36] Many Catholic school students would benefit from hearing that message from a queer educator. Catholic leaders who are committed to the evangelization mission of the school would be wise to retain these committed queer role models as an asset toward that mission.

Second, regarding the task of building community, queer educators are also uniquely equipped to look out for students who are particularly vulnerable. Participants in Everitt's study described ways they specifically support queer students through pastoral support, mentoring, and safe spaces like Gay-Straight Alliances. Some of these educators have to advocate for the existence of these safe spaces.

In our research, we noted that many queer educators seek to serve as the role models that queer students need. One respondent of the survey stated, "Although I am not openly gay, I think some students know, and it is unspoken between us. . . . I think being an LGBTQ+ educator has made me a more empathetic teacher to all minorities and students who don't 'fit in.' "[37] Another participant identified as a blessing "the ability to relate to students that are not the norm."[38] Furthermore, one stated, "My identities have helped me to better understand, empathize, and support my students and their needs. I have become an unofficial support for LGBTQ+ students to come to and share their story with."[39] It is clear that these educators perceive a lack of role models for queer students and have taken it upon themselves to act as those role models for this vulnerable population.

In addition to the welcome of queer students, queer educators, as members of the larger LGBTQ+ community, have a sense of what it means to establish communities against difficult odds. The LGBTQ+ community has a long history of establishing safe spaces for its members in the face of hostility and exclusion.[40] This may enable queer educators to create safe spaces for queer students and staff, establish a queer culture within the Catholic culture of the school, and contribute to the diversity of the Catholic community. One participant in Stockbridge's study expressed, "I wish that people could see that we are more than our sexuality, we are a culture!"[41] Such a diversified understanding of the Catholic faith helps the Catholic tradition make more sense of the human condition. Furthermore, that sense of community helps queer educators build communities within the Catholic school as a matter of justice.[42]

Third, regarding the task of Christian service, the presence of queer educators in Catholic schools can promote the school's mission of justice and work toward the common good, a trait central to the mission of Catholic education.[43] This is significantly showcased in Stockbridge's work, where participants were very aware of the diverse experiences within their school environments. Stockbridge observes, "In many ways, these queer teachers see themselves as acting in concert with the deepest heart of the Catholic mission by pushing against oppressive forces. They do this in ways that masterfully negotiate the world they inhabit."[44] These educators were committed to fighting against oppressive forces that expect members of their community to conform to a singular conception of goodness.[45] The queer teachers stated,

"We are a safe space for those who don't fit into the norm. . . . We can help others who are caught in a binary tension to live in the grey of this world."[46] This awareness allows them to fight for the liberation of their students (and colleagues) and empower them to fight for justice in the world.

Queer educators are exceptionally aware of the oppression because of their personal social location. Stockbridge states, "Because the queer experience questions the boundaries of cisgendered [sic] and heteronormative assumptions of human ontology, queer teachers enter the Catholic classroom with very particular vantage points."[47] This vantage point brings about awareness of the oppression queer people face in Catholic environments.

Furthermore, Stockbridge sees "doing queer" as a form of liberation in Catholic schools because queer educators who learn to survive in this setting are posing a radical challenge to forces of oppression in the school, which creates ripples that affect other members of the community.[48] Thus, by virtue of their queer identity, these educators serve to liberate those who are oppressed. A queer educator in Stockbridge's research stated, "Our very presence in schools in the midst of the oppression is a light of hope and a work of activism."[49]

Queer Cornerstones in Catholic Education

It is clear from these testimonies that many queer educators in Catholic schools are following a vocational call to serve God, their school communities, and the common good. These ministers are a blessing to Catholic education and are role models for their students in faith, community, and service. Although data on queer Catholic school educators is limited so one cannot make generalized claims about this population, even these limited experiences highlight the unique potential present in queer Catholic school ministers to advance the Catholic mission of the schools.

I call upon Catholic school leaders to cease the dismissals of these educators and seek ways to build an LGBTQ+-inclusive Catholic community. If Catholic leaders want to foster commitment to Catholicism among youth, they should look to the witness of queer Catholic school educators. Students who think about abandoning the Church could benefit from the testimonies of queer role models who have every reason to leave yet choose to stay. These educators have a deep spirituality and relationship with God through their beautiful baptismal vocation, are expert community builders despite the rejection they face, and are committed to social justice against risky odds. They have already been a crucial part of Catholic education. The stones that have been rejected have been cornerstones of Catholic schools for many years. Recognition of this reality is long overdue.

Notes

[1]Francis DeBernardo, "Employees of Catholic Institutions Who Have Been Fired, Forced to Resign, Had Offers Rescinded, or Had Their Jobs Threatened because of LGBT Issues," *New Ways Ministry*, last modified December 21, 2019, https://www.newwaysministry.org.

[2]I use the term "Catholic leaders" to refer to school administrators or diocesan officers, including bishops, who exercise authority over the dismissal of a Catholic school employee.

[3]Pope John Paul II, *Catechism of the Catholic Church* (1992), www.vatican.va, 873.

[4]Second Vatican Council, "Constitution on the Sacred Liturgy, *Sacrosanctum Concilium*" (1963), www.vatican.va; and Second Vatican Council, "Dogmatic Constitution on the Church, *Lumen Gentium*" (1964), www.vatican.va.

[5]United States Conference of Catholic Bishops, *Co-workers in the Vineyard of the Lord: A Resource for Guiding the Development of Lay Ecclesial Ministry* (Washington, DC: USCCB, 2005), 18.

[6]Ibid., 25–26.

[7]Ibid., 31.

[8]Ibid.

[9]Ibid., 10, 12.

[10]Edward P. Hahnenberg, "Theology of Lay Ecclesial Ministry: Future Trajectories," in *Lay Ecclesial Ministry: Pathways toward the Future*, ed. Zeni Fox (Lanham, MD: Rowman & Littlefield, 2010), 73.

[11]Richard R. Gaillardetz, "The Theological Reception of Co-Workers in the Vineyard of the Lord," in Fox, *Lay Ecclesial Ministry*, 22.

[12]See *Our Lady of Guadalupe School v. Morrissey-Berru*, 19–267 US 1 (2020).

[13]United States Conference of Catholic Bishops, *To Teach as Jesus Did: A Pastoral Message on Catholic Education* (Washington, DC: USCCB, 1972), 24; emphasis mine.

[14]Ibid., 30.

[15]Ibid.

[16]Ibid., 31.

[17]Melanie M. Morey and John J. Piderit, *Catholic Higher Education: A Culture in Crisis* (New York: Oxford University Press, 2010), 29–31.

[18]Ibid., 31–32.

[19]Ibid., 254.

[20]Ibid., 110–22, 227–28.

[21]Thomas Groome, *Educating for Life: A Spiritual Vision for Every Teacher and Parent* (Allen, TX: Thomas More, 1998), 59–60.

[22]Ibid., 12.

[23]Ibid., 42.

[24]Regina Bechtle, "Spirit Guides and Table Companions: Saints as Models for Lay Ecclesial Ministers," in Fox, *Lay Ecclesial Ministry*, 128.

[25]In this section, I draw from three studies. See James Everitt, "The Experience of Catholic, Gay and Lesbian, Secondary School Teachers within Northern California: A Participatory Action Research Study" (PhD diss., University of San Francisco, 2010), https://repository.usfca.edu; Kevin Stockbridge, "Queer Teachers in Catholic Schools: The Cosmic Story of an Easter People" (PhD diss., Chapman University, 2017), 153; and Ish Ruiz and Jane Bleasdale, "Mixed Blessings: Understanding the Experience of LGBTQIA+ Educators in Catholic Schools," *Journal of Homosexuality* (October 6, 2021): 1–19. I sometimes refer to this last study as "our study" or "our research." The survey was spread through word of mouth and snowball sampling to approximately 100 identified queer educators and received eighty responses across the United States, though less than half of the respondents answered all the questions. Although all three studies represent a small portion of the overall population of queer educators in Catholic schools, this data showcases the potential for all queer educators to serve as suitable ministers. Furthermore, the responses are indicative of a unique set of gifts these educators offer Catholic schools by virtue of their queerness.

[26]Ruiz and Bleasdale, "Mixed Blessings."

[27]Seventy-five percent of survey participants reported having been at their Catholic school for five or more years. See ibid.

[28]Everitt, *The Experience*, 94–96.

[29]Ibid., 87–88.

[30]Ibid., 83.

[31]Stockbridge, "Queer Teachers," 155.

[32]Everitt, *The Experience*, 85.

[33]Ibid., 99.

[34]Ibid., 100.

[35]Various studies showcase the diverse reasons teenagers leave the Church. See Christian Smith and Melinda Lundquist Denton, *Soul Searching: The Religious and Spiritual Lives of American Teenagers* (New York: Oxford University Press, 2005); Michael Lipkia, "Why America's 'Nones' Left Religion Behind," *Pew Research Center*, last modified August 24, 2016, https://www.pewresearch.org; and John M. Vitek, *Going, Going, Gone: The Dynamics of Disaffiliation in Young Catholics* (Winona, MN: Saint Mary's, 2017).

[36]Everitt, *The Experience*, 99.

[37]Ruiz and Bleasdale, "Mixed Blessings."

[38]Ibid.

[39]Ibid.

[40]Richard Peddicord outlines the history of the Gay Liberation Movement in his work and argues that the correct treatment of LGBTQ+ people is a

question of social justice and not of sexual morality. See Peddicord, *Gay and Lesbian Rights: A Question: Sexual Ethics or Social Justice?* (Kansas City, MO: Sheed & Ward, 1996), 3–26.

[41] Stockbridge, "Queer Teachers," 177.

[42] A full discussion of justice and Catholic education is beyond the scope of this essay, but there is a rich tradition of how Catholic schools serve the common good. See Anthony S. Bryk, Valerie E. Lee, and Peter B. Holland, *Catholic Schools and the Common Good* (Cambridge, MA: Harvard University Press, 1993).

[43] Ibid.

[44] Stockbridge, "Queer Teachers," 164.

[45] For these educators, oppression refers to the mechanisms of isolation the school uses to prevent them from authentically expressing their sexual identity. Stockbridge uses a Foucauldian analysis of these methods of oppression in his dissertation. See ibid., 18, 45–48.

[46] Ibid., 243.

[47] Ibid., 160.

[48] Ibid., 166.

[49] Ibid., 200.

PART III

THEOLOGIES AND PRACTICES

FOR RESISTING DEHUMANIZATION

Love for the Annihilated

A Black Theological Reading
of Angela of Foligno's *Memorial*

Andrew L. Prevot

As I consider how we might develop new approaches to theological anthropology, one central goal comes to mind. That goal is to discover a divine love that may bring new life to those whom this world annihilates. I am thinking of people whom regnant social ontologies, epistemologies, geographies, genealogies, imaginaries, normativities, and so on consign to the status of nonbeing, nonperson, or nonhuman.[1] I am thinking of people who are treated like their lives do not matter, like they are disposable objects, like their bodies can be used for any purpose without their consent, like they are an evil to be feared and controlled, like their deaths are ungrievable, and like they do not deserve healthcare or clean water or a safe place to stay or opportunities to flourish. I am thinking not only of those who are killed and whose material existences in this world are thereby obliterated. I am also thinking of those who are forced by persistent forms of underrepresentation, stigmatization, and oppression to doubt whether there are any positive, life-sustaining answers to the question of who or what they are—people who must struggle every day to believe they are worthy of love.

In particular, I am thinking about the cry "Black Lives Matter!" which resists the murdering of Black bodies and souls.[2] While protesting the fact of unjust killings by police and other governmental and nongovernmental agents, this cry also combats the annihilative positioning of Blackness within contemporary society. It challenges any language, culture, or institution that explicitly or implicitly associates Blackness with nothingness. It opposes all those material and conceptual structures that pressure the self-reflective Black person to confront the possibility of nihilism, by which I mean the possibility that his or her life means nothing to this world.[3] I recognize that the annihilative force of modern anti-Blackness is only one among many interlocking forces of this type. In connection with race, one must also consider questions of class, coloniality, gender, sexuality, ability, nationality, and so on.[4] The dehumanized are everywhere. They are diverse. And, arguably, they are the majority of this world's population. But I focus on Blackness in this essay because that is the position of nothingness to which my body, despite its caramel color and mixed genetic history, has been most regularly assigned and because this negative symbolic use of my body prior to me and without my consent has filled me with questions to which I have struggled to find answers—questions that are relevant to the present period of racial reckoning in the US and abroad.

The central question that I take up in this essay is whether sources from the Christian mystical tradition might remind us of a divine love that could bring hope and joy to such annihilated lives. To be sure, any number of mystically informed approaches to theological anthropology are conceivable. I cannot hope to catalogue and evaluate them all. But for me this will be their test: Do they search for this divine love and do they retrieve it for the sake of such negatively positioned communities and persons? What makes an anthropology "theological" is the effort to perceive human beings as God perceives them, which is to say with the sort of love that was present in their very creation, that denounces their sinful failures to love, but that also calls them to a more perfectly loving way of life which, through God's help, they can in fact achieve. Theological anthropology interprets the human being as created, fallen, and graced.[5] Mysticism, in turn, reveals the incredible fullness of such grace.[6] It attests to the possibility of a transformative union with divine love that takes place in this very historical, corporeal life. I suggest that the divine love that mystics reveal to us is the same love that the annihilated of this world desperately need and desire and that, in some cases, they have already found.

Methodological Considerations

As I look back to the Christian past, I sometimes use a Black lens forged by modern structures of racial violence and the activist movements that resist them. I ask what a self-reflective Black person who is tempted by nihilism because of his or her lifelong exposure to anti-Black racism might find in nearly forgotten fragments of a more theologically saturated premodern culture. With this Black retrospective my agenda remains futural. I am interested in recovering a divine love that might be consoling and energizing for people living now and for future generations. In response to critics, whether historians or contemporary theorists, who might consider this method to be unhelpfully anachronistic, I can only ask that it be judged according to its fruits. I hasten to add, moreover, that my Black theological interpretation of certain mystical sources in medieval Europe is but one way to seek divine love for the annihilated. Another indispensable strategy, which I and many other Black scholars such as Albert Raboteau, James Cone, and Diana Hayes pursue elsewhere, is to study the mystical aspects of Black cultures and freedom struggles, which contain a blend of elements drawn from Christianity, African traditional religions, and sometimes other religions and attest in their own distinctive ways to a liberative divine love.[7] The argument I make here is meant to supplement such endogenous Black theological efforts by showing how they might be connected with another contextually specific expression of the Christian mystical tradition which many theologians, perhaps especially Catholics, regard as more normative.

For much Catholic theology, the European Middle Ages is not just one context among others. The experiences and theories of divine love that come to us from this time and place enjoy a certain elevated authority. In some neo-scholastic quarters, it may be debated whether medieval mystics, including women who were denied access to formal theological training, deserve to be recognized as part of the revelatory theological tradition that Pope Leo XIII's *Aeterni Patris* influentially argues reaches an apex in Thomas Aquinas. Nevertheless, one can make a strong case, as Hans Urs von Balthasar and other *ressourcement* theologians do, that medieval mystics are sufficiently attached to this tradition to

be recognizable mediators of the Christian truth or way of life that
theologians of this sort are presently anxious to retain amid the
pressures of modern secularity. For such thinkers, the normative
canon is larger than neo-scholasticism presumes, while still being
weighted toward a glorious occidental past.[8]

In addition to outright denials of God, secularity includes
modern tendencies to reduce the meaning of faith to its attendant
politics or operations of power, whatever those might be. Even so,
a political turn in theology need not amount to its secularization.
Many theologians, whether favoring a more nearly *ressourcement*
or liberation-oriented method, persuasively argue that there is no
need to make a choice between contemplative immersion in the
tradition and active involvement in the world, because the two
can and must go together. To defend this point, scholars rang-
ing from Henri de Lubac to Gustavo Gutiérrez seek support for
contemporary political struggles in authoritative premodern theological sources.[9] This is a common feature of much constructive
Christian theology over the last half century or more, including
among many non-Catholic Christians who have their own ways
of shaping and inhabiting a tradition.

This strategy is particularly evident in feminist theologians
such as Barbara Newman, Grace Jantzen, Wendy Farley, Amy
Laura Hall, Elizabeth Dreyer, Catherine Hilkert, Sarah Coakley,
and others who use the witness of medieval women mystics and
theologians as a basis to argue for the greater inclusion of women
in church leadership and theology—and, indeed, simply in our
understanding of what it means to be fully human.[10] As a Black
Catholic theologian, I suggest that a similar strategy is conceivable for my community—again, not as a substitute for the study
of Black religious sources but as a supplementary effort to clarify
what certain premodern strands of the Christian mystical tradition
look like through a Black lens.

The move I make in this essay from a feminist to a Black theological engagement with medieval mysticism is not an attempt
to supersede feminist analysis but rather a proposal for a more
complex critical theological discourse that is poised to address in-
terrelated questions of gender and race, among other topics. Black
women are at the heart of the Black community and its theology
as well as the drivers of the intersectional turn in feminism that
first found expression in Black feminist and womanist sources.[11]

Any mystically informed theological anthropology that hopes to resist dehumanization must be prepared to think about femaleness, Blackness, and their various intersections and divergences.

Although constructs of gender are to some degree context-specific and, in any case, more plural and fluid than binary, essentialist accounts recognize, the feminist use of the Middle Ages is facilitated by the fact that women are prevalent in medieval sources as authors and celebrated saints and by the fact that sexual difference is an explicit topic of discussion.[12] By contrast, the peoples of Africa remain at a certain remove from the theologians of medieval Europe, and "Blackness"—in the modern sense derived from the transatlantic slave trade and its aftermath—had not yet been invented (though the first signs of it were starting to emerge through the intercultural encounters and shifting attitudes toward skin color occasioned by the Crusades).[13] For these reasons, it is not immediately obvious with whom or with what contemporary Black readers ought to identify when reading medieval mystical texts. Should they read themselves into the figures of poverty and illness to whom some mystics show extravagant largesse? Should they read themselves into the darkness that functions as an equivocal metaphor of both evil powers and the sort of unknowing that one experiences in contemplation? In either instance, they are at risk of identifying with something that will reinforce their sense of nothingness relative to a world derived from a supposedly normative (which is to say, medieval, European) Christianity.

One might be tempted to forgo any effort to do a Black theological reading of medieval mystics, on the assumption that Black people have no place in such literature and the culture it represents. Black people could be inclined—or encouraged even—to seek divine love exclusively in their own traditions—that is, in places and texts marked as specifically Black: hush arbors, spirituals, slave narratives, independent Black churches, movements of protest and racial uplift, or perhaps only in African indigenous materials that reflect what African life was like prior to European Christian incursions. But what are the implications of assuming the impossibility of a Black theological reading of medieval mysticism? Does a white Christian living today inherit the whole tradition but a Black Christian only a racially defined and temporally recent part of it? Is there a hidden presupposition that persons of European descent are more capable of under-standing and connecting with medieval mystics because of an allegedly shared geography, history, or bodily appearance, which is in fact highly dubitable? Black theology must actively question whether medieval sources provide a more authoritative witness to the gospel than comparable African American ones do and thus whether they actually deserve the elevated authority they often enjoy. At the same time, Black theology must not be expected to study only its own designated sources—which suffer, at least in their quantity, by a racially discriminatory lack of institutional support—while the rest of theology is implicitly encouraged to offer new interpretations of whatever materials it finds valuable. Black theology is not just a way to read certain things. It is a way to read everything. By engaging sources that one might not expect it to touch, Black theology may both clarify its relevance to a wider array of theological conversations and gain insights helpful to its own aims.

At the end of *Black Skin, White Masks*, Frantz Fanon argues that the inhumanity of the anti-Black colonial order is best coun-teracted not by a repristinated Black past to which Black people would have to adhere slavishly but by the recognition of a shared, corporeal, and endlessly questionable humanity, enveloping past, present, and future and a limitless variety of cultural achieve-ments. Fanon claims the Peloponnesian War, the invention of the compass, and Immanuel Kant's wonder at the night sky as much as he claims jazz. He refuses racially objectifying restrictions on his practices of identification and belonging. He emphasizes the freedom and responsibility to think creatively about history as a whole and to invent new ways of imagining life together. In short, Fanon—the great progenitor of Black studies and anticolonial rebellion—insists on the humanizing possibility of a Black read-ing of nonblack sources.[14]

The Black Catholic womanist theologian M. Shawn Copeland illustrates this possibility in her theological work, including in her creative use of medieval Christian mystics such as Catherine of Siena. In *Knowing Christ Crucified*, Copeland reads Catherine's *Dialogue*—particularly Catherine's description of a spiritual ascent from the feet of the crucified Christ to his head—through lenses provided by the Black spiritual, "Jacob's Ladder," and by Josiah Henson's slave narrative. Henson identifies himself as "a poor, despised, abused creature, deemed by others fit for nothing but unrequited toil." He is one of the annihilated. Yet he finds purpose in the love that Christ shows him on the cross and in his own efforts to follow Christ's example through compassionate love of others. Copeland likens Henson's discovery of a nihilism-defeating mystical discipleship not with any poor people whom Catherine serves or any metaphors she uses but with Catherine's own interior life.[15]

In the spirit of Fanon and Copeland, I offer a Black theological reading of Angela of Foligno's *Memorial*. I hope that this reading both honors the lasting significance of Angela's Christian witness and affirms the lives of Black people who continue to face annihilation because of the anti-Black forces of modernity. Angela was an Italian Franciscan laywoman who lived from the middle of the thirteenth century to the early fourteenth. Despite significant differences in context, I contend that Black readers may be able to identify with her experiences of inner torment and receive encouragement through the messages of love that God speaks to her troubled soul. It is important for theologians to acknowledge that Black readers can identify with the protagonists of Christian mystical texts and not only with marginalized recipients of charity or metaphorical uses of darkness. The fact that Angela is European is less significant, as far as the question of relatability goes, than certain facts about her inner struggles and the ways that her growing consciousness of divine love helps her overcome them. What she cared about most, namely God's empowering grace in her life, is more valuable to a Black theological reading than any contingent facts about her externally visible identity.

Angela has recently received some positive attention in Francophone postmodern theory and its Anglophone offshoots thanks to Georges Bataille's reading of her in the last part of his *Inner Experience* and thanks to the sympathetic interpretation that Amy Hollywood makes of Bataille's work in her *Sensible Ecstasy*. Bataille identifies with Angela's experiences of torment and ecstatic unknowing. To him, these experiences suggest not only the nothingness of Angela as a sinful creature but also the nothingness of the infinite darkness that transcends her knowledge and will, which she interprets theologically but he interprets atheologically. He also prizes her meditations on the crucified Christ insofar as they seem to dramatize the dissolution of the subject, and he performs his own meditations on photos of a Chinese torture victim in search of a similar effect. Bataille's response to the annihilation that he perceives all around him at the height of the Second World War is not to seek solace in an ever-greater divine love but to seek communion with others by contemplating the condition of nothingness or radical vulnerability that he shares with them. Although Hollywood is troubled by certain aspects of Bataille's at times wildly pornographic work, she values his struggle to create a mysticism not of totality and self-glorification but of intimate relationship through imagined self-laceration.[16]

If Bataille can read Angela within his own context, which, despite being European, differs in countless ways from hers, then Black theologians can do their own contextually informed readings of her—and, for that matter, any other sources they like. The Black theological interpretation I develop in these pages arguably remains closer to the heart of Angela's mysticism than Bataille's does insofar as it retains her Christian faith commitments and refocuses attention on the healing words of love that God speaks to her. In contrast to Bataille's postmodern reduction of mysticism to a condition of inner-worldly communion made possible through the annihilation of subjectivity, Black theology prioritizes a type of mysticism that builds up subjects who have been torn down. Black theology does not invite human beings to plunge themselves into the ecstatic horrors and pleasures of the world but to seek embodied, communal ways of honoring the God of love who created the world and promises to save it. Its message to the annihilated is not that their potentially hellacious experiences of carnal life simply reflect what it means to be human. Rather, its message is: God loves you and wants you to be free.

The Reading

Now that I have clarified some of my reasons for attempting such a reading, let me turn to Angela herself. She began her mystical path as a person of enough privilege and wealth to partake in an indulgent, luxurious lifestyle. Although we have very few details about her early years, we know she was of relatively high social standing and that she was part of a well-connected family.[17] We also know, however, that she was unhappy. She suffered from an increasingly painful awareness of her sinfulness, and this distress prompted her to change everything about her life. The first thirteen steps of her path, as reported by her confessor and amanuensis, the Franciscan friar known in the text as "Brother A," involved feelings of intense guilt, harsh penances, anguished visions of the cross, and fledgling efforts to embrace a life of poverty despite the wishes of her family. In the fourteenth step, she received another vision of Christ crucified, but this one was slightly different. In it, Christ invites her to drink the blood from his side, and she tastes it. She reports, "At this I began to experience a great joy, although when I thought about the passion I was still filled with sadness."[18] This is the first time that anything like joy bursts through her grief and self-recriminations.

Going forward, a pattern emerges in which she is very judgmental and punishing toward herself, but God is very sweet, gentle, and loving toward her. For example, one day while washing lettuce, she begins to feel like she is unfit to do even this menial task. She says, "I am only worthy that God send me immediately to hell, and I am likewise only worthy to collect manure." She speaks at the beginning of her *Instructions* about being "plunged into an abyss of deep humility," and she exclaims, "See what a devil I am and what malice is in my heart!" She feels like a "total fraud" and sinks into a state of extreme despair.[19] This sort of abusive self-talk and its attendant feelings of lowliness and wretchedness occur frequently throughout her text, even as she advances to higher stages of prayer.

What I am struck by is that these are not the sorts of messages that God gives her. In fact, precisely the opposite is the case. On one occasion, the Holy Spirit comes to her and addresses her with these affirming words: "My daughter, my dear and sweet daughter, my delight, my temple, my beloved daughter, love me because you are very much loved by me; much more than you could love me." And again, the Holy Spirit says to her: "Your whole life, your eating, drinking, sleeping, and all that you do are pleasing to me." Similarly, at one point while she is meditating on the crucified Christ, he begins to converse with her, saying, "My love for you has not been a hoax"; "I have not served you only in appearance"; "I have not kept myself at a distance, but have always felt you close to me"; and, echoing Augustine, "I am deeper within your soul than your soul is to itself." Although Angela endures excruciating physical and mental torments for two years, she attributes these to the actions of demons, not to God. Her union with divine love does not torture her. Rather it gives her a "joy that greatly surpasses all measure." She "swims" in her experiences of such divine elevation and finds indescribable delight in them. Insofar as such experiences prompt her to compare her weak and sinful soul to the extraordinary goodness of God, they sometimes do make her feel worse about herself, but she is the one doing this comparing. The outcome that God wants for her and that she experiences in the highest stages of her mystical path is an overwhelming condition of happiness, a feeling of being completely loved and welcomed into the triune life of God. Reflecting back on how this grace felt, she says, "I was so joy-filled, and my body felt so agile, healthy, [and] invigorated, that I had never experienced anything like it." The joyful effects of divine love are not merely spiritual or psychological for her. They also implicate her body.[20]

To be sure, when reading Angela, it is possible to worry about certain masochistic or sadistic tendencies. She makes herself suffer, and she desires it. The institution of the Franciscan Order, represented by Brother A., and the Catholic Church more broadly seem to endorse some measure of this self-crucifying behavior. It would not be unreasonable to view this whole ascetical system with suspicion, critiquing it in Nietzschean fashion as a form of life-negating violence.[21] However, it may help to note that God does not encourage Angela to suffer in these ways but rather to experience joy. It may also help to recognize that the joy Angela receives from God is given to her "without any merit" on her part.[22] She does not have to earn it through her self-mortifying asceticism, and in fact it would be impossible for her to do so, since this joy is a sheer grace.

Moreover, some of Angela's excessive behavior may be interpreted not as an ascetical or sadomasochistic effort to win God's approval but as a divinely inspired act of intimate solidarity with those annihilated by the cruelty of the world. She participates in the love of God not merely by enjoying it but also by sharing her life with others, especially those who have been discarded as dangerous and worthless. We can see this through her practice of washing the hands and feet of lepers and then drinking the water she used.[23] For her, to consume this water is to receive a gift of divine communion, just as she does when she receives the

Eucharist. She believes herself to be united with Christ precisely in her loving, body-and-fluid sharing, though in this case strictly non-sexual relationships with these physically and socially annihilated people.

Another example of an apparently excessive behavior that may not be ascetical in a sadomasochistic sense but possibly a genuine practice of love would be Angela's distribution of her goods to the poor. Granted, she gives all of her possessions away with the explicit goal of freeing herself "to experience the riches of God."[24] She thus appears to emphasize the spiritual value that her impoverishment has for herself more than the material benefits that accrue to others. More generally, her texts do seem, like others on the more radical side of the Franciscan tradition, to presuppose a competitive Creator-creature relationship in which the creature's status must be reduced in order for the Creator's love to be made manifest, and perhaps that is not quite right. Perhaps God does not need Angela to lose everything and annihilate herself in order to bless her with divine joy. Perhaps this is not the right way to understand the cross or the practice of holy poverty.

Yet one cannot deny that Angela's early life of hoarding wealth and her later life of donating it are strikingly different and that the latter is much more clearly an expression of love for those treated like nonbeings. If we take Angela as an example of a privileged person who discovers the meaning of love by giving of herself to others and by entering into close relationships with them, then her practices of self-denial may be less troubling and more attractive to us. It occurs to me, for instance, that if white Christians in the US followed Angela's lead, they would offer reparations to Black people and find communion with God by joining together in the struggle for Black lives. They would not keep their distance; they would not cross the street or turn away in fear. They would pour themselves out in solidarity. This is not a bad way to read Angela—namely, as a model for the sort of radical conversion that a truly divine love would demand of white Christians living in white supremacist societies.

However, it may be more important for Black Christians to read Angela as someone who suffers from feelings of self-hatred and worthlessness similar to those experienced by people whom this world treats as nonbeings, people who are branded as guilty and made to feel ashamed simply because of their bodies or their social status. Angela's *Memorial* is the story of a person with an unbearable sense of her own vileness, which seems to have at least partly been instilled in her by then-dominant cultural attitudes toward her gender and her body. It is a narrative about how divine love counteracts this annihilating and culturally reinforced self-perception and gradually empowers her to see herself in a different light as the very dwelling place of the Trinity and as one endowed with a great capacity for freedom and delight.[25] Black readers of her text need not identify primarily with the lepers whose feet she washes or the poor to whom she gives her goods. They can identify with her, the main character. They can relate to her interior yet contextually conditioned struggles. And they can find comfort and strength in the loving words that God addresses to her and in the blessings of joy that God imparts to her.

Now it may be the case that Angela was in fact sinful, that she was doing something malicious that needed correction. But the excessiveness of her negative self-descriptions suggests to me that there was very likely a great disproportion between any actual wrongdoings on her part and her ferociously judgmental feelings about herself. I think something similar could be said with respect to Black people who, precisely as people living in a fallen world, tend not to be perfect. We know that the demonization of Black life by anti-Black racism is a terrible thing. But in my mind, it would also be problematic to romanticize or idealize Black life by suggesting that it is impeccable through and through, nothing but pure goodness. This too is a life-negating distortion. Our goal must not be to insist on the innocence of Black people but to address the great disproportion that exists between any actual shortcomings any of them may have as fallible human beings and the annihilative ways their lives are regularly perceived by others and, perhaps to some degree, also by themselves. This great disproportion, which makes an ordinary imperfect person feel like trash, or like they deserve to die, or like they are not worthy of love, is a spiritual crisis that Angela shares, at least at a formal level, with many members of the Black community. For this reason, as a Black person, I can see myself in her struggles. I can relate to the experience of hearing one set of voices in my interior monologue that try to tear me down and another set, which seem to come from some higher truth or goodness not simply from the world, and which lift me up, sanctify my existence, and promise me a joy greater than I can conceive. To this latter set belong the locutions of divine love.

More specifically, Angela's mysticism offers me one helpful way to resist the nihilistic conclusions of Afro-pessimist theorists such as Frank Wilderson and Calvin Warren.[26] To be clear, I do not think one has to turn to the mystics in order to find some such means of resistance. Afro-pessimism is vulnerable to various sorts of critique. For one, it relies on a structuralist definition of ontology, which unpersuasively suggests that the meaning of being is exhaustively determined by the ways dominant social imaginaries and discourses configure it, as though one's real and living experiences of oneself as a body that is not nothing had no ontological weight. Black life itself, Black *flesh* itself—that is, the living and breathing bodies of Black people—already defy the structuralist assumptions undergirding Afro-pessimism. One, therefore, does not need to invoke Angela's God in order to push back. A better phenomenology would suffice.

A second way to critique Afro-pessimism, more on its own terms, would be to note that even at a structural level, this theory selectively absolutizes the most negative instances of signification—the instances that identify Blackness with nothingness—leaving aside or disregarding other parts of language and culture which give Black life positive representation. Again, one need not call upon Angela's God to critique this theory. The interdisciplinary field of Black studies already offers a much richer account of the meaning of Blackness that makes such a critique possible, even inevitable. A reduction of Blackness to its most extreme determination by anti-Black racism—that is, a nihilistic interpretation of it—is not convincing to anyone who reads Black literature, listens to Black music, worships at a Black church, has relationships in the Black community, or studies Black theorists, including the Afro-pessimists themselves.

Nevertheless, I do believe that there is some truth in Afro-pessimism. This theory is correct to claim that there are structural features of white supremacist cultures that are annihilating of Black life. These structural features contribute to the murdering of Black bodies and souls. Unless resistance occurs at this fundamental level, unless Blackness is freed from its deeply ingrained role of symbolizing nothingness, then no number of civil rights victories or Black cultural achievements will suffice to overcome the threat of nihilism. To the extent that the Afro-pessimists are right about the structural nothingness of Blackness, a systemic condition which negatively affects the psychological self-perceptions and physical well-being of Black people, there is a need not merely for a critique of this theory but also for a way of coping with and responding to its harshest implications.

My perhaps counterintuitive suggestion is that Angela of Foligno, a white woman before the invention of whiteness, a mystic who knows nothing about our current racial politics, actually has a helpful message to offer here. To access this message, one must give less weight to her own disparaging words about herself, however faithfully or unfaithfully they have been transmitted by Brother A, and more weight to the consoling divine words that are given to her. These contain a powerful repudiation of nihilism. These words of love open up a non-ontological ontology hidden from the world, according to which those who appear to be nothing may in fact be deeply united with the All-Good. Such an alternative, mystical perspective, whether articulated by Angela or by another medieval or even non-Western source, may not be the only way to fight the annihilative power of anti-Blackness, but, as a Black Christian and Catholic theologian, I have found this to be one very effective and energizing approach.

I should acknowledge that the close connection Angela draws between torment and darkness in the sixth supplementary step of her mystical itinerary does complicate my reading to some degree. If part of my goal is to overcome cultural identifications of Blackness with nothingness, then her highly negative comments about darkness in this part of her book may become a serious stumbling block. This is what she says:

> While I am in this most horrible darkness caused by demons it seems to me that there is nothing I can hope for. That darkness is terrible; vices which I knew to be dead are reawakened from the outside by demons, and along with those, some vices which had never been there before come alive in my soul. My body (which nevertheless suffers less than my soul) experiences such burning in those places— the shameful parts—that I used to apply material fire to quench the other fire, until you [brother A] forbade me to do so. When I am in that darkness I think I would prefer

to be burned than to suffer such afflictions. I even cry out
for death to come in whatever form God would grant it. I
beseech him to send me to hell without delay.[27]

In this passage, Angela uses darkness as a metaphor for her
suffering and her supposed sinfulness, which she believes to be
caused by demons. We find out that what she thinks of as sinful
seems in fact to be mere erotic desire and that she is ashamed of
her own body parts.

In addition to the likely gendered erotophobia and somato-
phobia that Angela experiences here, there is also a problematic
act of signification whereby darkness is made to stand for dia-
bolical affliction and evil. Angela's choice of imagery expresses a
certain spiritual fear of the dark or "nyctophobia" which, within
the indistinct associative flows of social imaginaries and public
emotions, can easily translate into a rampant "negrophobia," as
it has done in modernity. In the white supremacist Christian and
post-Christian societies of the West, Blackness becomes an object
of terror and fascination because it is something dark, therefore
presumably dangerous, and probably in a sexual way. In such
anti-Black cultures, whose effects have now spread globally, these
sorts of phobic significations form the conscious and unconscious
habits that make countless people of various racial backgrounds
recoil from darkly colored bodies whenever and wherever they
encounter them. These sorts of phobic significations, in turn,
pressure Black people to feel ashamed of their bodies and to undergo interior torments and depressions similar to those endured
by Angela—though, of course, some Black people may be less
susceptible to these pressures than others.

Angela's seventh supplementary step in which she uses darkness as a metaphor for a very high, unknowable, nonvolitional,
Dionysian stage of union with God may help matters a little, but
it also comes with its own problems. She explains that she sees
God "in a darkness precisely because the good that he is is far
too great to be conceived." Although this dark experience is a
sublimely positive event in which she beholds and is elevated into
the divine nature, the meaning of darkness in this case remains
at least somewhat privative. Darkness here is an image of the
"negative" in negative theology. It signifies the infinite difference
between Creator and creature, a difference which implies that

"the light, the beauty, and the fullness that are in God" are so high above the creature that its normal perceptual and intellectual capacities must be transcended or suspended.[28]

A Black reader of this text might want to identify with such divine darkness precisely in order to escape the threat of being identified with the morally and affectively negative darkness of Angela's worst demonic tribulations. Fred Moten attempts something similar to this in his mystical response to Afro-pessimism. He does not draw on Angela or any comparable figure in the Christian mystical tradition but rather on the Japanese Buddhist philosopher Nishida Kitarō. Yet Moten's association of Blackness with the "paraontological," with an elusive presence beyond being and knowledge beyond the sovereignty of the subject, beyond the world as it is ordinarily constructed in space and time, performs a similar operation. Black life is affirmed and the worst nihilism is avoided by reading the aesthetic sociality of Blackness into the exalted position of a divine darkness or, more precisely in Moten's case, a quasi-divine emptiness.[29]

Although like Moten I am inclined to use mystical sources to express love for Black life, I am wary of a strategy whereby one attempts to do this by deifying, or quasi-deifying, the nothingness that has been attributed to such life. That is, I am wary of reading Blackness into the "paraontological" position of divinity or elaborating a poetics in which Blackness and divinity function more or less interchangeably. My hesitation about this way of employing or imitating mysticism is that Black people are not God; nor are they any other approximately absolute reality that holds a quasi-divine place in nontheistic mystical traditions. In the perspective of theological anthropology, they are creatures in a fallen world who, like everyone in this world, must struggle to receive the transformative workings of divine grace. Blackness itself—which, for Moten, refers to the absorptive experience of Black life in music, community, and fugitivity—remains a condition of human vulnerability, a condition that leaves its bearers exposed not merely to suffering but also to a potential complicity in sinful acts and structures of violence, a condition in which grace may appear but also be refused.

What I would like to argue for, then, is not a paraontological Blackness but a paraontological love, a love that reveals its ecstasy beyond being by favoring, comforting, and empowering those who have been treated like nonbeings. The unknowable God that, in some sense, takes Angela beyond her self-seeking love is nevertheless the very source of love—that is, the All Good. This is the same God she enjoys in her less opaque union with Jesus.[30] If, as a Black person, I read myself into the *Memorial*, it seems best to do so not by identifying myself immediately with its divine darkness but rather by relating myself to Angela herself: the fallen yet graced creature. The joy-inducing love that I might receive, if I am in her position, powerfully counteracts the potentially anti-Black signification whereby the darkness of my supposed race would be identified with demonic nothingness, and this counteraction happens without requiring the blackness of my life to be something like the ineffable ground of all things. In Angela's place, I may become one with the divine, but the test of this oneness will not be the mere structural fact of my racial nothingness but the paraontological love that may flow into and through me, if in fact I love others who are annihilated. What elevates my body and soul is not Blackness per se but *love for nothing*—and in two senses: Love without asking the cost or seeking a reward. And love for those who have been discarded as if they were nothing at all.

In conclusion, I want to reiterate that my Black theological reading of Angela is but one example of a more general possibility available to critically minded theologians who are busy addressing a range of intersecting forces of dehumanization. This is the possibility of searching within the Christian mystical tradition for insights about the nature of divine love that may be politically, psychologically, and spiritually beneficial for various annihilated peoples of the world. These sorts of readings are meant to supplement, not replace, important studies in subaltern cultural traditions and their own internal mystical features. Theological anthropology is enhanced by a mystical understanding of the transformative presence of divine love. This presence—which is nothing other than grace, and which I believe is operative in our world, even if we cannot always detect it—animates the living bodies of those who resist annihilative structures of sin and calls these bodies into an experience of joy that knows no bounds. As a Black person and therefore as a human being, because that is quite simply what a Black person is, I take great comfort in Angela's experience of such love.

Notes

[1]Gustavo Gutiérrez, *A Theology of Liberation: History, Politics, and Salvation,* 15th anniversary ed., trans. Sister Caridad Inda and John Eagleson (Maryknoll, NY: Orbis Books, 2005), xxix; and Sylvia Wynter, "Unsettling the Coloniality of Being/Power/Truth/Freedom: Towards the Human, After Man, Its Overrepresentation—An Argument," *New Centennial Review* 3, no. 3 (Fall 2003): 257–337.

[2]Olga M. Segura, *Birth of a Movement: Black Lives Matter and the Catholic Church* (Maryknoll, NY: Orbis Books, 2021), 13–18.

[3]Cornel West, *Race Matters,* 25th anniversary ed. (Boston: Beacon, 2017), 11–20.

[4]Patricia Hill Collins and Sirma Bilge, *Intersectionality* (Cambridge, UK: Polity, 2016).

[5]Mary Ann Hinsdale, IHM, and Stephen Okey, eds., *T&T Clark Handbook of Theological Anthropology* (New York: Bloomsbury, 2021).

[6]Julia A. Lamm, ed., *The Wiley-Blackwell Companion to Christian Mysticism* (Malden, MA: Blackwell, 2013).

[7]Albert J. Raboteau, *Slave Religion: The "Invisible Institution" in the Antebellum South* (New York: Oxford University Press, 2004); James H. Cone, *The Spirituals and the Blues: An Interpretation* (Maryknoll, NY: Orbis Books, 1991); and Diana Hayes, *No Crystal Stair: Womanist Spirituality* (Maryknoll, NY: Orbis Books, 2016).

[8]Hans Urs von Balthasar, "Understanding Christian Mysticism," in *Explorations in Theology,* vol. 4, *Spirit and Institution,* trans. Edward T. Oakes, SJ (San Francisco: Ignatius, 1995), 309–35.

[9]Henri de Lubac, *Christian Resistance to Anti-Semitism: Memories from 1940–1944,* trans. Elizabeth Englund, OCD (San Francisco: Ignatius, 1990), and Gustavo Gutiérrez, *We Drink from Our Own Wells: The Spiritual Journey of a People,* 20th anniversary ed., trans. Matthew J. O'Connell (Maryknoll, NY: Orbis Books, 2003), 128–35.

[10]Barbara Newman, *Sister of Wisdom: St. Hildegard's Theology of the Feminine* (Berkeley: University of California Press, 1997); Grace Jantzen, *Power, Gender, and Christian Mysticism* (New York: Cambridge University Press, 1995); Wendy Farley, *The Thirst of God: Contemplating God's Love with Three Women Mystics* (Louisville, KY: Westminster John Knox, 2015); Amy Laura Hall, *Laughing at the Devil: Seeing the World with Julian of Norwich* (Durham, NC: Duke University Press, 2018); Elizabeth A. Dreyer, *Accidental Theologians: Four Women Who Shaped Christianity: Hildegard of Bingen, Catherine of Siena, Teresa of Avila, and Thérèse of Lisieux* (Cincinnati, OH: Franciscan, 2014); Mary Catherine Hilkert, *Speaking with Authority: Catherine of Siena and the Voices of Women Today* (Mahwah, NJ: Paulist, 2001); and Sarah Coakley, *God, Sexuality, and the Self: An Essay "On the Trinity"* (New York: Cambridge University Press, 2013).

[11]Traci C. West, "Is a Womanist a Black Feminist? Marking the Distinctions and Defying Them: A Black Feminist Response," in *Deeper Shades of*

Purple: Womanism in Religion and Society, ed. Stacey Floyd-Thomas (New York: New York University Press, 2006), 291–96.

[12]Barbara Newman, "Gender," in *The Wiley-Blackwell Companion to Christian Mysticism*, ed. Julia A. Lamm (Malden, MA: Blackwell, 2013), 41–55.

[13]Willie James Jennings, *The Christian Imagination: Theology and the Origins of Race* (New Haven, CT: Yale University Press, 2010); and Geraldine Heng, *The Invention of Race in the European Middle Ages* (New York: Cambridge University Press, 2018), 181–256.

[14]Frantz Fanon, *Black Skin, White Masks*, trans. Richard Philcox (New York: Grove, 2008), 198–206.

[15]M. Shawn Copeland, *Knowing Christ Crucified: The Witness of African American Religious Experience* (Maryknoll, NY: Orbis Books, 2018), 119–23.

[16]Georges Bataille, *Inner Experience*, trans. Leslie Anne Boldt (Albany: State University of New York Press, 1988), 99–157, and Amy Hollywood, *Sensible Ecstasy: Mysticism, Sexual Difference, and the Demands of History* (Chicago: University of Chicago Press, 2002), 60–190.

[17]For additional context, see Bernard McGinn, *The Flowering of Mysticism: Men and Women in the New Mysticism (1200–1350): The Presence of God, Vol. 3: A History of Western Christian Mysticism* (New York: Crossroad, 1998), 142–51; Paul Lachance, OFM, Introduction to Angela of Foligno, *Complete Works* (Mahwah, NJ: Paulist, 1993), 15–117; and Mary Walsh Meany, "Angela of Foligno: A Eucharistic Model of Lay Sanctity," in *Lay Sanctity, Medieval and Modern: A Search for Models* (Notre Dame, IN: University of Notre Dame Press, 2000), 61–75.

[18]Foligno, *Complete Works*, 128.

[19]Ibid., 172, 219–20.

[20]Ibid., 139, 142, 177, 198, 205, 206, 210, 281.

[21]Friedrich Nietzsche, *The Birth of Tragedy* and *The Genealogy of Morals*, trans. Francis Golffing (New York: Anchor, 1956), 231–99.

[22]Foligno, *Complete Works*, 140.

[23]Ibid., 163.

[24]Ibid., 129–30.

[25]Ibid., 185 and 215.

[26]Frank B. Wilderson III, *Red, White, and Black: Cinema and the Structure of US Antagonisms* (Durham, NC: Duke University Press, 2010); and Calvin L. Warren, *Ontological Terror: Blackness, Nihilism, and Emancipation* (Durham, NC: Duke University Press, 2018).

[27]Foligno, *Complete Works*, 198.

[28]Ibid., 202.

[29]Fred Moten, "Blackness and Nothingness (Mysticism in the Flesh)," *South Atlantic Quarterly* 112, no. 4 (Fall 2013): 737–80.

[30]Foligno, *Complete Works*, 202, 205.

From Sister and Brother
to Patient and Client

Is the "Therapeutic Frame" Dehumanizing?

Todd Whitmore

There is currently an ongoing debate as to whether addiction is a disease. Arguments that it is have led to what has been called the "medicalization of deviance": that is to say, a significant portion of meaning-brokers in American society has shifted addiction, previously identified as a moral and legal issue to be adjudicated in religious and juridical contexts, to a biological and psychological matter to be addressed in medical and therapeutic contexts. The rhetorical concern in appealing to medical language is to destigmatize addiction and mental illness more generally.[1]

As important as such arguments are, they often fail to assess whether the medical-therapeutic model of mental health and addiction has its own liabilities and limitations. It is the aim of this article to identify and assess those liabilities and limitations through a specific case, that of Oaklawn Psychiatric Center in northern Indiana. Oaklawn is a particularly interesting case for theologically oriented persons because it was founded by Mennonites with the specific aim to offer persons the love that the latter so often fail to receive in other mental health settings. In what follows, I first detail Oaklawn's Mennonite beginnings. Then, I show how the decision to go with a clinical model—the "therapeutic frame"—for addressing mental health has set limits on the love that can be offered to persons with substance use disorders. Finally, I point toward recent developments that hold out the promise of a more robust approach to persons with such disorders.

Mennonite Beginnings

The Mennonite Church is one of the historic "peace churches" emerging out of the Radical Reformation in the sixteenth century: "Conforming" themselves to Christ as embodied in Jesus of Nazareth, Mennonites have historically refused to take up arms on behalf of the state. During World War II, this refusal involved participation in alternative Citizen Public Service, or CPS. As part of CPS, fifteen hundred Mennonites requested assignments in mental hospitals in order to practice direct service modeled after Christ.

What is noteworthy is the *kinship-oriented* nature of their Christ-conforming love. Kinship terms are central to Mennonite understandings of love, such that there is a German word, *Geschwister*, for how they consider each other as "brothers and sisters" or "siblings." The original Anabaptists referred to themselves simply as "brethren" and to their first somewhat official statement, usually described as the *Schleitheim Confession*, by the more informal phrase, "Brotherly Agreement."[2] And like kinship groups generally, they practiced mutual aid.

Kinship, as I understand it, is a bond of love facilitated through such practices as shared meals, finances, and living space. While recognizing that kinship often organizes itself along biological or marital lines, these are insufficient for claiming kinship; there are kinship relationships among persons not related to each other by blood or marriage. Marshall Sahlins's definition of kinship as a "mutuality of being," where persons "participate intrinsically in each other's existence; they are members of one another," is perhaps closest among anthropologists to what I mean by the term.[3]

Post–World War II, the Mennonite Church founded eight mental health facilities as alternatives to the horrid conditions that they witnessed in the state hospitals. Abraham Nussbaum describes the kinship ethos.

These centers provided humane care modeled upon a therapeutic version of Mennonite communal life, which is tight-knit and centered around the family. The initial facilities were designed to resemble a Mennonite family home rather than the state-run institutionalized facilities in which the CPS veterans served, so these were unlocked facilities with a much smaller census than that of state hospitals and were decorated to resemble a home rather than a hospital. To encourage peer relationships, the facilities had low staff-patient ratios and a flat organizational hierarchy.[4]

In keeping with this lay, kinship-like atmosphere, the Mennonite Voluntary Service provided three thousand volunteers from congregations for the mental health centers. Oaklawn itself had a community support program in which patients who otherwise would have had to travel great distances for day treatment lived with local Mennonites.[5]

An extended biblical exegesis will have to wait until another time, but for now I suggest that the Mennonites are correct in viewing the Gospel's social ethics as a kinship-based social ethics. In short, Gospel social ethics is the audacious proposal that we ought to treat *everyone* as our sister and brother, even in social spheres—namely the economic and political spheres—most often constructed in opposition to kinship. We see the political (regarding violence) and the economic (regarding property) played out when Jesus says, "You have heard that it was said, 'An eye for an eye and a tooth for a tooth.' But I say to you, Do not resist an evildoer. But if anyone strikes you on the right cheek, turn the other also; and if anyone wants to sue you and take your coat, give your cloak as well" (Mt 5:38–40). These are among the so-called "hard sayings" of Jesus, which much of Christianity has set aside as simply "ideals" not meant to be lived out in public life. However, if we read this passage and others in kinship terms, we see that we are to respond to all others truly as if they are our sisters and brothers: Don't hit back; give in what is usually considered excess. The hard sayings are thus not only not to be set aside but rather are the very center of Gospel social ethics.

However, as the Mennonite community turned to clinical psychotherapists for guidance, the community's ideas for mental health practices, both little by little and all of a sudden, turned away from a kinship approach.

The Therapeutic Frame

For four hundred years, an agrarian way of life gave practical underpinning to the kinship self-understanding of the Mennonite community. The image of the barn raising is a common enough indicator of the intertwining of rural life and mutual aid. However, the first half of the twentieth century saw dramatic changes in the demographics of North American Mennonites as a largely rural farming population became more urban, with more members seeking higher education and professional degrees. In 1936, 85 percent of North American Mennonites lived in rural areas, with most of these directly involved with farming; by 1972, only 11 percent were farming.[6] In 1963, the church published a pamphlet titled "Discipleship in the Mental Health Professions: A Survey of Psychiatric Professions Open to the Christian Student, Your Guide to Choosing a Vocation in the Context of Christian Commitment." The pamphlet's Christian focus is evident on the cover showing Jesus carrying the cross with three men behind Him, following and conforming themselves to Him by carrying their own crosses.

In trying to meld Christian witness with professional psychotherapy, the Mennonites enlisted the psychiatrist Karl Menninger as a consultant, who, though not Mennonite, placed love at the center of his approach. A quote from Menninger appears repeatedly in the Mennonite literature: "If we can love: this is the touchstone. This is the key to all the therapeutic programs of the modern psychiatric hospital. . . . To our patient who cannot love, we must say by our actions that we do love him."[7]

The limits of that love become evident, however, when we compare the practices of psychotherapy to those of kinship. Again, practices giving shape to kinship love include a shared knowledge of each other that develops through practices such as shared abode and household responsibilities, common meals, and gift exchange. However, virtually all modes of professional therapy carry strong disapprobations against such practices, considering them to involve "boundary crossings" and even "boundary violations." To see how and why this is the case, we need to look more closely at the practice of therapy.

There is a myriad of schools of psychotherapy. For the sake of simplicity, we can contrast two dominant trends, each developing out of a particular understanding of the relationship between therapist and client.[8] The psychoanalytic school, indebted to Freud, views therapy as the process whereby the patient's unconscious desires are brought to light so that they can be addressed. Here, the ideal is of the therapist as a "blank screen" on which the patient projects his desires in a process called "transference."[9] Freud insisted, "The doctor should be opaque to his patients and, like a mirror, should show them nothing but what is shown to him."[10] Practices such as shared meals, where people disclose themselves to each other, interfere with the transference process and thus the therapy. "Therapy over lunch," write psychiatrists Thomas Gutheil and Archie Brodsky, "is the quintessential example of what to avoid."[11] The humanist school, indebted to Carl Rogers,[12] views therapy as a process whereby the clinician faces the client[13] not with the ideal of a blank screen, but with a "genuineness," in Rogers's words, where the therapist presents "freely and deeply himself." The aim is to make the client feel safe enough to disclose his "authentic" self. However, this does not mean that there are not strong limits on therapist self-disclosure. "Certainly the aim is not for the therapist to express or talk out his own feelings, but primarily that he should not be deceiving the client as to himself."[14] The therapist is only to disclose certain feelings specifically toward the client when these interfere with the therapist's ability to approach the client with what Rogers calls "unconditional positive regard" and "empathy."[15] Interestingly, the extant literature shows that even addiction counselors who identify as in recovery themselves and share that piece of information with addiction clients become more reticent regarding self-disclosure as they become more experienced.[16]

As different as the psychoanalytic and humanist schools are, both significantly confine their practices in terms of space and time—what is sometimes called the "therapeutic frame"—in order to further the therapeutic endeavor. The *space* is the therapist's office, such that any encounter, even an accidental one, with the patient outside the office becomes a boundary crossing.[17] The therapist then needs to consider whether the boundary crossing constitutes a boundary *violation* of the relationship or not and whether, in the next session of therapy, she needs to do repair work with the client. The goal is to preserve and, if necessary, restore the "safe space"—the sanctuary—of the office. Even parts of the office—in particular the space between the client's chair and the door, where informal talk can creep in—constitute danger zones such that the American Psychological Association makes recommendations for office dimensions.[18] The *time* boundaries in the therapeutic frame are constructed around the scheduled session to the extent that a therapist needs to consider whether going overtime in a session constitutes a boundary violation.[19] Oaklawn addictions therapists follow this pattern, with even group sessions being scheduled in special on-campus rooms dedicated for that purpose. When we look more closely at the therapeutic frame, then, we can see that the description of the humanist approach as involving "unconditional positive regard" can be misleading. There are all sorts of conditions placed on how the therapist regards and interacts with the client.

Freud himself knew that the therapeutic frame is a construct formed for a very specific purpose. Constructing the frame is, he said, a "technique."[20] And it is a peculiarly modern one. Psychiatrist Paul Genova argues that the therapeutic frame is a compensatory construct in the face of the loss of the mutual aid that persons provided for each other in earlier epochs. Genova adds the observation that such a loss overburdens the therapeutic relationship. That relationship is not built to take on the responsibility of making up for all of the losses of modernity:

> In the modern professionalized situation, the bottom drops out of small-group reciprocal altruism. As isolated and anonymous individuals encounter each other, having little past or future together, two things happen. The first is that, without the support of a true community, the limits of an individual helper's resources are reached sooner and more often. There are not enough helpers to go around. The second is that the help-seeker often brings a greater backlog or depth of unmet need, as well as depth of frustration if current needs are not met, to each encounter.[21]

Genova highlights the fact that the therapeutic frame itself is designed to *lessen* the strain of taking on such a burden. It is designed not only to safeguard the client and the therapeutic process from boundary violations; it also serves to protect the therapist from what Genova calls "the undiluted, overwhelming needs of limitless numbers of patients."[22] In the terms of the theme of this Annual Volume, it is not that the therapeutic frame dehumanizes the client; it is rather that that frame, absent other kinds of social support, is inhumane to—that is, dehumanizes—not only the client but the therapist as well.

It is clear that the therapists need help. One possibility is for organizations like Oaklawn to revisit a kinship model to mental health and addictions. The professional therapeutic model purposely *suppresses* the possibility of a kin-like relationship between therapist and client, and it does so for strategic reasons: The client's own prior kinship relations are typically themselves problematic. What the therapeutic model cannot then do, however, is *model* what a generative kin relationship might look like.[23] Without denigrating the real successes of therapy, it is clear that a more comprehensive approach to addictions requires a broadening of the kinds of relationships community mental health centers facilitate as a complement to the therapeutic relationship. Fortunately, there are two developments in the addictions field that hold real promise for just such an expansion: the rise of the addiction recovery coach and of the sober living home.

The Addiction Recovery Coach and the Sober Living Home: Retrieving a Kinship Frame

The recent development of what are being called "recovery coaches" or "recovery specialists" has taken place in the last twenty or so years as an institutional correction to an addictions services model that has focused too exclusively on clinical treatment. The response has been to professionalize peer-based recovery by giving non-clinical training to persons well into sobriety themselves to provide recovery support for persons still in active addiction. Reflective of the rapid growth of the recovery coaching field, two years ago Oaklawn had one recovery specialist; it now has twenty-three and plans on adding fourteen more in the near future.

The most succinct way to think about recovery coaches is that they are life coaches for persons with substance use disorders. As life coaches, they focus not only on the disorder but first and foremost on the broad components of the recoveree's life: health, housing, education, employment, relationships, and more. Early on, the coach engages with the recoveree in what is called "motivational interviewing"—basically an open-ended conversation about what the recoveree desires in life.[24] Once coach and recoveree have a sense of the latter's aspirations, the coach can then ask how the recoveree views his or her drug use in relation to those goals. The recovery coach is at once a role model of what recovery can look like, a provider of both affirmation and truthtelling, and an institutional navigator. Throughout, the coach's own experience is, unlike in the case of the therapist, one of the resources that the coach explicitly draws on when discussing recovery with the recoveree. That is part of the added value that coaches bring to addiction services.

While there is a practical literature about what coaches *do* as distinct from a therapist or a twelve-step sponsor, there is nothing yet more theoretical conceptualizing the role of the coach in terms of *their* "frame" as distinct from the therapeutic frame.[25] Such conceptualizing can serve as a grounding for thinking through the detailed activities. Theoretical conceptualization is necessary not least because in the rapid development of the use of recovery coaches in community mental health centers, there is a danger of framing coaches simply as auxiliaries of the clinicians rather than as having a professional integrity of their own. As a result, such mental health centers can miss out on the full range of service opportunities that recovery coaches can provide—including the opportunity to reopen the kinship dimension of recovery in a way that clinicians cannot.

I discussed the therapeutic frame above in terms of space and time, and it helps to approach the "coaching frame" in like manner. In the therapeutic frame, the office is a "safe space" from the world structured in a way that allows the unique, constructed therapist-client relationship to take place. Any encounter outside of the office is a boundary crossing that must be assessed as to whether it is a boundary violation. Recovery coaches, in contrast, serve in a variety of contexts, meeting recoverees quite literally and not just figuratively "where they are." Oaklawn's placement of recovery coaches is indicative. They serve, for instance, in local hospital emergency departments so that when overdose victims are revived, they are not simply sent home but are asked if they would like to work with a coach toward recovery. Coaches also serve in what is called the "Motels4Now" program, where a housing-first program offers rooms for homeless persons, the majority of whom have substance use problems. There is also a mobile response unit that goes out to overdose calls in the community; if the revived person refuses transport to a hospital, they are still offered the option of a recovery coach. What these examples make clear is that for the recovery coach, the office is less a safe space *from* the world than, to use an outdoors metaphor, a "base camp" from which to move *into* the world. Coaches are, in this sense, the itinerants of recovery services. This means that encountering the recoveree outside of the office does not necessarily constitute a boundary crossing, let alone a boundary violation; it is, in cases like those just mentioned, exactly where the coach is supposed to be. The office still has a function—there are notes to enter and service hours to file—but that function is to enable the coach to better encounter recoverees in their *Sitz im Leben* or "setting in life," to use a term from biblical studies. Similarly, with regard to the time aspect of the "coaching frame," there is a role for scheduled appointments and for helping recoverees get to their other appointments, but many—and in some settings most—of the encounters with recoverees are not scheduled and do not have a strict time limit whereby the coach has to worry if they go "over." Such encounters are more serendipitous but no less serious.

The coaching frame's distinct spatial and temporal settings do not mean that coaches need not concern themselves with boundaries. In fact, because the settings within which coaches operate are more in social flux (other people often coming and going) and involve more active social inputs (surrounding noise, for instance) than the therapist's office, the keeping of helpful boundaries is all the more difficult. Given the flux and inputs, the rules cannot be as hard and fast as for the therapist, thus requiring much more on-the-spot practical judgment. The advantage, however, is that, when done well, the coach-recoveree relationship can develop across a variety of settings. Some of those settings can include the kind of activities that take place in kinship groups, like giving the recoveree a ride to an appointment or sharing a meal. In such settings, like a parent or older sibling, the coach—unlike the office-bound therapist—can model for the recoveree how to be in the world.

Coaches active in sober living homes can extend the kinship aspects through the practices of shared housing, household responsibilities, and daily meals. Oaklawn has yet to take this step. It has number of group homes for persons with mental illnesses, but there are no homes specifically for persons with addictions. Oaklawn also staffs an eighteen-unit small apartment building as a housing-first approach for the homeless, many of whom have substance use disorders, but the apartments are separated off from each other and there are not, for instance, shared meals or chores.

It is widely recognized that stable recovery requires a wide array of social supports, including close relationships of love and solidarity that would qualify as kinship relationships. There is also evidence that recoverees living in sober living homes under conditions of shared expenses, responsibilities, and meals develop kin-like relationships and even use kin terms like "sister" to refer to their housemates.[26] How coaches maintain professional boundaries in a kinship-like setting is a difficult question to be considered and lived, but to dodge that question for the sake of preserving a seemingly "safe space" is to prematurely delimit the kind of humanizing services that a place like Oaklawn can offer. To return to Marshall Sahlins's understanding of kinship as a "mutuality of being," recovery coaches in the context of sober living homes can help facilitate the kinds of practices where, in Sahlins's words, persons "participate intrinsically in each other's existence" and so become "members of one another."

Notes

[1] Alan I. Leshner, "Addiction is a Brain Disease, and It Matters," *Science* (October 3, 1997): 45–47.

[2] Cornelius J. Dyck, *An Introduction to Mennonite History* (Scottdale, PA: Herald, 1993), 50, 57–58.

[3] Marshall Sahlins, *What Kinship Is—And Is Not* (Chicago: University of Chicago Press, 2013), ix.

[4] Abraham M. Nussbaum, "The Mennonite Mental Health Movement: Discipleship, Nonresistance, and the Communal Care of People with Mental Illness in Late 20th-Century America," *Journal of Nervous and Medical Disease* 200, no. 12 (December 2012): 1091.

[5] Ibid., 1091, 1090.

[6] Leo Driedger and Donald B. Kraybill, *Mennonite Peacemaking: From Quietism to Activism* (Scottdale, PA: Herald, 1994), 46–48.

[7] Quoted in William Keeney, "Experiences in Mental Hospitals in World War II," *Mennonite Quarterly Review* 56, no. 1 (January 1982): 16.

[8] Michael Kahn, *Between Therapist and Client: The New Relationship*, rev. ed. (New York: Henry Holt, 1997), xii.

[9] Most Freudian therapists now acknowledge that the "blank screen"

is a construction that itself has a lot of content in it. A screen conveying "neutrality" toward the patient is still an ideal for which there are concrete recommendations made by professional organizations. For the case for a modified "blank screen" approach, see Thomas G. Gutheil and Archie Brodsky, *Preventing Boundary Violations in Clinical Practice* (New York: Guilford, 2008), 108ff.

[10]Sigmund Freud, "Recommendations to Physicians Practicing Psycho-Analysis," in *The Freud Reader*, ed. Peter Gay (New York: W. W. Norton, 1989), 361. Notably, Freud himself did not always follow his own rules on interaction with patients.

[11]Gutheil and Brodsky, *Preventing Boundary Violations in Clinical Practice*, 63.

[12]Barry Farber, *Self-Disclosure in Psychotherapy* (New York: Guilford, 2006), 107–8.

[13]Rogers insisted on the term "client" in contradistinction with the psychoanalytic use of the term "patient."

[14]Carl R. Rogers, "The Necessary and Sufficient Conditions of Therapeutic Personality Change," *Journal of Consulting and Clinical Psychology* 60, no. 6 (1992): 828–29.

[15]Ibid., 829.

[16]Carson C. Ham, Kai Dawn Stouffer LaMasson, and Jeffrey A. Hayes, "The Use of Self-Disclosure Lived Experiences of Recovering Substance Abuse Counselors," *Alcohol Treatment Quarterly* 31, no. 3 (2013): 348–74.

[17]"As a rule, therapy is conducted in the therapist's office or in a suitable institutional setting." Gutheil and Brodsky, *Preventing Boundary Violations in Clinical Practice*, 60.

[18]Ibid., 61.

[19]Ibid., 56–57.

[20]See Sigmund Freud, "On Beginning the Treatment: Further Recommendations on the Technique of Psychoanalysis," in *The Freud Reader*, 363–77.

[21]Paul Genova, "Boundary Violations and the Fall from Eden," *Psychiatric Times* 18, no. 6 (June 1, 2001), www.psychiatrictimes.com.

[22]Genova, "Boundary Violations and the Fall from Eden."

[23]Most therapists reject the controversial practice called "reparenting," where the therapist deliberately takes on the role of surrogate parent for the client in order to correct the client's distorted experience of being parented. See Tori Marlan, "A Most Dangerous Method," *Chicago Reader* (August 10, 2000), www.chicagoreader.com.

[24]William R. Miller and Stephen Rollnick, *Motivational Interviewing: Helping People Change*, 3rd ed. (New York: Guilford, 2013).

[25]Melissa Killeen, *Recovery Coaching: A Guide to Coaching People in Recovery from Addictions*, 2nd ed. (Somerdale, NJ: MK/RC, 2020), 125–37.

[26]Kevin C. Heslin et al., "Alternative Families in Recovery: Fictive Kin Relationships Among Residents of Sober Living Homes," *Qualitative Health Research* 21, no. 4 (2011): 477–88.

Decolonization as a Humanizing Practice

The Importance of Storytelling in Constructing a Community Identity for Natives and Settlers

Colleen Mary Carpenter

Imagine, if you will, a star. Now picture as the central design on a black quilt an artistic depiction of a stylized, multicolored, eight-pointed star surrounded by eight constellations outlined in sparkling crystals. Your imagination might or might not approximate Dakota artist Gwen Westerman's gorgeous 2014 quilt, titled "Star Knowledge." Unfortunately, a black-and-white photo of the quilt cannot begin to do justice to the spectacular pattern of colors Westerman used, and so I strongly urge you to find an image online.[1] The quilt serves as a guiding image for this essay for several reasons: First, the artist is a Dakota woman, and the Dakota people are central to this essay. Second, I chose the quilt for its beauty—and to remind us that intricate, complex, beautiful art is central to Native American cultures despite the dehumanizing judgment that Native art is simply "primitive." Finally, I chose this particular quilt because of its subject and title: "Star Knowledge." Again, this was specifically to combat the dehumanizing assumptions that commonly in the past and still sometimes today dismiss Native knowledge—about science, history, religion, farming, business practices, child rearing, and many other subjects—as inferior or sometimes even nonexistent. White supremacist culture does not take seriously Native knowledge—nor Native people and especially Native claims to the land on which American settlers live.

All the work discussed in this essay was done at St. Catherine University (St. Kate's) in St. Paul, Minnesota, which is located on Dakota land. This land was supposedly ceded to the United States in an 1805 treaty—a treaty that the US Senate later determined had never been promulgated, had not been considered binding on the Dakota, and whose terms were never fulfilled by the US.[2] St. Kate's is only a few blocks from the Mississippi River and three miles from the confluence of the Mississippi and Minnesota rivers: We are within the scope of a place known to the Dakota as Bdote. As a general term, bdote refers to the coming together of two bodies of water—but the bdote of the Mississippi and Minnesota rivers is special. It is not simply *a* bdote but *the* Bdote, the center of the world, where creation itself began and where the Dakota people began.[3]

It is also where the US built Fort Snelling, a nineteenth-century military post designed and built to further both fur trading and the colonization/settling of what would later become the state of Minnesota.[4] And it was here that the state of Minnesota imprisoned over sixteen hundred Dakota people, mostly women and children, after the US-Dakota war of 1862. Hundreds died there in what is now recognized as a concentration camp.[5] Thus Bdote, once revered as a holy and life-giving place, is now, in the words of the Reverend Jim Bear Jacobs, a site of "both genesis and genocide."[6] My work took shape in the context of this place, its history, and its many people and nations, and my intent, though without doubt imperfectly fulfilled, is to honor that.

One might argue, of course, that the only true way to honor the fact that much of Minnesota is Dakota land (and the rest belongs to the Anishinaabe, or Ojibwe people) is to simply *give the land back*. Honoring the treaties would also be a possible response, although many of them were signed under coercion, incorporated unjust terms that were added but not discussed before signing, or are otherwise deeply flawed. Still another response would be to follow the suggestion of Dakota author and activist Waziyatawin, who has argued that taking down Fort Snelling is the first thing that settler Minnesotans need to do if they truly want to move toward justice.[7] Any of these concrete, material steps is, unfortunately, unlikely if not flatly impossible. However, there is a lot of room between "doing nothing" and having five-and-a-half million settler Minnesotans renounce their ownership of the land and leave. I would like to focus our attention on that space, that quite large space, and how we enter into it in order to start moving from "doing nothing" or even doing small things like land acknowledgments to doing something concrete—and then something more, and then something more. We can move the window on what seems possible and what indeed *is* possible—and I argue that the way we do that is through storytelling.

Stories shape us, both as individuals and as societies: We learn the stories of our family and of our nation, and we come to understand who we are (and who other people and other nations are) in the terms set out by those stories. "The truth about stories is that that's all we are," says Native author Thomas King,[8] who goes on to claim that "[s]tories are wondrous things. And they are dangerous."[9] That danger lies not just in the formative power of stories, however, but also in the fact that stories can change. They are not set in stone: Stories shift and adapt as communities grow and change through time. Moreover, communities can actively choose how their foundational stories grow and change, and the high stakes involved in making changes to those stories is evident in the passions unleashed when someone starts telling a competing story or suggests that the story we all know and treasure is somehow inadequate. The current debate over removing Confederate memorials is a dramatic example of this dynamic.

Therefore, storytelling—especially the telling of new stories—is a powerful social force. Theologian Charles Villa-Vicencio recognizes this and has seen it play out in his own country. Villa-Vicencio is a South African theologian whose scholarship focuses on justice and reconciliation in societies ripped apart by civil war or ethnic or racial conflict; beyond academia, he served as the National Research Director for South Africa's Truth and Reconciliation Commission.[10] Villa-Vicencio argues that it is "only by sharing our stories with one another that we can hope to transcend the boundaries of our past and reach toward a shared future."[11] Sharing stories is exactly what needs to happen in Minnesota, just as in South Africa: we need to build a unifying memory that incorporates the partial memories that each community holds. This, however, is incredibly difficult because some stories are too painful to bring adequately to speech. That is certainly true in Minnesota, where Dakota memories of the 1862 US-Dakota War (and the mass hanging of thirty-eight Dakota men after the war,

and the experiences of the women and children in the concentration camp at Fort Snelling, and the experiences of all the Dakota
exiled from Minnesota because of the war) are still raw—and they
are still largely ignored by the wider settler culture.

Similarly, Georges Erasmus, a First Nations political leader in
Canada, also points to the importance of storytelling. Quoting
H. Richard Niebuhr, he makes the link between memory and
community: "Where common memory is lacking, where people
do not share in the same past, there can be no real community.
Where community is to be formed, common memory must be
created."¹² Both South Africa and Canada have sought to do this
through Truth and Reconciliation Commissions. Minnesota has
not set up a Truth and Reconciliation Commission, but there
are a variety of things happening here that are clearly efforts
to change the story, to build a new common story. And it is in
building that new common story that Minnesotans will not only
affirm both the history and humanity of the Native communities
of Minnesota but also open up the possibility of creating a just
community—of finding ways to move toward justice, to step into
that space between doing nothing and doing everything.

Before turning to what is happening in Minnesota, however,
I need to make clear that storytelling, and especially the work of
telling new stories that are more accurate or truthful than the older
stories, is not merely a social force that builds community, important as that is. The work of telling new stories, more truthful stories, also needs to be understood as a spiritual practice, especially
for Christians. Sacramental theologian Bernard Cooke points to
the importance of storytelling when he describes how the interpretation of our experience is key to recognizing the presence of
God in our lives. As human beings trying to understand ourselves
and our lives, we usually begin with "the particular mythology"
of our culture and social group.¹³ We narrate the isolated events
of our individual experience into stories—and these are of course
stories that locate our own experience within the boundaries of
the stories and mythology of our family, nation, and social group.
These stories never fully capture the truth of complex reality but
can be more or less accurate, more or less true to what is really
happening. If we are to tell stories that recognize the presence and
transforming power of God's grace in our lives, Cooke argues, then
we need to examine the stories we tell about our lives quite care-

fully: We need to live reflectively, work to interpret our experience correctly, and allow ourselves to be shaped not just by family or cultural scripts but also and even more so by the Christian story. Moreover, in order to sort through the clashes and contradictions between the Christian story and the other stories within which we were raised, we need a hermeneutic of experience: that is, "a set of principles, insights, and critical judgments that equips us to interpret our experience in a more accurate and more profound way."[14] To truly live a Christian life requires the continuing work of examining the stories through which we are interpreting our lives. "How adequate, or perhaps misleading, are the models according to which we have been educated to view reality?" Cooke asks.[15] Asking that question and being able to answer it through the telling of new and better stories are significant parts of living a life of Christian discipleship.

In the remainder of this essay, I will introduce you to several things that are happening in Minnesota with respect to telling new stories—stories about Minnesota's past and its present, about who counts as a Minnesotan, and about how the diverse communities that live here are indeed a single (if diverse and complex) Minnesotan community. I argue that these stories and the practices involved in creating and telling them are *humanizing* practices, practices that are aimed at recognizing the humanity and dignity of the Dakota and Anishinaabe people. It is only when we recognize our common humanity and include one another in a unified story of who we are as a people together that we will be able to adequately address the problems in our community—including the historical problems that are still playing out today in the very concrete ways that the Native people of Minnesota continue to suffer, physically, socially, economically, and spiritually.

The first significant thing happening here in Minnesota is that we are in the midst of updating and changing what is being taught in the schools. Every ten years, Minnesota updates its K–12 curriculum standards. Knowing this and knowing how inadequate the current standards are, one of the Dakota communities in Minnesota has been working to raise awareness among educators. The Shakopee Mdewakanton Sioux Community has invested millions of dollars in curriculum and training, focusing particularly on the fact that *they are still here.*[16] The idea that "all the real Indians died off" is a common one,[17] and it is unfortunately reinforced by school lessons that focus on nineteenth-century history but never mention, for example, that Native nations are the largest employers in several Minnesota counties today.[18] The new standards will directly address this idea that Native people are still here and are a significant part of Minnesota today. Unfortunately, the proposed new standards have received significant pushback from some conservative groups. The Center for the American Experiment has attacked the standards for their "disproportionate emphasis on Indigenous people" and warns that they are "rewriting history in a way that will profoundly affect our state's future."[19] That warning is of course exactly the point: if Minnesota's schools teach the history of the state in a way that significantly incorporates not only the past but also the present of the Native peoples who live here, then both settler and Native children will grow up learning that they are all part of a single, shared Minnesota.

The Minnesota Historical Society (MHS) is also working to "rewrite history" in ways that are causing controversy even as they strive to build new community. The MHS runs Fort Snelling, which holds a special place in the teaching of Minnesota history, as evidenced by the fact that most elementary schools within driving distance schedule annual field trips there. Until recently, visiting Fort Snelling was all about the soldiers and the cannons and even the muskets: it was focused exclusively on military history—specifically, on good old-fashioned *patriotic* military history. In the past few years, however, the Minnesota Historical Society has begun to make a significant effort to promote "a new vision" for Fort Snelling, one that incorporates much more than military history and which also focuses on a variety of minority communities in Minnesota whose connection with the Fort had previously been ignored. This new approach can be seen even in the photograph featured on the homepage for Fort Snelling.[20] Instead of soldiers or cannons or even the fort itself (which is visible, but only in the distance), the main photo at the top of the webpage is of the meeting of the two rivers below the fort. In other words, it is a picture of Bdote. In fact, in 2019 the historical society even tried to rename the fort from "Historic Fort Snelling" to "Historic Fort Snelling at Bdote," but this caused significant protest from people who were afraid that this was "revisionist history" that would erase the military history that they saw as "unifying" Minnesotans.[21] Republicans in the state legislature threatened to cut the historical society's funding by millions of dollars and even passed a budget with that provision. The historical society removed the new signs, and their funding was restored.[22]

Despite not being able to add to the name of the fort, the Minnesota Historical Society is clearly moving to tell the story of Fort Snelling in a new and more inclusive way. The "essential stories of our shared past"[23] include not just Dakota stories of Bdote and of the 1862 US-Dakota war but also African American stories of enslavement and freedom (Dred Scott lived at Fort Snelling from 1836 to 1840, and witnessed several successful freedom lawsuits by other illegally enslaved people at the fort),[24] and Japanese American stories of a secret language school at the fort during World War II.[25] All of this is in service of expanding the story of Minnesota to include many voices that have too long been left unheard.

Turning from Fort Snelling to other initiatives happening around the Minneapolis-St. Paul metro area, the Hennepin Theater Trust in downtown Minneapolis has partnered with NACDI, the Native American Community Development Institute, to support public art along Hennepin Avenue.[26] The overall theme of the public art project is "We Are Still Here," recalling the Shakopee Mdewakanton Sioux Community's similar emphasis. Billboards, murals, animations, and building-size projections are all part of the project. One particular billboard, designed by Jonathan Thunder, a member of the Red Lake Nation of Ojibwe people in northern Minnesota, references the Dakota phrase from which Minnesota took its name: Mni Sota Makoce, the Land Where the Waters Reflect the Clouds. The Dakota phrase is written out in bright yellow letters over a scene of a variety of Minnesotans biking and walking outdoors, and there is also a tagline along the bottom of the billboard: "All Minnesotans Speak a Little Dakota." This clever and inviting phrase reminds viewers that not only the state but also a significant number of cities, towns, and lakes have Dakota names, or at least names rooted in the Dakota language. If their goal is building community between settler Minnesotans and Native Minnesotans, then pointing out that settlers are already participating in Dakota language and community is a good way to do it.

Another initiative, this one sponsored by the Minnesota Council of Churches, is titled "Healing Minnesota Stories."

"While many people and institutions contributed to [the trauma suffered by Native people in Minnesota]," the Council states, "it happened with the full participation of Christian churches."[27] This acknowledgment of the involvement not just of individual Christians or Christian ideas but also of churches is fascinating and powerful. In other words, the problem was not just the Doctrine of Discovery, promulgated by the faraway Vatican hundreds of years ago;[28] it was not just long-ago Christian missionaries; no—it was the churches of Minnesota, faith communities that are still here today. Moreover, these churches today have work to do here and now to respond to their destructive past: they can invite Native speakers to their church, or they can learn about Native spirituality or about Minnesota history or even about current controversies about how we tell the story of the state through the art displayed at the State Capitol.[29] Again, this is working to do what Charles Villa-Vicencio and Georges Erasmus spoke about: telling a story that creates community in a new way.

And we cannot forget that telling stories to create community is an activity with profound and quite tangible consequences. These stories help shape our social imagination, which in turn shapes not just our ideas about our community but also the material conditions through which our community exists. Theologian William Cavanaugh tells us that "the imagination of a society is the sense of what is real and what is not; it includes a memory of how the society got where it is, a sense of who it is, and hopes and projects for the future. . . . [I]t is the condition of possibility for the organization and signification of bodies in a society.[30] The social imagination, then, is about the past and the future—and about our bodies, our physical existence in a particular place. This is incredibly important: our social imagination shapes the lives that we are able to live. This plays out in Minnesota in the homelessness rate for Native people, the poverty rate, the premature death rate, and the cancer rate; all of these and more are significantly higher than, and sometimes several times as much as, what they are for white Minnesotans.[31] *Bodies matter, and our imagination shapes what is possible for bodies.* Right now, what is possible for the bodies and lives of Native Minnesotans has been sharply limited and deeply distorted by the inadequacies and injustice that mark the social imagination of settler Minnesotans. Developing a new and more adequate social imagination through the telling of new stories is an absolute necessity if we are to move toward a more just society.

And so, with the development of a new social imagination in mind, let us return to the quilt described at the opening of this essay. The beauty of the quilt, the talent of the quiltmaker, and the different kinds of "star knowledge" referenced in the title all speak to the glorious and rich humanity of the Dakota people and Dakota culture. In speaking about her quilts, Gwen Westerman said, "As Dakota people, we have a long, rich history that explains not only where we came from, but also our responsibilities in this world to each other and to the universe. My art is grounded in Dakota culture and tradition, history, oral tradition, and language recovery—and the continuation of our story."[32] The continuation of the Dakota story in a state that tried to erase that story and eliminate the people is an amazing if not flatly miraculous thing. And looking to all the ways that the stories of Native people in Minnesota are now being told is heartening. It is also making room for new things to happen, for a newly shaped social imagination—guided by a hermeneutic of experience that calls us toward justice and to the equal dignity of all people—to develop new hopes and projects for the future. There are humanizing things happening here in a place that dehumanized people for far too long. And I would argue that the work being done here in Minnesota is not an isolated or parochial project but is instead a case study for what needs to happen throughout Turtle Island if all people here today are to recognize one another as human and live together in a single human family.

Notes

[1]Beautiful color images of this quilt are easily found online by searching the artist, Gwen Westerman, and the title of the artwork, "Star Knowledge." The quilt was featured in an exhibit at the Minnesota History Center in 2019. News articles about this exhibit, including commentary from the artist, photos of the quilt, and historical background/context, can be found online at Peter Diamond, "Behind Minnesota's Native History," *Minneapolis-St. Paul Magazine* (December 3, 2019), www.mspmag.com, and at Jessica Kohen, "Exploring Indigenous Minnesota," *Minnesota Good Age Magazine* (December 3, 2019), www.minnesotagoodage.com.

[2]See the description of the 1805 Dakota treaty at www.treatiesmatter.org or at www.mnhs.org.

[3]For a full explanation of bdote and Bdote, see www.bdotememorymap.org or www.mnhs.org.

[4]See "The Expansionist Era (1805–1858)," *Minnesota Historical Society*, accessed September 27, 2021, www.mnhs.org.

[5]See "The US-Dakota War of 1862," *Minnesota Historical Society*, accessed September 27, 2021, www.mnhs.org.

[6]Margie O'Loughlin, "Sacred Sites Tours Seek Healing through Storytelling," *Longfellow Nokomis Messenger* (December 1, 2019), longfellownokomismessenger.com.

[7]Waziyatawin, *What Does Justice Look Like: The Struggle for Liberation in Dakota Homeland* (Saint Paul, MN: Living Justice, 2008).

[8]Thomas King, *The Truth about Stories: A Native Narrative* (Minneapolis: University of Minnesota Press, 2003), 2.

[9]Ibid., 9.

[10]See "Charles Villa-Vicencio," *Conversation*, accessed September 27, 2021, www.theconversation.com.

[11]Charles Villa-Vicencio, "Telling One Another Stories: Toward a Theology of Reconciliation," in *The Reconciliation of Peoples: Challenge to the Churches*, ed. Gregory Baum and Harold Wells (Eugene, OR: Wipf & Stock, 2009), 31.

[12]Mark Charles and Soong-Chan Rah, *Unsettling Truths: The Ongoing, Dehumanizing Legacy of the Doctrine of Discovery* (Downers Grove, IL: InterVarsity, 2019), 204.

[13]Bernard Cooke, *Sacraments and Sacramentality*, rev. ed. (1983; New London, CT: Twenty-Third, 1994), 33.

[14]Ibid.

[15]Ibid.

[16]Kelly Smith, "Shakopee Sioux Announce $5 Million Campaign to Boost Indian Education in Minnesota Schools," *Minneapolis Star Tribune*, October 11, 2019, www.startribune.com.

[17]There is even a book by that title: Native American scholars Roxane Dunbar-Ortiz and Dina Gilio-Whitaker are authors of "*All the Real Indians Died Off*": And 20 Other Myths about Native Americans* (Boston: Beacon Press, 2016).

[18]Smith, "Shakopee Sioux Announce $5 Million Campaign."

[19]Katherine Kersten, "Woke Revolution Looms for Minnesota Schools." *Minneapolis Star Tribune*, February 6, 2021, www.startribune.com.

[20]See "Historic Fort Snelling," *Minnesota Historical Society*, accessed September 27, 2021, www.mnhs.org.

[21]Jennifer Brooks, "State Senators Try to Slash Minnesota Historical Society's Budget over Sign at Fort Snelling," *Minneapolis Star Tribune*, April 25, 2019, www.startribune.com.

[22]David Chanen, "Fort Snelling Signage Opens History Debate among Officials at Minnesota Legislature, Local Level," *Minneapolis Star Tribune*, May 24, 2019, www.startribune.com.

[23]This language is from "Historic Fort Snelling."

[24]Ibid.

[25]Ibid.

[26]"NACDI and Hennepin Theatre Trust Collaborate to Launch We Are Still Here, an Initiative to Uplift Native Voices in the Hennepin Theatre

District," *Hennepin Theater Trust News*, December 8, 2020, www.hennepintheatretrust.org.

[27]See "Healing Minnesota Stories," *Minnesota Council of Churches*, accessed September 27, 2021, www.mnchurches.org.

[28]For more information about the Doctrine of Discovery and the role of theology in settler colonialism, see Charles and Rah, *Unsettling Truths*. The three papal bulls at the heart of the Doctrine of Discovery are *Dum Diversas* (1452), *Romanus Pontifex* (1454), and *Inter Caetera* (1493), which together authorized European explorers to conquer and claim land not inhabited by Christians and to enslave the inhabitants of those lands. In addition, the Doctrine of Discovery lies at the heart of the American legal understanding of property ownership, as laid out in the 1823 Supreme Court decision Johnson v. McIntosh.

[29]Each of these activities is suggested at "Healing Minnesota Stories," *Minnesota Council of Churches*, www.mnchurches.org.

[30]William Cavanaugh, *Torture and Eucharist* (Malden, MA: Blackwell, 1998), 57.

[31]This is discussed in Greta Kaul, "Across a Range of Measures, Minnesota's American Indians Fare Worse Than Other Groups. So Why Isn't It Talked about More?" *MinnPost*, October 10, 2018, www.minnpost.com. In addition, detailed demographic data can be found at the "Populations of Color and American Indians" in *The Community Health Services Administration Handbook*, rev. ed. (2014), www.health.state.mn.us.

[32]"Great Plains Museum to Host Native American Textiles Artist," *N-Announce*, accessed September 27, 2021, www.newsroom.unl.edu.

"Holiness Is Wholeness"

The Influence of Jewish and Catholic Anarchism on Judith Malina's Artistic Challenge to Dehumanization

Marjorie Corbman

In the summer of 1957, three women gathered on the roof of the New York Women's House of Detention, the prison to which they had been sentenced to thirty days' incarceration. A six-foot-high wall blocked their view of the city, but, standing on the brightly painted benches in front of the wall, they could see "all of [Greenwich] Village, and much of Manhattan."[1] Surveying the view, they realized that all of them had spent about ten years frequenting the Village's bars, though these periods of time had not overlapped.[2] The oldest of the women was Dorothy Day (1897–1980), the co-founder of the Catholic Worker, a movement based on a Catholic philosophy of radical hospitality and nonviolence.[3] The youngest of the three, Day's cellmate, was the Jewish actress and theater director Judith Malina (1926–2015).[4] All three of the women had been imprisoned for refusing to participate, as committed pacifists, in the city's Cold War–period air raid drills.

In light of Malina's friendship with Day, this essay examines Malina's religiously informed artistic critique of dehumanization and her contrasting vision of a politics based on personal encounter. As will be shown, Day's influence was crucial for Malina in emboldening her to conceive of her art in religious terms, drawing on Jewish traditions and thinkers to craft a framework of "holy encounter" facilitated through performance.[5] For Malina, theater was a form of ritual that instantiates direct encounters between individuals, thereby empowering participants to dismantle dehumanizing structures. Because of the intense, affective, and embodied relational context between actor and spectator, she asserted, theatrical performance can cultivate the kinds of personal encounters necessary for a truly human politics.

This stress on personal encounter is notable for Catholic theologians in light of Pope Francis's call to build a "culture of encounter" in response to the gospel call to "run the risk of a face-to-face encounter with others, with their physical presence which challenges us, with their pain and their pleas, with their joy which infects us in our close and continuous interaction."[6] The foregrounding of radical confrontation of evil in Day's and Malina's understanding of personal encounter underscores what Bradford Hinze has identified as Pope Francis's recognition of the "reality and role of conflict" in these risky face-to-face encounters.[7] Malina argued that theatrical performance could serve as a model for this kind of spiritual and political vision, as drama is uniquely capable of maintaining the tension between confrontation of injustice and loving, personal encounter. As theatrical performance necessarily relies on direct, immediate contact, it anchors even the most stringent critique of social evil in personal relationships. This essay will use the Living Theatre's 1963 staging of *The Brig* as an exemplary expression of Malina's understanding of theater as both loving encounter and confrontation of dehumanizing structures.

Anarchism, Political Theater, and the Catholic Worker

After Malina was arrested for the first time, which took place along with Dorothy Day and others in 1955, she reflected: "How blithely I went! It was new to me."[8] Along with her husband, Julian Beck, Malina was the founder of the Living Theatre, the longest-running and one of the most influential experimental theater troupes in the United States. While nonviolent direct action was largely new to her, she was not a novice in political action. It was simply that, beginning in childhood, her previous political engagement had been theatrical.

As she explained in a 2013 interview with John Bredin, she had been doing political theater since she was four years old (3:47–3:54).[9] Her father, Max Malina, an idealistic, intellectual rabbi, moved their family from Germany when she was three years old as a result of ascendant anti-Semitism in the country.[10] In New York, her father tirelessly advocated for Jewish communities in Germany. Malina told Bredin:

> My father was concerned with explaining to the American people what was happening to the Jews in Germany and for this there were rallies and meetings, and I would recite German poetry about the suffering of the Jewish children in Germany, and I didn't know it was political theater. I thought I was just reciting poetry. But I've always done political theater and I've always been political and I've always been concerned with the people that are suffering more than we do. (3:55–4:38)

At the age of twelve, to her father's dismay, she began identifying fervently as a pacifist, committed to the principle of acting without bitterness toward all people, even the Nazi officials then dedicating themselves to the genocidal annihilation of her people.[11] As a young adult, Malina studied under the legendary German theater director Erwin Piscator, who understood theater as a means of political communication. Malina's and Beck's intention with the Living Theatre was "to create a theater that would present pacifist and anarchist ideals" (4:38–4:51).[12] By anarchism, Malina primarily meant a social structure based on egalitarian, voluntary cooperation rather than coercive state violence,[13] a view that aligned with Day's understanding that "to be opposed to State is to be an anarchist" and that anarchism at best offers "visions of a new society 'where it is easier to be good.'"[14]

Given Malina's earlier background, it may be surprising to note that she credited Day with teaching her everything she knew about the "theatricalization of politics."[15] She was especially awed by Day's capacity to transform moments of political confrontation into opportunities for loving encounter. Malina described what she learned from Day about theater and politics to journalist Lewis MacAdams: "Whenever you organize mass demonstrations, whenever you have a public protest, it is likely to take its natural form, which is to end up in riot and battle. But the leap from confrontation to violence is cooled out by theatricalization."[16] For Day, this emphasis on loving confrontation had a religious basis; she understood political demonstrations as embodiments of the traditional Catholic spiritual works of mercy. "To go on picket lines to protest discrimination in housing, to protest the draft," she wrote, "is one of the works of mercy, which include 'rebuking the sinner, enlightening the ignorant, counseling the doubtful.'"[17] Thus, in Day's understanding, political action was inseparable from the other forms of spiritual and corporal almsgiving that constitute the works of mercy.[18]

Malina described a play that the Living Theatre performed whenever someone was executed in the United States, which she said always reminded her of Dorothy Day. The actors, gathering in Times Square, would "confront total strangers and try to get them to promise not to kill anybody."[19] Malina explained: "If you confront someone, the problem becomes immediately to make it a loving relationship."[20] These anti–death penalty plays were typical expressions of the Living Theatre's later style, in which the troupe sought out nontraditional theater environments—from Brazilian slums, to a Pennsylvania steel mill, to a gathering of homeless neighbors on the Lower East Side—to collaborate with audiences in performance.[21] Malina's explicit linking of the Living Theatre's innovative approach to crafting personal encounters with Dorothy Day's influence raises questions about the relationship between art, political action, and spiritual experience.

Personal Encounter, Holiness, and Ritual

Malina was deeply moved by witnessing Day enact her intensely personal form of loving confrontation during their time together in prison. In her diary, Malina wrote: "I see now that I cannot write down the essence of Dorothy's influence on me. Only that I felt myself to be in the presence of someone in whom I could have complete faith, someone who does the right thing, even the holy thing, at every moment."[22] In their shared cell, they read to each other from the liturgies of their respective Catholic and Jewish traditions.[23] When Malina argued with a prison guard about his complicity, Day gently reflected on the importance of meeting everyone with love.[24] When Malina became overwhelmed by the suffering of other prisoners, Day reminded her that they could not change everything.[25] "What she did," wrote Malina, "remains the mystery of sanctity. She was there and heard them and talked to them of the work in prison, of the problems of earning a living, of her world, of their homes and their children, and through it all, without too many words, of the great goodness of God."[26]

In essence, as Malina later explained in an interview with Rosalie Riegle, what she learned from Day was that political work and spiritual commitment must necessarily be aligned. "All the time we were in jail," Malina said,

> she tried to teach me that anarchism is holiness, which I had never understood. I had thought there was much more contradiction between anarchism and holiness. . . . Dorothy's human generosity could include the most pitiful person and the finest in the same embrace, and so I finally learned what she'd been trying to teach me, that anarchism is holiness. It's a holiness here and now which consists in treating each other as holy beings. No dividing into good ones and bad ones.[27]

This insight would become key to Malina's interpretation of the role of theater in politics: Through performance, a profound connection between actor and spectator is made possible. This encounter is the necessary spiritual posture for the building of a world founded not on violence and exploitation, but on what Malina termed "the kinship of our physical empathy."[28]

In her understanding of theater as essentially a ritual experience, Malina was by no means unique; as theater scholars such as Christopher Innes and David Callaghan have shown, the Living Theatre's conflation of theater with the sacred was typical of the twentieth-century avant-garde.[29] As David Callaghan writes, "The Living Theatre essentially used performance, including extensive audience participation, as a contemporary act of secular ritual that could provide spiritual sustenance to a decaying culture it believed needed new myths and rites of worship."[30] While Callaghan's characterization of the Living Theatre's art as "secular ritual" was true in many respects, it is at the same time important to note the influence of actual religious communities on Malina's understanding of theater.

Judith Malina's Jewish Influences

Malina's recognition, after her time in prison with Dorothy Day, that anarchism *is* holiness empowered Malina to revisit the religious influences of her childhood. At times, reliance on Jewish concepts was explicit in her work, as in *Korach: The Biblical Anarchist* (2010) or in the influence of Martin Buber's thought and Jewish texts on the groundbreaking *Paradise Now* (1968).[31]

But beyond these explicitly Jewish themes, Malina described her overall understanding of theater in Jewish terms. In 1993, in an oral history interview with Cindy Rosenthal, Malina offers an extended discussion of the spiritual meaning of art in relationship to the central prayer of Judaism, the *shema*, recited twice daily by observant Jews, and particularly the words "*adonai ekhad*," God is one. Malina interpreted this phrase as meaning that "God is that oneness, that God is that unity." For her, "holiness is wholeness" because "unification is the goal of religion and the goal of art." Art's role is to facilitate this unification through immediate encounter between persons:

> And the work of art is to create an ambiance in which that holy encounter is heightened. . . . You have a moment of epiphany or a moment of enlightenment, or a moment even of pleasure and joy on a level where it changes you. . . . [O]ne has communicated something to the other and this bridge has been made of a common language, of a bond in our isolation, loneliness and our alienation, to overcoming that in a moment of profound contact. I think it's in this that the religious experience exists. I think it exists in the theater and I think it exists in the temple and I think it exists . . . I would hesitate to draw very strict lines between a religious experience and the theatrical experience.[32]

Immediately before this passage in the interview, Malina referred to *I and Thou* (1923), the influential work of her father's friend Martin Buber, himself also a Jewish anarchist and pacifist. Summarizing Buber, she reflected on how drama emerges from the "twofold" character of our being, as essentially alone and essentially together. Art, she asserted, bridges the gap between our irreducible, concrete individuality, and our fundamental togetherness.[33] God, for Buber as for Malina, can only be found in the relational matrix between individual beings: "[T]he authentic assurance of constancy in space consists in the fact that men's relations with their true *Thou*, the radial lines that proceed from all the points of the *I* to the Centre, form a circle."[34]

In addition to the influence of Buber's view of God found in relationality, Malina's concept of unification as the goal of religious and artistic experience also was likely shaped by Buber's and Malina's father's friend Eric Gutkind. (Malina described Gutkind as "the beautiful philosopher who used to sit talking for hours with my father, of the spirit and the world, of the Kabbalah, of the Chassidim, and of the horrors of war.")[35] In Gutkind's *Choose Life: The Biblical Call to Revolt* (1952), which Malina read in April 1953,[36] he claimed that "the supreme aim of the Jewish people is the restoration of the broken unity between God and the manifestation of God in the world."[37] This act of unification is made possible through ritual, which, in the Jewish tradition, consists of words and physical actions rather than images, thus making "the body transparent to the Divine Light" and establishing "the vision of the 'Holy Flesh.'"[38]

Gutkind saw this uniquely Jewish process of personal and social integration through ritual as a potential path for all humanity, if Jews who avoided both (in his view) the limitations of traditionalist "petrification" and the "disastrous fallacies" of liberal assimilationism would blaze the trail.[39] "If the Jew would undertake to free the ritual discipline from its present frustrating narrowness, he might reach unparalleled heights and pave the way for all mankind towards the vertical ascent."[40] Like these other twentieth-century Jewish thinkers engaged in philosophizing and universalizing the Jewish tradition, Malina aimed to communicate a Jewishly grounded insight (the connection between ritual and unification) in a medium accessible to all.

The Brig: Staging and Disrupting the Inhuman

One of Malina's most in-depth reflections on producing and heightening what is holy in the encounter between actor and spectator can be found in her production notes to the Living Theatre's staging of *The Brig* (1963), a play by Kenneth Brown about life in a military prison. In Robert Knopf's summary of the play:

> The guards, under the command of the warden and the Marine Corps manual, use the environment, rules, and ritualistic actions to dehumanize the prisoners. They beat the prisoners into submission as punishment for unspoken crimes, stripping them of their names, identities, and senses of self. Prisoners must live by the Marine code and nothing else; their only hope of survival is to be a Marine.[41]

Malina's directorial approach to the play was to create a context in which the actors and the audience would enact bodily, in her words, "the price of the chaos under which we suffer."[42] Malina urged her actors to hear the sounds they were making as they embodied these rituals of cruelty: that the music they were making was "clashing, disorganized, disordered, confused, tumultuous."[43]

The goal of the play was to expose violence in its actuality. "Violence is the darkest place of all," wrote Malina. "Let us throw light on it. In that light we will confront the dimensions of the Structure, find its keystone, learn on what foundations it stands, and locate its doors. Then we will penetrate its locks and open the doors of all the jails."[44] By "jails," she did not mean only literal prisons but also, she wrote, "a school or a factory or a family or a government or The World As It Is."[45] And yet this insight derived from her own experience as a prisoner, quite literally. As she wrote in *The Brig*'s production notes, "the month that I spent in the Women's House of Detention was not only instructive, but it enables me to count myself as always among the prisoners."[46] This statement echoes a passage she wrote immediately after her release from prison in 1957:

> I was not ever again to be free while prisons exist, and I am not free now. I am not free because I am in the street that surrounds and encircles the prison. . . . "In the street" is on that narrow strip around the walls that enclose the secret sins of the world and the elemental human. Here we hide away our untamed part, instead of letting our minds know how our hearts feel, free and unashamed and compassionate.[47]

Malina aimed, with help of the heightened encounter of the drama, to dismantle the walls that imprison our naked, fleshy, compassionate, animal humanity, the "kinship of our physical empathy."[48]

Conclusion: Towards a Theology of Personal Encounter

Malina's statement in *The Brig*'s production notes that exposing violence through drama could lead to concrete actions such as the dismantling of prisons reflects her sincere belief in the role of the individual in political change. In Malina's view, political change would always be insufficient without "integrating the ideal social situation with the real, individual, human factor."[49] By "throw[ing] light" on violence and reconnecting the spectators of a drama to their primal kinship with other beings, Malina believed that radical transformation would be made possible.[50] The Living Theatre could offer justification for this claim in citing responses to their plays, most notably in the role the troupe played in the 1968 uprisings in France but also in the final performance of *The Brig* itself, which was performed illegally after the Internal Revenue Service had seized the building.[51] When *The Brig* "was closed by the state because the theatre could not meet its financial obligations," Malina wrote, "the actors, the author, the stage hands, the box-office workers, the stage manager, the house manager, and the technicians were joined by some members of the audience in volunteering to be arrested on the stage with us rather than leave without protesting that this play should not continue to speak."[52] Yet Malina and Beck also insisted that the value of political theater could not be measured in terms of how the audience *does* respond but rather in how it offers the possibility of *a different kind of response* than was previously imaginable.[53]

Malina and Day had discussed the limits of political action and the importance of personal connection in their prison cell. In *Loaves and Fishes*, Day reflected on this further. "When I lay in jail . . . thinking of war and peace and the problem of human freedom," Day wrote,

I was all the more confirmed in my faith in the little way of St. Thérèse [of Lisieux]. . . . Young people say, What good can one person do? What is the sense of our small effort? They cannot see that . . . we can be responsible only for the one action of the present moment. But we can beg for an increase of love in our hearts that will vitalize and transform all our individual actions, and know that God will take them and multiply them, as Jesus multiplied the loaves and fishes.[54]

For Day, the urgency of political critique was ultimately inseparable from the lifelong struggle to view others—despite how unlovable, selfish, and repellent we can appear to one another—as Jesus Christ, human and divine.[55] For Malina, anarchism meant "treating each other as holy beings. No dividing into good ones and bad ones."[56] As can be seen in the example of *The Brig*, one profound contribution "theatricalization" makes to politics is its capacity to confront the full horrors of a social system geared toward violent dehumanization while also maintaining the centrality of encounters with other individual beings—a prisoner, a guard, a bystander. Malina's mobilization of Jewish and artistic sources to build on Day's Catholic understanding of political action as a "work of mercy" demonstrates the crucial role of engaging non-Christian and non-theological sources in developing a Christian theological response to dehumanization. Drawing on the diverse influences of philosophers, activists, religious leaders, and dramatists, and grounded in her friendship with Dorothy Day, Judith Malina's theatrical work offers a rich resource for a theology of personal encounter.

Notes

[1]Judith Malina, *The Diaries of Judith Malina, 1947–1957* (New York: Grove, 1984), 450.

[2]Ibid., 454.

[3]On Day's conversion, see James Fisher, *The Catholic Counterculture in America, 1933–1962* (Chapel Hill: University of North Carolina, 1989), 1–24.

[4]Malina, *Diaries*, 454. The other woman on the roof was Deane Mowrer.

[5]Day's emphasis on personal encounter, as has frequently been noted, derived from the influence of francophone personalist philosophers. See, e.g., Nancy L. Roberts, *Dorothy Day and the Catholic Worker* (Albany: State University of New York Press, 1984), 7–8.

[6]Pope Francis, *Evangelii Gaudium*—The Joy of the Gospel (2013), www.vatican.va, para. 88. See also paras. 87, 171, 220, 239.

[7]Bradford Hinze, *Prophetic Obedience: Ecclesiology for a Dialogical Church* (Maryknoll, NY: Orbis Books, 2016), xx.

[8]Malina, *Diaries*, 368.

[9]Judith Malina with John Bredin, "A Conversation with Judith Malina," *Public Voice Salon*, January 13, 2013, YouTube video, 56:50, www.youtube. com.

[10]Stéphanette Vendeville, *Le Living Theatre: De la toile à la scène, 1945–1985* (Paris: L'Harmattan, 2007), 19–20; Malina, *Diaries*, 30; Interview with Judith Malina by Cindy Rosenthal, "Judith Malina," Dorot Jewish Division, *New York Public Library Digital Collections*, Tape 1-4, Tape 1-42, https:// digitalcollections.nypl.org.

[11]Rosenthal, "Judith Malina," Tape 1-9, 1-10; Malina, *Diaries*, 175.

[12]Malina with Bredin, "A Conversation with Judith Malina."

[13]Judith Malina with Harold Channer, "Judith Malina 01-14-10 Airdate," Harold Channer, January 8, 2010, YouTube video, 57:41, www.youtube.com.

[14]Dorothy Day, *The Duty of Delight: The Diaries of Dorothy Day*, ed. Robert Ellsberg (Milwaukee, WI: Marquette University Press, 2008), 601–2.

[15]Lewis MacAdams, *Birth of the Cool: Beat, Bebop, and the American Avant-Garde* (New York: Free Press, 2001), 213.

[16]Ibid.

[17]Dorothy Day, *On Pilgrimage* (1948; Grand Rapids, MI: Eerdmans, 1999), 207.

[18]See, e.g., Thomas Aquinas, *Summa Theologica*, II-II, Q. 32, Art. 2.

[19]MacAdams, *Birth of the Cool*, 213.

[20]Ibid.

[21]See Terrell W. Marrs, "The Living Theatre: History, Theatrics, and Politics" (master's thesis, Texas Tech University, May 1984), 74–89.

[22]Malina, *Diaries*, 446.

[23]Ibid., 446, 451, 457–58.

[24]Ibid., 456.

[25]Ibid., 453–54.

[26]Ibid., 454.

[27]Rosalie Riegle Troester, ed., *Voices from the Catholic Worker* (Philadelphia: Temple University, 1993), 82, 86.

[28]Judith Malina, "Directing *The Brig*," in *Theater of the Avant-Garde, 1950–2000: A Critical Anthology*, ed. Robert Knopf (New Haven, CT: Yale University Press, 2011), 172.

[29]See David Callaghan, "Ritual Performance and Spirituality in the Work of the Living Theatre, Past and Present," *Theatre Symposium* 21 (2013): 36–53; Christopher Innes, *Holy Theatre: Ritual and the Avant Garde* (New York: Cambridge University, 1981).

[30]Callaghan, "Ritual Performance and Spirituality," 36.

[31]Marrs, "The Living Theatre," 67; Jennifer Buckley, *Beyond Text: Theater and Performance in Print after 1900* (Ann Arbor: University of Michigan Press, 2019), 108–10.

[33]Rosenthal, "Judith Malina," Tape 1-20, Tape 1-21.

[34]Ibid., Tape 1-19.

[35]Martin Buber, *I and Thou*, trans. Ronald Gregor Smith (1958; New York: Scribner Classics, 2000), 108.

[35]Malina, *Diaries*, 140.

[36] Ibid., 276.

[37] Eric Gutkind, *Choose Life: The Biblical Call to Revolt* (New York: Henry Schuman, 1952), 102.

[38] Ibid., 202

[39] Ibid., 78.

[40] Ibid., 91.

[41] Robert Knopf, *Theater of the Avant-Garde, 1950–2000: A Critical Anthology*, ed. Robert Knopf (New Haven, CT: Yale University Press, 2011), 95.

[42] Malina, "Directing *The Brig*," 172.

[43] Ibid, 171–72.

[44] Ibid., 172.

[45] Ibid., 158.

[46] Ibid., 157.

[47] Malina, *Diaries*, 441.

[48] Malina, "Directing *The Brig*," 172.

[49] Malina, *Diaries*, 42.

[50] Malina, "Directing *The Brig*," 172.

[51] Emeline Jouve, "The Living Theatre and the French 1968 Revolution: Of Political and Theatrical Crises," *E-rea* 15, no. 2 (June 15, 2018): http://journals.openedition.org/erea/6370.

[52] Malina, "Directing *The Brig*," 159.

[53] See Jouve, "The Living Theatre and the French 1968 Revolution," para. 25.

[54] Dorothy Day, *Loaves and Fishes* (1963; Maryknoll, NY: Orbis Books, 1997), 175–76.

[55] Ibid., 181–82.

[56] Troester, ed., *Voices from the Catholic Worker*, 86.

Reframing Consumption
in Environmental Ethics
to Empower Agents

Sara Bernard-Hoverstad

It is clear that human beings are consuming at a rate that is unsustainable for planetary health and for our flourishing as a species. In the era of Amazon Prime delivery and groceries that can be ordered without leaving our couches, it has never been quicker or easier to have new consumer goods delivered directly to our doorsteps. The current period of consumption also has well-documented consequences: increasing demand for non-renewables facilitated by extractive industries; widespread exploitation of land and people, particularly in the global south; and enormous piles of waste—including the now immeasurably large floating islands of trash in the Pacific Ocean.[1] The attitudes that lead to this kind of overconsumption are sharply critiqued in Pope Francis's encyclical *Laudato Si'*, in which he derides the ideology of "compulsive consumerism" that has led to "throwaway culture"—which presumes the disposability of goods, of natural resources, and of people—and promotes instead a program of integral ecology for living more sustainably on the earth.[2]

Whereas Francis focuses his remarks about consumerism on the environmental and social impacts of consumption, and rightly so, this essay seeks to situate consumption within the setting of consumer practices. Only by better understanding consumer practices and their social implications will the market be a site capable of reforming the practices that have proved to be so destructive. First, this essay briefly lays out Francis's evaluation of consumerism in *Laudato Si'* and the limitations of this framework. It then situates consumption within the wider context of the consumer practices that structure today's economic activity. The final section argues that a pragmatic strategy to empower agents to engage in market reform is a necessary next step for environmental theology and ethics and is ultimately compatible with Francis's vision of integral ecology.

Consumerism is described in a variety of ways throughout theology and ethics but increasingly is used to indicate a sinful social force at odds with the values promoted by religious practice.[3] Theologian Laura Hartman defines consumerism as "an ideology that sees consumption as an identity-forming, meaning-making activity that rivals religious practice in its importance for humans' sense of self and community."[4] Consumerism, as an ideology or way of life, is then distinct from consumption, which describes the acts or sets of practices by which an agent acquires goods and services. Defining consumerism as an ideology in binary opposition to modes of religious belief identifies it as a moral threat; this is consistent with the many critiques of consumerism lodged by environmental theology and ethics.[5] Though he does see opportunities for sustainability within economic systems, Pope Francis's challenge to consumerism in *Laudato Si'* identifies it as the identify-forming, rival religious ideology in Hartman's definition. Francis refers to consumerism as a culture, one which "prioritizes short-term gain and private interest" at the expense of the long-term common good and suggests it promotes a lifestyle of indifference.[6]

Francis reasons that this lifestyle is fueled by a misguided anthropology and built up by anthropocentrism, practical relativism, and disordered desire.[7] This anthropology is framed by human beings who incorrectly place themselves at the center of being, prioritizing their immediate convenience and assisted by technologies that provide near-immediate gratification while the common good is marginalized. This anthropocentric way of life, Francis finds, illustrates a failure to adequately understand, with humility, that human beings are participants in and not masters of the natural world, and to recognize the ecological and economic limits to the growth we can attain.[8] When people are wrapped up in their own comfort, convenience, and way of life, sinful desire turns inward and greed increases. This further reinforces a lifestyle of insatiable overconsumption.[9]

Because consumerism is fueled by a misguided anthropology, Francis's solution is to turn away from this ideology and prioritize a new way of living. He proposes that human beings "replace consumption with sacrifice, greed with generosity, wastefulness with a spirit of sharing" and recommends ascetic practices to move away from worldly desires and toward God.[10] Throughout the encyclical, Francis articulates the need for personal and communal self-discipline to set limits on growth and to restrain ourselves from overconsuming.[11] Overcoming consumerism requires reorientation and conversion toward a dramatically different anthropology, spirituality, and lifestyle, ones that promote care for others and for the earth.[12]

Laudato Si' makes an important contribution by diagnosing some of the particular values held by consumer culture that are environmentally and socially destructive while envisioning a more just and humane way of life. However, Francis primarily considers the problem of consumerism to be a spiritual crisis, which is insufficient if it is the only frame for diagnosing and mitigating the environmental impact of consumption. Positioning an authentic Christian worldview in opposition to a culturally embedded ideological consumerism makes it difficult to identify a path forward and begin the work of reform within our current system.[13] Religious ethicist Willis Jenkins observes that "an interpretation of market consumerism as a rival religious system . . . can make concrete economic reforms appear less meaningful, perhaps even complicit" in perpetuating a destructive ideology.[14] If the global economic order is so deeply entrenched in the culture of consumerism, then attempts to reform it, rather than replace it, will be considered suspect.

Similarly, an overemphasis on the economic values of another era, for example, the exemplar of St. Francis of Assisi's life of voluntary poverty in the thirteenth century, can present a false perspective of a lost "golden age" of consumption to which we can simply return.[15] Such accounts do not adequately contextualize St. Francis's life within a feudal economic system that bore gross inequalities of its own.[16] Environmental theological and ethical discourse need practical, contemporary examples of reform that are possible to implement in today's economy in order to foster creative opportunities for agents to engage the current system.

Theologian Vincent Miller's account of consumption also challenges perspectives that present consumerism as a competing belief system or as a corruption of Christian doctrine. If this were truly the case, he remarks, Christianity theology would be well prepared to defend itself against the corruptive influence of consumerism, as it has against heresies past. Rather, Miller finds consumerism to be "a cultural system that shows little interest in censoring, editing, or corrupting the contents of religious belief. Any belief, even those most radically critical of capitalism, are embraced with enthusiasm."[17]

Miller's observation that the current economic system tends to absorb critical feedback rather than be threatened by it is evident in the way that the market has responded to challenges from environmentalists. Environmentalists' challenges did little to damage market operations, but did produce a massive new array of consumer goods and services designed to present the market as more environmentally friendly. Since 2000, markets have been flooded with "sustainable" and "green" products, some of which represent genuine changes in production practices and many of which fail to meet basic sustainability standards and compound environmental-economic injustices in the global south.[18] Miller argues that current problems in consumption stem not from veneration of consumerism that supplants authentic Christian religious belief but from a failure of the Christian tradition to adequately connect belief with practice.[19] He finds that Christian believers are trained to be passive consumers of belief, and this passivity leaks into subsequent market relations: Christian consumers who have been moved to act by arguments for sustainability are now able to choose a "green" product on the shelf with little inconvenience rather than insisting on real, systemic reform. Francis acknowledges this problem in *Laudato Si'*: even as ecological sensitivity grows, consumer practices known to be environmentally damaging have not changed.[20] This lends credibility to Miller's claim that an agent's changed belief is not enough to connect them to the practices it would take to enact environmental justice. Miller's diagnosis is to reinscribe agency in both religious belief and consumer practices. In order to do so, theology must better understand how consumption practices operate and how change occurs in the market.

Therefore, environmental theology ought to move away from the loaded language of consumerism, an ideology fueled by a malignant anthropocentric anthropology, to focus on consumption and the practices related to acquiring goods and services. As Jenkins points out, "Consumption is not intrinsically bad or impoverishing, but it is always morally and theologically significant."[21] Treating consumption as significant but not necessarily morally bankrupt gives consumers tools to understand how and why their consumption practices are shaped and enacted. Further, it can empower agents to join in reform movements by opposing certain market practices or engaging in new ones.

There are several different models for understanding consumer behavior. The conventional approach of neoclassical economics makes several key assumptions about consumer society: First, consumers are rational, in that they ascribe to a particular set of values which continuously motivate their choices over time and across market sectors; next, consumers are deliberative and operate to maximize personal utility or well-being; and finally, consumers are independent, in that their consumption choices are based on preferences they have cultivated.[22] According to this model, agents may know that their consumption practices are harmful to others or to the environment, but they continue to selfishly maximize utility for themselves anyway.

In presuming a rational, deliberate, and independent consumer, the conventional model fails to describe certain key patterns in consumer behavior. Competing models challenge consumer independence by arguing that consumption is not independent but social and is not always rational and deliberative but influenced by specific social pressures. Sociologist Pierre Bourdieu found that family and social class play a key role in forming an agent's taste for consumer products. He describes the phenomenon of "conspicuous consumption"—consumption intended to be seen by others—and shows that consumer choices are not just personal but are socially consequential in gaining, maintaining, or losing class status.[23] The social stakes of consumption, for Bourdieu, are not just about egoism and personal utility but have real consequences for an agent's future educational, professional, and familial prospects.[24] Bourdieu's account of consumption is helpful in understanding the value disconnect between those who have ecological or social justice concerns but continue to consume in excess: these concerns do not outweigh competing stakes or structural barriers. Theological accounts of consumption should, therefore, better interrogate the social and cultural dimensions that produce this tension between environmental values and consumer practices.[25] Reforming consumption in these contexts involves finding new and creative opportunities for agents to enact their environmental values.[26]

In the United States, a nation often considered paradigmatic of the materialist and selfish consumption practices leading to environmental degradation, one norm impacting consumption trends is the relationship between the American worker and time. Sociologist Juliet Schor argues that, in recent decades, Americans have increasingly devoted their time to market activities in the following ways: "working longer hours, filling leisure time with activities that require more income per unit of time, and buying, rather than making, more of what they consume."[27] As hours at work increase, wages during this period remain stagnant, which induces the need to work even longer to maintain a lifestyle.[28] More time spent at work means less leisure time to develop skills or to produce goods for oneself, leading to increasing reliance on convenience goods and services. The gig economy was on a growth trajectory even before the COVID-19 pandemic due to trends constraining time and income. This sector of the economy includes workers not traditionally considered in the corporate or institutional structures—artists, musicians, freelance web designers—as well as those whose "gigs" are replacing traditional occupations, such as the prevalence of rideshare app drivers overtaking taxi drivers and on-demand services replacing personal assistants and care workers.[29] In 2018, Gallup reported that 36 percent of the US workforce engages in gig work for full-time employment or supplementary income.[30] While awaiting to see the full impact of COVID-19 on the gig economy, there were early reports in May 2020 of significant booms in grocery delivery services like Instacart.[31]

No circumstances, including trends in work hours in the United States, necessitate the use of gig economy services, a market sector that is fraught with intersecting justice issues.[32] However, this is a good illustration of some of the trade-offs consumers face. Decisions regarding how and what to consume are made in a social context with peers and neighbors who are also navigating similar trade-offs. Therefore, an important job for theology and ethics is to help agents define and attend to the values that inform their everyday consumption practices in the present moment.[33] When we become better informed about how and why we consume, this in turn can motivate us to reform the practices that have destructive social and environmental impacts.

Given the social context in which consumption choices are negotiated, the market should be viewed as a potential site for reforming practices. The social nature of consumption is not reflected in accounts of consumerism that decry it as an ideology opposed to Christian values by emphasizing cultures of anthropocentrism, selfishness, and atomistic individualism. Instead, environmental theology and ethics ought to assist agents in making consumption choices in line with their values in ways that are sensitive to the structural opportunities and constraints consumers face. We can rely on dimensions of Christian anthropology that describe the human being as fundamentally social and relational throughout the whole range of social praxis, including in market relations. For Christian ethics, an important opportunity for consumption reform is employing new strategies within the communities we inhabit, including our faith communities.

A pragmatic strategy targeting environmental justice begins with the sustainable practices of communities.[34] As Jenkins notes, sustainable practices are already employed in many communities of faith and provide the opportunity to understand how communities craft moral responses to social problems. Such engagement with social problems invites communities into new practices, which subsequently influence the way they relate to the market and to one another. The resources they cultivate foster "opportunities for moral agency to bear responsibility for unprecedented problems, and thereby permit moral agents to sustain the meaning of life carried by their tradition of faith."[35] Employing a pragmatic strategy in environmental ethics does important work empowering agents who might, as individuals, feel dwarfed by the scale of the crisis by connecting them with social groups engaging similar shared values. Drawn from communities of faith and broader environmental movements, what follows are four preliminary criteria for a pragmatic, values-led strategy to reform consumer practices.

First of all, environmental movements should focus on making specific interventions to contemporary consumer practices rather than on shifting ideologies. There is value in considering the scale and threat of the environmental crises we face today, but the theological and secular arguments highlighting consumerism as an ideology fail to sufficiently motivate agency and change the practices and systems at fault.[36] An overuse of ideological critiques that identify the present system as corrupt can undermine the legitimacy of consumer movements and economic reforms by leading agents to believe that economic and environmental justice is only possible in a new system, limiting opportunities for engagement in the present.[37] Further, actually involving agents in the work of ecological and social justice can help shape moral imaginations in more impactful ways than rhetoric alone.[38] Finally, a pragmatic approach has the benefit of being able to quickly respond to the urgency of the climate crisis; without needing to reformulate worldviews, new strategies and consumer movements can be implemented with relatively greater ease to address specific problems.

This approach also invites those who are less engaged in ecological and economic justice issues to "buy in" by providing tangible evidence of reform projects in their communities and reasonable opportunities to participate.[39] This approach is not oriented toward changing the aggregate of individual behavior—i.e., more people bringing their canvas bags to the supermarket—but encouraging social movements in specific segments of the market. As Francis indicates, "Social problems must be addressed by community networks and not simply by the sum of individual good deeds. . . . The ecological conversion needed to bring about lasting change is also a community conversion."[40] One example of a community network advocating for change is the Boston Cyclists Union, which successfully lobbied for the expansion of protected bike lanes throughout the city of Boston to prevent accidents involving motor vehicles and bicycles, thereby make biking a safer and more enticing option for the city's commuters.[41] Though perhaps originally motivated by an underlying environmental concern—reducing carbon emissions—the group identified the need to address the public safety concern by rebuilding specific infrastructure to make a non-emitting commuting option more feasible for more people.

Second, a pragmatic strategy recognizes that economic and environmental justice are closely linked.[42] Though environmentalists may be suspicious of market-based responses to the climate crisis, it is critical that the market is viewed not only as an obstacle to environmental justice but also as a site for change. Furthermore, environmental justice rhetoric sometime fails to compel those who are not already activists when they highlight problems that are faraway geographically and temporally.[43] For example, decades of "Save the Polar Bears" campaigns from environmental groups in the United States captivated the attention of the white middle class but failed to adequately motivate lower-income communities and people of color.[44] Leveraging multiple strategies and relating intersecting justice issues allows for greater participation and engagement.

Community Supported Agriculture, or CSA, programs often articulate a dual motivation of environmental and economic justice. The nonprofit organization New Entry Food Hub articulates its mission as aiming "to build long term economic self-reliance and food security among farmers in eastern Massachusetts and their communities, and to expand access to healthy and culturally appropriate foods in underserved areas through production of locally grown foods."[45] This organization addresses the economic justice issues faced by small farmers who experience increased price competition from industrial farms as well as the needs of low-income and migrant communities who often lack access to affordable, healthy food. It also promotes environmental standards by emphasizing low-pesticide farming methods and, by growing a local distribution network, reduces the distance that produce usually travels from conventional farms to our grocery stores and homes.

Third, shifting from language of moral or spiritual conversion to focus on practices mirrors trends within environmental movements to limit language of "sacrifice" and "consuming less" in favor of "consumption equity." It is possible for an individual concerned about their own environmental impact to spend an enormous amount of time scrupulously reducing their own carbon emissions, sourcing food locally, dramatically reducing waste, and only acquiring new goods from used or second-hand stores.[46] While such practices are laudable, they over-accentuate the responsibility borne by individuals to reduce their personal consumption and can lead to a culture of competitive ecopiety available only to those with the time and the means to pursue such a lifestyle.[47] Shifting from emphasis on individual sacrifice of certain consumer goods and practices to consumption equity— ensuring that everyone has access to the basic goods and services they need to survive— is an important narrative change and a means to link environmental and economic justice movements. Expanding access to affordable food and housing are critical environmental and economic issues worth the time investment an agent might otherwise spend reducing personal consumption.

And fourth, political consumption movements are an additional strategy in a repertoire of resistance employed to disrupt conventional modes of consumption. They can include opting out (boycotting) or opting in ("buycotting") to purchasing certain consumer goods and services. Theologian Luke Bretherton refers to political consumption as a "nonrevolutionary attempt to restructure [consumer practices] by utilizing what is at hand."[48] Political consumption movements attempt to reform, rather than replace, the current economic system by pointing out moral contradictions in the current system. Francis voices his support for boycotts in that they are "successful in changing the way businesses operate" by interrogating corporate environmental footprints and social impact.[49] Political consumption movements are often motivated by a combination of economic and environmental justice concerns—fair wages, public health, and sustainability standards—and seek to impose different values in the marketplace. The clear articulation of values motivating political consumption movements has made these movements particularly successful in engaging faith communities in this type of resistance.[50]

A pragmatic strategy aimed at shifting consumption practices through social and consumer movements employs a different point of departure from the ideological strategies but is ultimately consistent with Pope Francis's goal of integral ecology. Francis insists that integral ecology has environmental, economic, and social dimensions. Just as ecological reality is connected in an intricate web of life, social, economic, and environmental concerns contribute to a complex crisis.[51] He draws attention to the importance of social institutions, including the family, in building relationships to address intersecting crises, indicating the insufficiency of individual conversion alone.[52]

By design, a pragmatic strategy employed in environmental ethics regarding consumption does not have an overarching cosmology or system of values. Pragmatic approaches, therefore, are sometimes critiqued by theology as instrumentalizing religious thought for secular ends.[53] Therefore, it is significant that a pragmatic strategy could be compatible with Francis's vision of integral ecology, as it is rooted in the Christian tradition. Integral ecology draws on integral development in Catholic social teaching, which asserts that Christian values play an essential role in building a good society and promoting authentic human development.[54] This view is rooted in a relational anthropology and views development of the whole person as essential to build up just societies.[55] Integral ecology also draws on Gustavo Gutiérrez's concept of integral liberation, which similarly challenges the rhetoric of economic development and affirms that environmental justice must hear *"both the cry of the earth and the cry of the poor."*[56] Drawing on the values expressed in liberation theology and Catholic social teaching can help social movements remain grounded in a Christian value system and a relational anthropology as they respond to the pressing concerns of ecological and economic justice.

Although it is important for environmental theology and ethics to work against the worldviews that produce environmental degradation, it is just as critical to understand how specific consumer practices are developed and identify possible strategies for change. The preliminary criteria for a pragmatic approach to reforming consumer practices remains limited in its ability to meet all of the structural barriers to environmental justice but gives a sample of what kinds of work are possible for agents who feel the call to work toward sustainability but have been frustrated in their efforts to live out this call in tangible ways. The market should therefore be considered an important site for reforming consumer practices in order to forward the work of ecological and economic justice.

Notes

[1]"Great Pacific Garbage Patch," *National Geographic*, revised July 5, 2019, https://www.nationalgeographic.org/encyclopedia/great-pacific-garbage-patch/.

[2]Pope Francis, *Laudato Si'* – "On Care for Our Common Home" (2015), www.vatican.va, §16, 22. Hereinafter *LS*.

[3]Kenneth R. Himes identifies three understandings of consumerism: as a favorable social movement upholding the rights of consumers; as a descriptor of the ideology by which market capitalism operates; and as a way of life, subject to moral scrutiny. He notes that this final way of understanding is of greatest interest to moral theology, and it is the operative use of consumer-

ism in this essay. Himes, "Consumerism and Christian Ethics," *Theological Studies* 68, no. 1 (2007): 133.

[4]Laura M. Hartman, "Consumption," in *Routledge Handbook of Religion and Ecology*, ed. Willis Jenkins, Mary Evelyn Tucker, and John Grim (New York: Routledge, 2017), 317.

[5]For a prominent take on this topic, see Sallie McFague, *Blessed Are the Consumers: Climate Change and the Practice of Restraint* (Minneapolis: Fortress, 2013). See also Mark Graham's challenge of the widespread critique of consumerism functioning as an ideology in Christian ecotheologies: Graham, "The Environmental Burden (Disaster?) of Catholic Act Analysis," *Political Theology* 10, no. 1 (2009): 101–14.

[6]*LS*, §§184, 232.

[7]*LS*, §§122, 123. Here, Francis draws from *Evangelii Gaudium* to define practical relativism as consistent with "acting as if God did not exist, making decisions as if the poor did not exist, setting goals as if others did not exist, working as if people who have not received the Gospel did not exist." See Francis, "On the Proclamation of the Gospel in Today's World, *Evangelii Gaudium*" (November 24, 2013), §80, www.vatican.va.

[8]*LS*, §§106, 116.

[9]*LS*, §204. Some economic theories revolve around this similar image of the human, going so far as to argue that the human species, *Homo sapiens*, are better considered *Homo economicus* in the modern era due to our obsession with consumption.

[10]*LS*, §9.

[11]*LS*, §105.

[12]*LS*, §208. In §217, Francis also refers to this as "ecological conversion."

[13]*LS*, §112. Francis argues here for a "non-consumerist model of life" which again frames consumerism as something antithetical to his project.

[14]Willis Jenkins, *The Future of Ethics: Sustainability, Social Justice, and Religious Creativity* (Washington, DC: Georgetown University Press, 2013), 257.

[15]See, for example, the sixteen references to St. Francis of Assisi in *Laudato Si'*.

[16]Anthropogenic (human-created) climate change is a problem of modernity, but a great number of other social injustices and inequities existed in the thirteenth century, which makes a cultural shift to those standards undesirable and impractical. Pope Francis acknowledges that he does not recommend turning back technological advancement to the "Stone Age" but does not offer much more by way of guidance when deploying moral exemplars from this period. *LS* §114.

[17]Vincent J. Miller, *Consuming Religion: Christian Faith and Practice in a Consumer Culture* (New York: Continuum, 2004), 4–5.

[18]This strategy is known as "greenwashing." Cynthia D. Moe-Lobeda, "Climate Change as Climate Debt: Forging a Just Future," *Journal of the Society of Christian Ethics* 36, no. 1 (2016): 30.

[19]Miller, *Consuming Religion*, 12.

[20]*LS*, §55.

[21]Jenkins, *The Future of Ethics*, 258.

[22]This is also known as the rational choice model. Juliet B. Schor, "Towards a New Politics of Consumption," in *The Consumer Society Reader*, ed.

Juliet B. Schor and Douglas B. Holt (New York: New Press, 2000): 452–54.

[23]Pierre Bourdieu, *Distinction: A Social Critique of the Judgement of Taste* (Cambridge, MA: Harvard University Press, 1984), 31.

[24]This model deeply implicates the social inequality of consumption practices. Bourdieu, *Distinction*, 106–12.

[25]David Cloutier's theological study of luxury in the Christian tradition does an adept job highlighting the social and political impact of consumer choices. Cloutier, *The Vice of Luxury: Economic Excess in a Consumer Age* (Washington, DC: Georgetown University Press, 2015).

[26]Jenkins, *The Future of Ethics*, 257.

[27]Juliet B. Schor, *Plenitude: The New Economics of True Wealth* (New York: Penguin, 2010), 4.

[28]We ought also to consider how difficult it can be in certain professions to transition from full-time to part-time work and/or to make decisions about one's home and family life without adequate parental leave and part-time work provisions.

[29]Some of these services include TaskRabbit for errands; Care.com for child, elder, or pet care; and the aptly named "PeoplePerHour" for freelance and consulting work.

[30]"The Gig Economy and Alternative Work Arrangements," *Gallup*, 2018, https://www.gallup.com/workplace/240878/gig-economy-paper-2018.aspx.

[31]Ellen Huet and Lizette Chapman, "Instacart's Frantic Dash From Grocery App to Essential Service," *Bloomberg*, May 6, 2020, www.bloomberg.com.

[32]Some of the justice issues at stake in on-demand services include the overproduction of waste through use of disposable packaging; lack of adequate personal protective equipment (PPE) and worker protections for grocery delivery workers during the COVID-19 pandemic; lack of sick and vacation leave; and variability in income, rendering some full-time workers unable to earn a living wage.

[33]Conor M. Kelly's recent monograph argues that what agents do in what is generally considered their private lives or free time is morally significant and should be integrated into social ethics. Kelly, *The Fullness of Free Time: A Theological Account of Leisure and Recreation in the Moral Life* (Washington, DC: Georgetown University Press, 2020). Additionally, Kate Ward's work on moral luck and the virtues extrapolates on the challenge of developing virtues in communities of constrained agency. Ward, "Toward a Christian Virtue Account of Moral Luck," *Journal of the Society of Christian Ethics* 38, no. 1 (2018): 133–34.

[34]The pragmatism indicated here draws on Cornel West's prophetic pragmatism, as adapted by Willis Jenkins. Jenkins, *The Future of Ethics*, 9.

[35]Jenkins, *The Future of Ethics*, 81.

[36]There is parallel literature in secular and philosophical environmental rhetoric encountering the same failure to motivate agency against the ideology of consumerism as seen in the theological account described here. See, for example, Douglas B. Holt, "Constructing Sustainable Consumption: From Ethical Values to the Cultural Transformation of Unsustainable Markets," *AAPSS* 644 (November 2012): 236–55.

[37]Jenkins, *The Future of Ethics*, 8, 257.

[38]Ibid., 74.

[39]Douglas B. Holt, "Why the Sustainable Economy Movement Hasn't Scaled: Toward a Strategy That Empowers Main Street," in *Sustainable Lifestyles and the Quest for Plenitude: Case Studies in the New Economy*, ed. Juliet B. Schor and Craig J. Thompson (New Haven, CT: Yale University Press, 2014), 222.

[40]*LS*, §219.

[41]The examples provided here are specific to the author's geographic location, but could be scaled to other regions via comparable programs and movements. "Mission, Vision, and Values," *Boston Cyclists Union*, accessed March 12, 2021, https://bostoncyclistsunion.org/.

[42]Cynthia D. Moe-Lobeda, *Resisting Structural Evil: Love as Ecological-Economic Vocation* (Minneapolis: Fortress, 2013), 197.

[43]Holt, "Why the Sustainable Economy Movement Hasn't Scaled," 223.

[44]Amanda J. Baugh, *God and the Green Divide: Religious Environmentalism in Black and White* (Oakland: University of California Press, 2017), 39.

[45]This nonprofit was previously known as "World PEAS." "New Entry Food Hub," *New Entry Sustainable Farming Project, Tufts University*, accessed March 12, 2021, https://nesfp.org/foodhub.

[46]Holt, "Why the Sustainable Economy Movement Hasn't Scaled," 224.

[47]The very useful phrase "ecopiety" is described by Sarah McFarland Taylor in *Ecopiety: Green Media and the Dilemma of Environmental Virtue* (New York: New York University Press, 2019). The "freegan" subculture in New York City is an example of such competitive ecopiety. Participants in the "freegan" movement distinguish themselves from other New York City residents by choosing not to purchase any goods but rely on a time-intensive strategy of dumpster diving, Craigslist, and Buy Nothing groups on social media to meet their material needs. This subculture is dominated by white people of means and is competitive and exclusionary based on its commitment to not purchasing. See Alex V. Barnard, "Making the City 'Second Nature': Freegan 'Dumpster Divers' and the Materiality of Morality," *American Journal of Sociology* 121, no. 4 (January 2016): 1017–50.

[48]Luke Bretherton, *Christianity and Contemporary Politics: The Conditions and Possibilities of Faithful Witness* (Malden, MA: Wiley-Blackwell, 2010), 178.

[49]*LS*, §206.

[50]Mark Dawson, "Justice and Demonstration of Christian Principles: Why Churchgoers Support Fair Trade," *Expository Times* 131, no. 8 (2020): 354.

[51]*LS*, §139.

[52]*LS*, §142, 232.

[53]Jenkins, *The Future of Ethics*, 68.

[54]Pope Benedict XVI, "On Integral Human Development in Charity and Truth, *Caritas in Veritate*" (2009), www.vatican.va, §4.

[55]Pope Paul VI, "On the Development of Peoples, *Populorum Progressio*" (1967), www.vatican.va, §14.

[56]*LS*, §49, emphasis in the original. This argument is developed by Daniel P. Castillo, "Integral Ecology as a Liberationist Concept," *Theological Studies* 77, no. 2 (2016): 353–76.

"The Shadow's the Thing"

Annie Dillard's Flinching Vision and Faltering Artistry

Andrew Staron

"Evolution loves death more than it loves you or me," Annie Dillard says in passing in *Pilgrim at Tinker Creek*. "This is easy to write, easy to read, and hard to believe. The words are simple, the concept clear—but you don't believe it, do you? Nor do I. How could I, when we're both so lovable?"[1] Such recoil is not particular to this passage, and as often as Annie Dillard's attention to pain, suffering, and death is called "unflinching," she does, in fact, flinch. She does not ultimately look away, to be sure, but neither is she comfortable. Her entire corpus works to draw our attention to that reactive flinch, the impact that such harrowing visions make upon our own spirits, and the language with which we try to describe them.

This essay looks to Dillard's three primary works (*Pilgrim at Tinker Creek*, *Holy the Firm*, and *For the Time Being*) and her insights into the creative process to consider the disconcerting and disorienting effect of her writing and what it asks of her readers.[2] It follows possible responses to two sets of questions. First, what might Dillard be saying about nature as creation? That is, how do we reconcile a brutal, excessively fecund, it-doesn't-care-about-you-and-me nature with the idea that we are created by a God who is not all-bad and has even peppered creation with real marvels, real beauty? These questions, older than the Book of Job, are inescapable when reading Dillard. However, Dillard offers no systematic attempt to justify suffering and death, nor does she suggest the possibility that her readers might come to some resolution to the tension between life and death, hope and fear, or, as Seamus Heaney puts it, the marvelous and the murderous.[3] What she does, though, is to confront her readers with their own desire to look away from that which is murderous and that which is marvelous (for she pauses before signs of life, too). Where excesses force themselves on us and there is no decisive meaning to be won, her artistry is in nimble navigation of that tension, performatively faltering where others might seek escape.

Second, what is Dillard asking of her readers? Even as Dillard stands fast against any conceptual reconciliation of these tensions, she does imply the need for a response on our part, for some work to embrace the world as it is—to redeem death (or at least our fear of its meaninglessness) and in so doing, redeem our humanity as well. I propose that this work begins with recognizing the goodness of "flinching" before excess. For there is danger in gazing unflinchingly, if nonetheless sympathetically, at the murderous, meaningless, unabated suffering of the world. An unflinching look is not compassionate, and it certainly does not itself impel us to act. I suggest that in her flinch and falter, Dillard offers her reader an image of God as a hidden artist, who, in turn, invites us not only to be attentive to this creation but also to bless and hallow it.

Throughout all her writing, Dillard's quick shifts in tone, topic, and mood are easy to recognize and feel. Sometimes harshly, often humorously, but never without a sharpness, she makes us *read* the tension she sees in the world, tension she wants us then *to feel*. What is present though perhaps less immediately pronounced—but what ultimately drives her point—is the frequency with which she addresses her readers directly. Her use of the second person is noticeable throughout her writing as she seems to continually ask us: *And you, what do you make of this? What do you fear, what do you hope, and what are you willing to overlook in order to be comfortable?* For instance, she inquires in *For the Time Being*, ostensibly offhandedly: "What were you doing on April 30, 1991, when a series of waves drowned 138,000 people? Where were you when you first heard the astonishing, heart-breaking news? Who told you? . . . Who did you tell? Did your anguish last days or weeks?"[4] Without saying it, she implies a self-condemnation: These deaths had no effect on you.

She begins *For the Time Being* rather shockingly with a summary of severe human birth defects—"bird-headed dwarfs" with "moderate to severe mental deficiency" who "cannot straighten their legs," whose six-year-old faces are the size of a doctor's thumb. She asks: Can we love these children who, themselves, are capable of love? Can we bless their creation, saying with the God of Genesis, *It is good,* even as they themselves realize their own fates, their futures?[5] She writes: "You cannot turn a page in *Smith's Recognizable Patterns of Human Malformation* without your heart's pounding from simple terror. . . . You cannot brace yourself. Will this particular baby live? What do you hope?"[6] The impact on the attentive reader is forceful. She asks us—you—to be honest about your own pretensions to care and the temptation to detachment masquerading as compassion: Do you hope that such a child lives, or is some part of you hoping for a so-called merciful death so that its life might no longer haunt you?

She asks you to imagine the rationale of life not your own. "You" she writes, " . . . are God. You want to make a forest, something to hold to soil, lock up solar energy, and give off oxygen. Wouldn't it be simpler just to rough in a slab of chemicals, a green acre of goo?" You are a retired railroad worker; you are a starling; you are a sculptor; you are a chloroplast.[7] She invites you to take seriously your apathy to beauty and terror. She concludes the description of a birth by asking, "How many centuries would you have to live before this, and thousands like it every day, ceased to astound you?"[8] She suggests, as noted above, that maybe you should experience some anguish at the death of 138,000 people.

As people often do standing beside the grave, Dillard turns to ritual for instruction both about what is actually happening and for direction toward a way of proceeding, concluding *Pilgrim at Tinker Creek*, with a turn to chapter 19 of the Book of Numbers and the "waters of separation."[9] These waters result from a ritual involving the mixing of a sacrificed, unblemished red heifer; cedar wood; hyssop; and scarlet yarn. They are splashed upon anyone who has become unclean by contact with human death—even contact with the least bone of the corpse. Perhaps it can be comforting to draw such a line of separation: the unclean there, the clean here. But Dillard insists that even as she might carefully avoid reaching out to a corpse, such separation is not possible. "[T]he bone touched me," she avows.[10] Death haunts life; the line we hope stands between life and death simply isn't there.

Dillard never turns apologetically to an already arrived messiah for salvation from death, which stubbornly maintains its sting. Whatever her own faith, there is no Risen Christ in her work, no accomplished defeat of death. When Christ does appear, it is through the luminous matter transfigured by his immanence[11] or as baptized, sanctifying and being sanctified by water.[12] He appears as the Eucharistic elements of growth and diminishment from Teilhard's "Mass on the World"[13] and while hanging on the cross.[14] He is the unsettlingly ordinary bottle of wine Dillard buys for a communion service ("Christ with a cork").[15] The only suggestion of a possible saving Jesus is in her hint that he might be the one who brings together immanence and transcendence, as the prototype of the artist, tying the heights of our hope to the "holy firmament" at the absolute base of creation.[16]

Instead of to a Christian messiah, Dillard's "holy" is as often as not rooted in Jewish mysticism. In her book, *A Literary Shema*, Lori A. Kanitz makes the convincing case that for all Dillard's embrace of Christian mystics, she is also deeply shaped by Kabbalistic and Hasidic traditions. Kanitz comprehensively illustrates Dillard's debt to Rabbi Isaac Luria's creation mythology in which God makes a "place" for creation by withdrawing Godself—by inhaling (a contraction which, among other things, allows for a "latent potential for evil").[17] The following movement of divine exhaling sets creation into motion. So God makes creation a visible manifestation of divine love by limiting Godself—presence revealed in absence. This exhaling, the Baal Shem Tov speculates, encases the sparks of divine light in the shells of created things, imbuing all of nature with immanent, if hidden, holiness. Dillard follows this mysticism in tying this process to God's own exile in creation—absent from Godself, wandering the world with us, breathing creation into being through withdrawing and giving of Godself over to the material world.

Elaborating on this divine contraction which makes space for creation, Dillard is attentive to the play of presence and absence. Early in *Pilgrim at Tinker Creek*, she reflects on stories of the first people to regain sight after the perfection of cataract surgery:

When a newly sighted girl saw photographs and paintings, she asked, "why do they put those dark marks all over them?" "Those aren't dark marks," her mother explained, "those are shadows. That is one of the ways the eye knows that things have shape. If it were not for shadows many things would look flat." "Well, that's how things do look," Joan answered. "Everything looks flat with dark patches."[18]

"The shadow's the thing," Dillard says elsewhere, perhaps playing on both the colloquial sense of "that which matters" and the sense of presence itself.[19] It is the darkness, the absence that gives shape to presence, certainly. But the shadow's value is not simply in its utility. She continues: "It could be that we are not seeing something,"[20] not that there is some *thing* that we are missing (if only we had the eyes to see!) but that the thing itself is a matter of *not seeing*. Somehow, what is to be seen is absence itself and not merely a lack of presence.

Kanitz's work is helpful here as she turns to the Jewish traditions of looking at both the dark letters of the Torah and the white spaces around them. "It came to be suggested that the Torah was 'black fire' written on the 'white fire' of the arm of God himself. The white spaces become synonymous with the Holy One."[21] Kanitz notes an echo of this in Dillard's own care for the appearance of every page in *Holy the Firm* and *For the Time Being*, both showing the author's deliberate choice for much more blank space on each page than in a comparable book.[22] The space serves not simply as an indifferent emptiness on which to print words, but it guides the reader in reading. It slows the eye, gives a moment for breath, and invites contemplation of that which is not word.

"The gaps are the thing," Dillard says later, summoning the reader's mind at various times to the gaps from which Moses sees the back of God (Ex 33:18–23), the "gap" in God in which creation appears, and in fissures in meaning that abide no matter the dedication and deftness of our attempt to repair our understanding.[23] Presence and absence, text and space, play throughout her work. We might consider, as an example, her description of the copperhead she noticed was sunning itself unsettlingly close to her as she sat on a rock:

I noticed its tail. It tapered to nothingness. I started back at the head and slid my eye down its body slowly: taper,

taper, taper, scales, tiny scales, air. . . . It was a thickening of the air spread from a tip, a rush into being, eyeball and blood, through a pin-hole rent. Every other time I had seen this rock it had been a flat sandstone rock over the quarry pond; now it hosted and bore this chunk of fullness that parted the air around it like a driven wedge. I looked at it from the other direction. From tail to head it spread like the lines of a crescendo, widening from stillness to a turgid blast; then at the bulging jaws it began contracting again, diminuendo, till at the tip of its snout the lines met back at the infinite point that corners every angle, and that space once more ceased being a snake.[24]

The fullness of the snake is revealed by—and reveals—the surrounding space that is not snake. The absence around the form takes its invisible shape in the snake's diminuendo. The invisible is not unmasked but revealed as invisible through the visible created world. With the messianic arrival always deferred, there no escaping the mediation of the material world. And yet even the idea of *mediation* is misleading, as there is no "hidden meaning" to uncover behind, underneath, or beyond creation but only a God whose apparent absence provokes questions about the possibility of God's meaningful touch.

By what sense, reason, or even faith can we hope in a hidden meaning of creation? One that is not to be discovered and presented for all to see but one *that stays hidden* and is only meaningful as mystery? In one of her final original published paragraphs, Dillard turns to theologian Pierre Teilhard de Chardin. She quotes: "In our hands, the hands of all of us, the world and life—our world, our life—'are placed like a Host, ready to be charged with the divine influence. . . . The mystery will be accomplished.'"[25] What does this mean, "to accomplish mystery"? Not, to be sure, to unravel it, to shine light on the shadows, to stop the tapering of the snake's tail into the full invisibility of the air. Perhaps this is a matter of accomplishing mystery *as* mystery.

Art suggests a possible path toward such accomplishment. Dillard observes:

[Intellectuals] discover that in order to write fiction that anybody might want to read, they must painstakingly conceal what is to them the very point. (Here is the germ of truth in that funny, sweet saying of the ignorant, that the function of criticism in general, and of freshman critical essays in particular, is to "find the hidden meaning.") In order to make a world in which their ideas might be discovered, writers embody those ideas in materials solid and opaque, and thus conceal them. In the process of fleshing out a thought, they brick it in. The more subtle they are as artists (not as thinkers, but as artists), the more completely their structures will vanish into the work, and the more grouchy they will become the more readers tell them what lovely, solid bricks they make.[26]

The way of the artist, Dillard insists, is one of vanishing through self-emptying. "One of the things I know about writing is this: spend it all, shoot it, play it, lose it, all, right away, every time. . . . Anything you do not give freely and abundantly becomes lost to you. You open your safe and find ashes."[27] Successful art is a matter of holding nothing back, not the smallest idea and particularly not a "self" protected from creative fire.

In what is perhaps her most acclaimed passage, Dillard turns to this annihilation of the self, provoking later reflection on the choice to so sacrifice. "One night a moth flew into the candle, was caught, burnt dry, and held."[28] Circling around fire, *Holy the Firm* weaves together the process of writing, the burnt face of a young girl (whom Dillard names Julie Norwich), and the burning of the moth, whose "moving wings ignited like tissue paper," whose "moth-essence"—a "spectacular skeleton—began to act as a wick." Dillard continues: "She kept burning. The wax rose in the moth's body from her soaking abdomen to her thorax to the jagged hole where her head should be. . . . The moth's head was fire. . . . She burned for two hours without changing, without bending or leaning, only glowing within."[29] She parries the already striking impact of the narrative itself, redirecting the story's power to a classroom where she asks her students, "Which of you want to give your lives to be writers?"[30] The reverberations of her question might unsettle the naïve and underprepared: Who can become faceless for the sake of the work's face? "How can people think that artists seek a name? . . . There is no such thing as an artist: there is only the world, lit or unlit as the light allows. When the candle is burning, who looks at the wick? When the candle is out, who needs it? But the world without light is wasteland and chaos, and a life without sacrifice is abomination."[31] If you hold on to what you can instead give, then the real abomination for the artist is desolate pretension of a self that can be kept in reserve and held back from creation. The artist gives themself over to the work, and the better the artist the more they are consumed by creative fire, the more the artist cannot be found apart from the work.

She returns frequently to the language of flame: "The whole show has been on fire from the word go. I come down to the water to cool my eyes. But everywhere I look I see fire; that which isn't flint is tinder, and the whole world sparks and flames."[32] If creation is aflame, then it might be that the creator is the wick. And the superlatively subtle divine artist gives everything over to the art and is, for better or often for worse, hidden within. There is no God accessible outside of the work—which is creation itself, perhaps here presented as both noun and verb.

Yet such accessibility is, itself, shadowed. A noticeably bewildered Dillard quotes Simone Weil: The evidence of divine mercy here below "is the complete absence of mercy here below." "How this proves his mercy," Dillard quips, "I don't understand."[33] The potent implication of Dillard's confession is the turn to the reader: Can *you* understand? Can you venture anything toward these gaps, toward accomplishing mystery as mystery which somehow might hint at God's merciful presence? Certainly, such accomplishment cannot be the "discovery" of meaning, not if we are looking for an idea upon which we can stand at the end of the day. There is nothing creation points *to* except, at the most, the shadows that give it its texture and form or the shadows that receive their textureless formlessness by the presence around them. There is no messiah who comes to sweep us from the gaps over which we hang suspended. Dillard's Christ hangs there, too, nailed beside us.[34] God burns in and through creation, or creation burns with God; either way, we get the flame.

So what, then, is our work? What is *your* work? Despite possible criticism that Dillard ignores the ethical implications of her observations,[35] and is only concerned with what is going on around her as a vehicle to consider what is going on in her head, her compact question late in *For the Time Being* is direct and practical: "How to live?"[36] Dillard asks, her writing tapering to a point at the end of *For the Time Being*. What happens when we are in the gap, when the shadows overtake us, when we touch death, or when the dead bone touches us? How to live now, when redemption is, itself, only a shadow of the death always already there, like the copperhead on the rock?

For all its attention to beauty and to stark desolation—to burnt earth, burnt moths, and a burnt little girl named Julie Norwich[37]—Dillard's work does not actually say anything new, not if we look for innovative answers to long-asked questions. But like much good art, the point is not so much the articulation of a new message to understand as the gift of an arresting vision to compel.

Her art flinches before suffering and falters in its path around meaning, refusing to reveal hiddenness except as hidden, except as the tearing which impels us to act. It flinches because there is no one else visible here to whom we can pass the responsibility to accomplish this mystery. We do not unveil holy hiddenness so we might point, confidently, to clean and pure *there* where God is visible, to a *there* where we might rest. "To accomplish mystery" is never an escape from death nor a completion of a task. It is a blessing of creation as it is—an affirmation with the God of Genesis and with an exhausted Job that this creation is ravaged by death, and it is, too, in some way passing understanding, good and holy.

But we are not left alone in this work; there is precedent. Dillard observes: "The Talmud specifies a certain blessing a man says when he sees a person deformed from birth. . . . The blessing for this occasion . . . is 'Blessed art Thou, O Lord, our God, King of the Universe, WHO CHANGES THE CREATURES.' "[38] We affirm the goodness of God and of our transformations, not for God's sake but for ours. Indeed, such blessing is also for the sake of others. We might even come to hope to be so changed—enkindled even—by repeating such a prayer that names creation—however different, damaged, frayed, or haunted—as holy just as its Creator, hidden, is holy.

Wrapping up *For the Time Being*, she writes: "Now, in striped prison clothes on his cot, Dietrich Bonhoeffer is writing a letter to express his—outdated and perhaps when all is said and done, even accurate—belief that the 'theological category' between God and human fate is 'blessing.' He hopes someone will find a moment to untie his thought."[39] Whatever the fullness of Bonhoeffer's vision, Dillard's involves ultimately a call to be changed into those who flinch and so still speak a blessing, not to transcend the tear but to sit with it, as we sit with a dying friend, through a ministry of presence with nothing to accomplish but to be there in the shadow. We bless amid suffering in shadows and the deathly gaps before the invisible presence of God hidden in the flames of creation. Such active creativity does not mend the rents in meaning. It does not make all things new. But the shadows give us the task to flinch and still speak a response to the shadows we cannot avoid: *Blessed are you, God, who changes us, the creatures, so that we might be merciful.*

Notes

[1] Annie Dillard, *Pilgrim at Tinker Creek* (New York: Harper Collins, 2013), 177–78.

[2] Ibid.; Annie Dillard, *Holy the Firm* (New York: Harper Perennial, 1998); Annie Dillard, *For the Time Being* (New York: Vintage, 2000).

[3] Seamus Heaney, "Crediting Poetry," *The Nobel Prize*, December 7, 1995, www.nobelprize.org.

[4] Dillard, *For the Time Being*, 107.

[5] Ibid., 63–66.

[6] Ibid., 6.

[7] Dillard, *Pilgrim at Tinker Creek*, 131–32.

[8] Dillard, *For the Time Being*, 36.

[9] Dillard, "The Waters of Separation," in *Pilgrim at Tinker Creek*, 265–77.

[10] Dillard, *Pilgrim at Tinker Creek*, 272.

[11] Dillard, *Holy the Firm*, 64–66.

[12] Ibid., 66–68.

[13] Dillard, *For the Time Being*, 202.

[14] Ibid., 169.

[15] Dillard, *Holy the Firm*, 63.

[16] Ibid., 68–72.

[17] Lori A. Kanitz, *A Literary Shema* (Eugene, OR: Pickwick, 2020), 17.

[18] Ibid., 28–29.

[19] Dillard, *Pilgrim at Tinker Creek*, 63.

[20] Ibid., 27.

[21] Kanitz, *A Literary Shema*, 127.

[22] Ibid., 93–94.

[23] Dillard, *Pilgrim at Tinker Creek*, 274.

[24] Ibid., 228–229.

[25] Dillard, *For the Time Being*, 202.

[26] Annie Dillard, *Living by Fiction* (New York: Harper Perennial, 2000), 155–56.

[27] Annie Dillard, *The Writing Life* (New York: Harper Perennial, 2013), 79.

[28] Dillard, *Holy the Firm*, 16.

[29] Ibid., 17.

[30]Ibid., 18.

[31]Ibid., 71–72.

[32]Dillard, *Pilgrim at Tinker Creek*, 11.

[33]Dillard, *For the Time Being*, 164.

[34]Ibid., 169.

[35]For instance, Dillard offers descriptive accounts of the dynamics of race, class, and gender in her memoir, *An American Childhood* (New York: Harper & Row, 1987), without venturing toward criticism of socioeconomic systems.

[36]Dillard, *For the Time Being*, 156.

[37]Dillard names the girl "Julie Norwich" in an oblique reference to the late-fourteenth/early-fifteenth-century mystic, Julian of Norwich, who encountered Christ in her suffering.

[38]Dillard, *For the Time Being*, 5–6.

[39]Ibid., 198.

Contributors

Sara Bernard-Hoverstad is a fourth-year doctoral candidate in theological ethics at Boston College. Her research focuses on ecological ethics, sustainability, and moral agency.

Derek Brown researches in contemporary political theology. Specifically, and as his dissertation explores, he is interested in contributing to the development of a political theology responsive to the theoretical and political challenges of postmodernity. His writing has been published in *Black Theology, The Journal of Speculative Philosophy, Philosophy and Theology,* and elsewhere.

Cynthia L. Cameron is the Patrick and Barbara Keenan Chair in Religious Education at the University of St. Michael's College at the University of Toronto. Her research focuses on adolescence, particularly female adolescence, in feminist theological anthropology, developmental psychology, and practices of Catholic schooling and religious education. Her most recent research will appear in the forthcoming volume *Conceptualizing the Outcomes of Religious Education,* edited by Jon A. Levisohn, which reflects on Catholic, Jewish, and Muslim approaches to religious education.

Colleen Mary Carpenter is a professor of theology and women's studies at Saint Catherine University in Saint Paul, MN. She holds an MA in English from the University of Wisconsin-Madison, and an MA in theology and PhD in religion and literature from the University of Chicago Divinity School. She is the author of *Redeeming the Story: Women, Suffering, and Christ,* and she is the editor of the 2015 CTS Annual Volume, *An Unexpected Wilderness: Christianity and the Natural World.*

Jessica Coblentz is an assistant professor in the department of religious studies and theology at Saint Mary's College in Notre Dame, Indiana. She is the author of *Dust in the Blood: A Theology of Life with Depression* (Liturgical, 2022). Her research on mental health in theological perspective and on feminist theology can be found in *Theological Studies, Horizons, Journal of Feminist Studies in Religion*, and *Journal of Moral Theology*.

Marjorie Corbman is an assistant professor in the theology and religious studies department at Molloy College. Her research focuses on the multireligious history of social movements in modern American history and the theological questions raised through encounters among Muslims, Jews, and Christians in the context of shared political struggle. Her work is also informed by her time living at a Catholic Worker community in Chicago and working with Jewish organizing and activist communities in Boston.

Julia Feder is assistant professor of theology at Creighton University in Omaha, Nebraska. She specializes in theological anthropology, theologies of suffering, sexual trauma, and human evolution. Her articles appear in *Theological Studies*, the *Journal of Religion and Society*, *Anthropology News*, and *Philosophy, Theology, and the Sciences*. Her current book project is *Trauma and Salvation: A Theology of Healing*.

Donna Freitas, PhD, has written more than twenty books, including *Consent: A Memoir of Unwanted Attention* (Little, Brown), *Consent on Campus: A Manifesto* (Oxford), and *Sex and the Soul* (Oxford). She's spoken at over 200 colleges and universities about her research related to sex/Title IX issues on campus, and her essays and opinion pieces have appeared in the *New York Times* and the *Washington Post*, on NPR's *All Things Considered*, and in many other places.

David de la Fuente is a doctoral candidate in systematic theology at Fordham University, a senior teaching fellow for the 2021–22 academic year, and a lay Catholic minister.

Daniel P. Horan, OFM, is a professor of philosophy, religious studies and theology and director of the Center for Spirituality at

Saint Mary's College in Notre Dame, Indiana. He is the author of fourteen books, including *All God's Creatures: A Theology of Creation* (Fortress/Lexington, 2018) and *Catholicity and Emerging Personhood: A Contemporary Theological Anthropology* (Orbis Books, 2019). A columnist for the *National Catholic Reporter*, he is also the author of more than 250 scholarly and popular articles and book chapters.

Karen Kilby is the Bede Chair at Durham University. She is the author of three highly regarded monographs: *Balthasar: A (Very) Critical Introduction* (Eerdmans, 2012); *A Brief Introduction to Karl Rahner* (SPCK, 2007); and *Karl Rahner: Theology and Philosophy* (Routledge, 2004). In addition to twentieth-century Catholic theology, Prof. Kilby is interested in a range of themes in systematic theology, including the doctrine of the Trinity, questions around sin and suffering, and the place of mystery in Christian thought—all of which feature in her most recent books, *Suffering and the Christian Life* (co-edited with Rachel Davis, T&T Clark, 2019) and *God, Evil and the Limits of Theology* (T&T Clark, 2021).

Jason King is professor of theology at Saint Vincent College in Latrobe, Pennsylvania. He received his PhD from The Catholic University of America. He is the author of *Faith with Benefits: Hookup Culture on Catholic Campuses* (Oxford), and he is the coeditor of *Sex, Love, and Families: Catholic Perspectives* (Liturgical) with Julie Rubio. It won first-place awards from the Association of Catholic Publishers (in theology) and the Catholic Media Association Award (in marriage and family living).

Martin Madar is an associate professor of theology at Xavier University in Cincinnati, Ohio. He specializes in systematic theology, particularly ecclesiology. He is the author of *The Church of God and Its Human Face*, which investigates the contribution of Joseph A. Komonchak to ecclesiology (Pickwick, 2019).

Jack Louis Pappas is a fourth-year doctoral student in systematic theology at Fordham University with primary research interests at the intersection of fundamental theology, continental philosophy of religion, and theological metaphysics. His dissertation focuses on the theological reception of phenomenology and the philosophy of Martin Heidegger in the thought of Karl Rahner and Hans Urs von Balthasar, and the ongoing significance of this reception for the so-called "theological turn" in contemporary French phenomenology.

Andrew L. Prevot is associate professor of theology at Boston College. His research spans the areas of spiritual and mystical theology, philosophical theology and continental philosophy of religion, and various forms of political, liberation, Black, and womanist theology. He is the author of *Theology and Race: Black and Womanist Traditions in the United States* (Brill, 2018) and *Thinking Prayer: Theology and Spirituality amid the Crises of Modernity* (Notre Dame, 2015), and he is the co-editor of *Anti-Blackness and Christian Ethics* (Orbis Books, 2017).

Julie Hanlon Rubio is a professor of Christian social ethics at the Jesuit School of Theology of Santa Clara University in Berkeley, California. She has published six books, including *Hope for Common Ground* (Georgetown), winner of the College Theology Society's book award. Her current project is *Catholic and Feminist: Is It Still Possible?* (Oxford). She is a principal investigator, with Paul Schutz, for "Taking Responsibility: Jesuit Educational Institutions Confront the Causes and Legacy of Clergy Sexual Abuse."

Ish Ruiz is a doctoral candidate at the Graduate Theological Union in Berkeley, a religious studies teacher at a Catholic high school in San Francisco, and a Fall 2021 adjunct professor at the University of Dayton. His dissertation explores how an ecclesiological model of synodality can help the Catholic Church embrace the gifts of LGBTQ+ educators in Catholic schools. His broader academic research interests include theology, ecclesiology, queer liberation theology, sexual ethics, and education.

Andrew Staron is an associate professor of systematic theology at St. Mary's Seminary and Graduate School of Theology in Cleveland, Ohio. He received his PhD from the Catholic University of America in 2013 and is the author of *The Gift of Love: Augustine, Jean-Luc Marion, and the Trinity* (Fortress, 2017).

Tracy Sayuki Tiemeier, PhD, is an associate professor of theological studies and the director of peace and justice studies at Loyola Marymount University in Los Angeles, CA. Her work focuses on classical and medieval Tamil literature; comparative theology; Hindu-Christian studies; Asian and Asian American religious thought and practice; multiracial, decolonial/postcolonial, and gender/sexuality studies; and interreligious dialogue.

Cristina L. H. Traina is the Avery Cardinal Dulles, S.J. Professor of Catholic Theology at Fordham University. Her research focuses on critical and constructive Christian feminist ethics, with a specialty in Catholic ethics. Areas of special expertise include sexuality, ethics of relationship, methodological questions, and moral agency, in particular children's moral agency. She has additional interests in bioethics, migration, intersectionality, and economic and political justice.

Todd Whitmore is an associate professor of theology and concurrent associate professor of anthropology at the University of Notre Dame. He uses ethnographic methods to raise theological questions. Professor Whitmore is author of *Imitating Christ in Magwi: An Anthropological Theology* (Bloomsbury/T&T Clark, 2019). He is also the co-editor of the book series T&T Clark Studies in Social Ethics, Ethnography, and Theologies (socialethicsethnographytheologies.com).